NEUROPSYCHOLOGICAL REPORT WRITING

Evidence-Based Practice in Neuropsychology
Kyle Brauer Boone, *Series Editor*

Clinical Practice of Forensic Neuropsychology:
An Evidence-Based Approach
Kyle Brauer Boone

Psychological Assessment:
A Problem-Solving Approach
Julie A. Suhr

Validity Testing in Child and Adolescent Assessment:
Evaluating Exaggeration, Feigning, and Noncredible Effort
Michael W. Kirkwood, Editor

Neuropsychological Report Writing
Jacobus Donders, Editor

NEUROPSYCHOLOGICAL REPORT WRITING

Edited by
Jacobus Donders

Series Editor's Note by Kyle Brauer Boone

THE GUILFORD PRESS
New York   London

Library of Congress Cataloging-in-Publication Data

Names: Donders, Jacobus, editor.
Title: Neuropsychological report writing / edited by Jacobus Donders.
Other titles: Evidence-based practice in neuropsychology (Series)
Description: New York : The Guilford Press, [2016] | Series: Evidence-based
    practice in neuropsychology | Includes bibliographical references and
    index.
Identifiers: LCCN 2015047550| ISBN 9781462524174 (pbk. : alk. paper) | ISBN
    9781462524259 (hardcover : alk. paper)
Subjects: | MESH: Neuropsychology | Medical Writing
Classification: LCC RC346 | NLM WL 103.5 | DDC 616.8—dc23
LC record available at *http://lccn.loc.gov/2015047550*

To Kenneth M. Adams,
for his critical support that allowed me,
as a graduate student from The Netherlands,
to come to the United States and embark
on a career in clinical neuropsychology
that I would not change for the world

—J. D.

About the Editor

Jacobus Donders, PhD, ABPP (CN, RP), is Chief Psychologist at Mary Free Bed Rehabilitation Hospital in Grand Rapids, Michigan. He is board certified in Clinical Neuropsychology, Pediatric Clinical Neuropsychology, and Rehabilitation Psychology through the American Board of Professional Neuropsychology. His main interests include validity of neuropsychological tests and prediction of outcome after brain injury. In addition to being an active clinical practitioner, Dr. Donders has served on multiple editorial and executive boards, has published more than 100 publications in peer-reviewed journals as well as six edited or coedited books, and is an associate editor of *Child Neuropsychology* and *Archives of Clinical Neuropsychology.* He is a Fellow of the American Psychological Association and the National Academy of Neuropsychology.

Contributors

Kira Armstrong, PhD, ABPP (CN), independent practice, Woburn, Massachusetts

Ida Sue Baron, PhD, ABPP (CN), independent practice, Potomac, Maryland

Jacobus Donders, PhD, ABPP (CN, RP), Mary Free Bed Rehabilitation Hospital, Grand Rapids, Michigan

Laura A. Flashman, PhD, ABPP (CN), Department of Psychiatry, Geisel School of Medicine at Dartmouth, Lebanon, New Hampshire

Thomas J. Gola, PhD, Department of Rehabilitation Psychology and Neuropsychology, Rehabilitation Institute of Michigan, Detroit, Michigan

Laura H. Lacritz, PhD, ABPP (CN), Department of Psychiatry and of Neurology and Neurotherapeutics, University of Texas Southwestern Medical Center, Dallas, Texas

Glenn J. Larrabee, PhD, ABPP (CN), independent practice, Sarasota, Florida

Shannon M. Lundy, PhD, University of California, San Francisco, Benioff Children's Hospital, San Francisco, California

William S. MacAllister, PhD, ABPP (CN), Alberta Children's Hospital, Alberta, Canada

Bernice A. Marcopulos, PhD, ABPP (CN), Department of Graduate Psychology, James Madison University, Harrisonburg, Virginia

Joel E. Morgan, PhD, ABPP (CN), independent practice, Morristown, New Jersey

Chris Morrison, PhD, ABPP (CN), Department of Neurology and Comprehensive Epilepsy Center, NYU Langone Medical Center, New York, New York

Heidi C. Rossetti, PhD, Department of Psychiatry, University of Texas Southwestern Medical Center, Dallas, Texas

Robert M. Roth, PhD, Department of Psychiatry, Geisel School of Medicine at Dartmouth, Lebanon, New Hampshire

Carrie-Ann H. Strong, PsyD, ABPP (CN), independent practice, Coral Springs, Florida

Kirk J. Stucky, PsyD, ABPP (CN, RP), Department of Psychology, Hurley Medical Center, Flint, Michigan

Marsha Vasserman, PsyD, ABPP (CN), Child Study Center, NYU Langone Medical Center, New York, New York

Series Editor's Note

Upon seeing the title of this book, *Neuropsychological Report Writing*, the reader might anticipate readability equivalent to that of a technical manual. However, what might have otherwise been a dry topic in other hands is instead, under the editorship of Jacobus Donders, a compendium of engaging and highly readable chapters, each written by respective experts in their specialties. Each chapter provides not only suggestions for report writing, but also the relevant "back story" (i.e., the relevant factors that need to be considered when selecting and interpreting tests in various patient populations). This book emphasizes practicality, with each chapter providing examples of "less desirable" and "more desirable" report-writing styles as well as illustrative case examples. The information provided is critical for students in the process of writing their first reports, but even experienced neuropsychologists will find many of the tips and suggestions to be of value.

In the first chapter, "General Principles of Neuropsychological Report Preparation," Jacobus Donders and Carrie-Ann H. Strong present a thorough and organized overview of the critical issues in neuropsychological report writing, including how report formats change depending on the age of the examinee, and also such important topics as overinterpretation of isolated lowered scores, use of interpretative labels, and common interpretation errors. Of particular value, Donders and Strong summarize the guidelines that American Board of Clinical Neuropsychology reviewers are asked to consider when grading applicant report samples, thereby providing an "inside peek" as to report parameters that the boarding organization for clinical neuropsychologists views as essential.

Kira Armstrong and Shannon M. Lundy, in their chapter, "Neuropsychological Reports for School-Age Children," summarize issues unique to pediatric assessments, including information critical to obtain in the interview, and the necessity of deftly navigating mismatches between parental perceptions and those of school personnel regarding child symptoms and interventions. The authors emphasize that pediatric evaluators must have a solid understanding of school administrative procedures, policies, and guidelines, as well as of the federal and state laws that govern special education services and the range of accommodations, modifications, and supports that public schools are mandated to provide. Armstrong and Lundy address the topic of evaluating for special education eligibility, and they point out how neuropsychologists are uniquely positioned to integrate data from multiple sources. The chapter's major emphasis is on how to produce reports that are useful to the educational system. Common flaws encountered in pediatric neuropsychological reports are also discussed, as well as useful resources to assist the beginning assessor.

In Chapter 3, "Neuropsychological Evaluation of the Medically Complex Child," Marsha Vasserman and Ida Sue Baron discuss the range of issues encountered in this population, such as testing in nonstandard environments, unique referral questions (e.g., lateralization or language and potential for decline postsurgery), and the effect of major family stresses precipitated by the child's typically chronic medical issues. The authors address report writing both in inpatient and outpatient contexts, and they list nine helpful "rules" when writing reports for this patient group.

In Chapter 4, "Differential Diagnosis in Older Adults," Laura H. Lacritz and Heidi C. Rossetti deftly cover the specific issues encountered in neuropsychological evaluations of older individuals, including consideration of patient stamina when selecting tests, presence of sensory and motor problems (vision, hearing, tremor, etc.) that may interfere with test administration and complicate test interpretations, importance of age-appropriate test norms (and the lack of sensitivity encountered with some norms), and the importance of functional assessment (i.e., how test scores directly translate into real-world function) that may require administration of measures specific to this issue. The authors discuss navigating consent issues and communication of results when testing is to be used to measure capacity and for competency/guardianship purposes. They also emphasize that evaluators of older patients should have knowledge of differing symptoms and cognitive patterns in various dementing disorders, and they discuss the use of serial assessments when tracking mild cognitive impairment. The chapter concludes with common report-writing mistakes.

In "Psychopathology and Psychiatric Comorbidity" (Chapter 5), Robert M. Roth and Laura A. Flashman summarize the types of cognitive deficits found in various psychiatric conditions, such as schizophrenia, major depression, bipolar disorder, attention-deficit/hyperactivity disorder, and posttraumatic stress disorder. They provide report-writing recommendations in these populations and discuss how to effectively write reports for, and collaborate with, psychiatrists. The authors emphasize that report recommendations must be practical, and, in particular, they should identify resources, services, and interventions to assist with independent functioning in the community.

In Chapter 6, "Personal Injury Forensic Neuropsychological Evaluation," Glenn J. Larrabee discusses how these reports differ from standard clinical reports. In particular, he notes that in forensic neuropsychological reports, the evaluator documents not only test findings but also the reasoning process by which the conclusions were reached, with particular focus on grounding reports in peer-reviewed published literature. He further points out that in medical–legal cases the focus should be on documenting the nature and extent of damages (i.e., functional loss) as well as cause, and that simply documenting cognitive impairment does not necessarily address the legal issue. Larrabee outlines recommended sections of the forensic neuropsychological report, as well as common errors encountered in medical–legal neuropsychological reports.

Joel E. Morgan and Bernice A. Marcopulos, in their chapter, "Criminal Forensic Neuropsychological Evaluation" (Chapter 7), define relevant terms in these assessments, the differences between civil and criminal assessment contexts, and types of referral questions in criminal cases (e.g., including questions of competency, diminished capacity, and not guilty by reason of insanity). Organization of criminal forensic neuropsychological reports is discussed, along with tips on writing for attorneys, judges, and juries. Neuropsychological assessment in death penalty cases is also addressed.

In "Pre- and Postsurgical Neuropsychological Evaluation" (Chapter 8), Chris Morrison and William S. MacAllister outline the unique types of information that neuropsychologists provide in their reports on these patients, such as language lateralization, ability to cope with surgery, and expected postsurgery cognitive function. Also covered in the chapter is repeat testing and measuring "reliable change" in test scores, the importance of providing raw data in reports (so that subsequent evaluators can quickly compare scores), and writing reports useful for neurosurgical and neurology colleagues.

In the final chapter, "Evaluation for Treatment Planning in Rehabilitation" (Chapter 9), Kirk J. Stucky and Thomas J. Gola discuss tailoring neuropsychological reports to the rehabilitation context, with emphasis on writing reports that are timely, succinct, and useful to the interdisciplinary treatment team. This focus should be on real-world functionality and address issues of safety, need for supervision, and whether accommodations and environmental modifications are indicated. The authors emphasize that prognostic statements should be carefully and appropriately worded, and that treatment commendations require knowledge of empirical data on treatment outcomes and availability of community resources.

The descriptors I would use to characterize this book are "sophisticated," while at the same time "practical" and "easily digestible," and the recommendations contained therein will push the written work products of both students and experienced neuropsychologists to higher levels. As such, *Neuropsychological Report Writing* represents a critical addition to The Guilford Press Evidence-Based Practice in Neuropsychology series. A comprehensive treatise on the "nuts and bolts" of neuropsychological report writing has not previously been available, and this book should be on the top of the "wish list" for all clinical neuropsychologists.

KYLE BRAUER BOONE, PhD, ABPP, ABCN
Alliant International University Los Angeles
Los Angeles, California

Preface

Clinical neuropsychologists routinely assess persons with known, suspected, or disputed neurobehavioral impairment and then provide a written report that presents the findings, conclusions, and recommendations. Neuropsychological reports provide a permanent record of the services that were provided. In addition, depending on the setting, these reports can be used for a variety of potentially important purposes, such as feedback to a referring physician regarding differential diagnosis and treatment planning, advocacy with the schools for special education services, or informing the trier of facts in a legal context about the mental state of the examinee.

The purpose of this book is to provide guidelines and methods for preparing neuropsychological reports that are evidence-based, yet intelligible and practically useful to the intended reader, while adhering to relevant ethical, legal, and professional standards. Considering that the format of the report will typically vary with the context and purpose of the evaluation, this book covers applications in various settings (e.g., educational, legal, medical) and pertaining to both adult and pediatric examinees. It is not intended to cover every possible scenario in which neuropsychological reports may be generated. Instead, it focuses on some of the most common practice settings of neuropsychologists who typically prepare written reports based on an in-person evaluation of an individual.

All chapters in this volume were written by known experts in their respective fields. They have all used material from actual cases (with all identifying details disguised) to address the unique variables that need to be addressed in each particular context. Throughout the volume, they have consistently used a format of illustrating specific points by means of contrasting problematic versus more effective ways of describing the findings in neuropsychological reports, ranging from describing how the background is presented all the way to discussing the results and providing conclusions and recommendations. Although this book contains many practical examples of how to present information in the most useful manner to the reader, it does not offer any simple cut-and-paste, cookie-cutter, or boilerplate material. There are no shortcuts to preparing neuropsychological reports. The ultimate responsibility for the content and quality of the report lies with the practicing clinical neuropsychologist who has to consider the unique brain–behavior relationships in each individual patient, with due regard to the context in which the evaluation occurs.

The various chapters will show that no single format for a neuropsychological report works equally well in any and all settings. I hope that the various illustrations of "less desirable" versus "more desirable" ways to present information in such documents will be helpful to practitioners in considering how to serve their examinees and referral sources most effectively and most efficiently.

Contents

1. General Principles of Neuropsychological Report Preparation   1

Jacobus Donders and Carrie-Ann H. Strong

Prerequisites Prior to Report Preparation   2
Technical Aspects of Report Preparation   6
Ethical and Professional Issues   8
ABCN Practice Sample Criteria   10
Lifespan Issues   13
Psychometric and Interpretive Issues   15
Case Example   17
APPENDIX 1.1. Sample Complete Neuropsychological Report for Jane   26

2. Neuropsychological Reports for School-Age Children   30

Kira Armstrong and Shannon M. Lundy

Developmental Neuropsychological Considerations
     and the Assessment Process   31
Understanding Special Education Law and Eligibility Criteria   33
Determining Eligibility for Special Education Services: The Distinction
     between "Disorder" and "Disability"   34
Writing for and Collaborating with School Professionals   35
Technical Aspects of Report Preparation   37
Common Mistakes   43
Final Thoughts Regarding Report Writing for School-Age Children   45
Case Examples   45

Abridged Sample Neuropsychological Report   51

APPENDIX 2.1. Abridged Sample Neuropsychological Report
    for Joe Bruin   54

3. Neuropsychological Evaluation of the Medically Complex Child   62
Marsha Vasserman and Ida Sue Baron

Complex Medical Conditions   63
Assessment Issues   66
Family Issues   68
Managing Long-Term Prognostic Issues   68
General Report-Writing Considerations   69
Writing for Medical Personnel   70
Other Considerations   73
Case Example   74

4. Differential Diagnosis in Older Adults   92
Laura H. Lacritz and Heidi C. Rossetti

General Geriatric Neuropsychological Considerations   92
Pretest Considerations   95
Spectrum of MCI to Dementia   96
Writing for and Collaborating with Neurologists   97
Sections of the Report   98
Case Example   99
Examples of Conclusions   104
Report Recommendations   106
Reevaluations   109
Common Report-Writing Mistakes   111

APPENDIX 4.1. Sample Neuropsychological Report for Ms. Smith   113

5. Psychopathology and Psychiatric Comorbidity   118
Robert M. Roth and Laura A. Flashman

Lifespan Issues   119
Neuropsychological Functioning in Selected Psychiatric Disorders   120
Collaborating with and Writing for Psychiatrists   127
Case Example   128

6. Personal Injury Forensic Neuropsychological Evaluation   143
Glenn J. Larrabee

The Nature of Forensic Neuropsychological Practice   143
The Forensic Neuropsychological Report   146
Common Errors in Forensic Neuropsychological Reports   155

Conclusions   161

APPENDIX 6.1. Sample Summary, Impressions, and Conclusion Sections
from a Criminal Forensic Evaluation Report   163

7. Criminal Forensic Neuropsychological Evaluation   166
Joel E. Morgan and Bernice A. Marcopulos

Civil and Criminal Forensic Exams   167
Typical Criminal Referral Questions   170
Writing for and Interacting with Lawyers, Judges, and Juries   175
Report Examples   180
The Death Penalty   188
Conclusions   189

8. Pre- and Postsurgical Neuropsychological Evaluation: 192
   Illustrations in Epilepsy
Chris Morrison and William S. MacAllister

Unique Aspects of Evaluating Patients with Epilepsy   193
Writing for and Collaborating with Neurological/
   Neurosurgical Teams   193
Measuring Reliable Change   196
Report Components and Analysis with Selected Examples   197
APPENDIX 8.1. Sample Neuropsychology Consultation Report   215

9. Evaluation for Treatment Planning in Rehabilitation   220
Kirk J. Stucky and Thomas J. Gola

Standard Rehabilitation Report-Writing Recommendations   221
Outpatient Report Commentary and Component Analysis   227
Summary   241
APPENDIX 9.1. Sample Outpatient Neuropsychological Report   244

Index   253

NEUROPSYCHOLOGICAL REPORT WRITING

CHAPTER 1

General Principles of Neuropsychological Report Preparation

Jacobus Donders
Carrie-Ann H. Strong

Clinical neuropsychology is the practice and science of dealing with brain–behavior relationships and their implications for the daily life of individuals and their families. Assessment of persons with known, suspected, or disputed neurobehavioral impairment is the mainstay of the practice of most clinical neuropsychologists. Such an assessment has many important components, such as proper interview techniques, standardized test administration, understanding of domains ranging from psychometrics to neuropathology to psychopathology, and consideration of cultural and ethical issues. However, the resulting written report is the document that formally presents the clinical neuropsychologist's integration and interpretation of all available information, along with a logical set of conclusions and recommendations. It is an important, though not exclusive, piece of feedback to the referring agent and/or the patient and family, provides a permanent record of the service, and often effectively serves as the clinician's business card.

The format and length of a clinical neuropsychological report will vary with variables such as the practice setting, the purpose of the evaluation, the primary target readership, and the clinician's level of professional expertise as well as personal preferences (Donders, 2001a, 2001b). This chapter reviews some core aspects of most reports. This review assumes that the clinician has sufficient competence in the specialty of clinical neuropsychology, as described in the Houston Conference model (Hannay et al., 1998). In addition, this review pertains primarily to narrative reports that are based on a comprehensive neuropsychological evaluation as opposed to the brief chart notes that may be more appropriate following a neurobehavioral status examination at bedside.

First, we discuss some issues that should be considered prior to any report preparation. Second, we comment on technical aspects of writing style, with an emphasis on organization, clarity and intelligibility. Next, we address specific ethical and professional considerations that should be made when preparing reports. This then leads to a review of the criteria that the American Board of Clinical Neuropsychology (ABCN) uses for consideration of professional practice samples as part of the board certification process. We then consider how the nature and format of the report may differ with examinees across the lifespan. Most of this chapter focuses on the key aspects of the way the neuropsychologist can integrate all the available information in a manner useful to the reader. This includes a discussion of psychometric and interpretive errors that are commonly found in reports. Throughout, we highlight the importance of an evidence-based approach that includes accurate interpretation of the data, leading in a logical manner to clear and defensible conclusions. In this process, we emphasize that in order to be useful, reports must not only address the referral question but also offer new insights as well as added value, and offer feasible recommendations that are supported by the available data.

PREREQUISITES PRIOR TO REPORT PREPARATION

It is important to conceptualize the content, purpose, and potential impact of a neuropsychological report, even before dictating or writing a single sentence. In this context, it must be realized that such a report can typically only be as good as the quality of the information on which it is based. That means that the clinician must have:

- A good understanding of the referral question.
- An accurate understanding of his or her professional role in the evaluation.
- Familiarity with the condition of interest.
- Access to relevant medical and (especially in pediatric cases) academic records.
- Conducted a thorough interview and history, obtaining information not only about the presenting complaint but also about other potentially important variables.
- Inspected results from a set of formal psychometric tests that were administered in a standardized manner, that are widely accepted in the professional field, and for which appropriate norms are available.

- Reviewed behavioral and other qualitative observations during both interview and formal testing.
- Considered results from freestanding and/or embedded performance and symptom validity tests.

If clear reasons for the evaluation were not provided at the time of the referral, the clinician should contact the referring agent to obtain them (Axelrod, 2000). This does not mean that the clinician cannot address other issues that emerge as relevant during the course of the evaluation. It does facilitate giving specific feedback to the referring agent in a way that may help that person with further decision making.

There are major differences between clinical evaluations, where a doctor–patient relationship is established, and forensic evaluations, where the client is typically not the examinee (for more details, see Donders, Brooks, Sherman, & Kirkwood, in press). It is important for the clinician not only to be aware of those differences and their implications, but also to make sure that the examinee or his or her legal guardian clearly understands the nature and purpose of the evaluation at the time of obtaining informed consent and/or assent, consistent with standard 3.10(a–d) of the ethics code of the American Psychological Association (APA, 2002).

Some degree of familiarity with the condition of interest is important because psychologists should only accept those cases that are within their area of expertise, consistent with standard 2.01(a–b) of the APA ethics code. Consultation with a colleague who has more experience with that condition is permissible and can be advantageous, particularly if the disorder or syndrome is rare or when there are confounding or complicating factors. A good understanding of the condition of interest will likely also guarantee that the tests selected are crucial to the nature and manifestation of the underlying pathology (e.g., inclusion of tests of speed/efficiency of processing in a case of traumatic brain injury [TBI]).

It is standard practice to review all relevant records with regard to the case at hand (Baron, 2004; Jasper & Capuco, 2001). The nature of which records are most crucial will vary with the presenting problem and referral question. For example, in a case of an educational evaluation of a school-age child, access to academic records is likely more important and feasible than when differentiating between mild cognitive impairment and dementia of the Alzheimer type in an elderly person. In some cases, it can also be informative to review additional records, such as those pertaining to employment or military service. If specific records were desirable for the evaluation but were not available, the report should state how this limits the scope of the conclusions that can be made. Especially in cases involving sudden disruption of cognitive processes, such as TBI and stroke, review of acute care medical records and neuroimaging reports is necessary in order to obtain accurate information about the nature and severity of the injury. Retrospective self (or family) report of injury variables is often not sufficiently reliable.

Although clinical neuropsychologists are often known for piling on test after test, the importance of a thorough interview and history cannot be overestimated. This interview should address both the origin and progression of the presenting complaint as well as a review of symptoms that could be pathognomonic to the condition in question. In addition, the interview should inquire about a range of other variables that can potentially be confounding factors. These include, but are not limited to, issues such as early developmental history, family medical history, current medications, and complicating premorbid (e.g., personal abuse) as well as comorbid (e.g., financial compensation seeking) factors (for more details, see Sbordone, 2000; Vanderploeg, 2000). Use of collateral interview information can also be highly informative, particularly with patients at the extremes of the age spectrum (Donders, 2005; Jasper & Capuco, 2001).

Whenever possible, neuropsychological tests should have been selected because they were known to be appropriately normed for the demographic background of the examinee, and validated for use in the condition of interest. A neuropsychologist working with a diverse population who fails to appreciate the potential influence of variables such as quality of education (Glymour & Manly, 2008) or level of acculturation (Boone, Victor, Wen, Razani, & Pontón (2007) on test scores is at risk of making interpretive errors. Particularly when new tests are used, it is important to avoid simply assuming that they measure the same constructs, or are as sensitive to cerebral impairment, as older or similar tests; particularly if there are no independent validation studies in samples with the condition of interest (Loring & Bauer, 2010).

Whether the neuropsychologist personally administered the tests or used a properly trained technician to do so, behavioral observations can be of considerable informative value, with both children (Baron, 2004) and adults (Vanderploeg, 2000). These observations can include basic facts such as physical appearance, as well as specific variables that may reflect pathognomonic processes that the standardized tests do not always reveal. Examples could be the inclusion of neologisms or semantic paraphasias in the spontaneous speech of a person who does not demonstrate severe deficits during a test of naming to confrontation, or the subtle neglect of the left side of space that is noted only in the relatively more crowded environment of the hallway to the office. Behavioral observations may affect both test selection and interpretation.

No neuropsychological evaluation is complete without considering the validity of the findings. Several professional organizations have advocated for the routine inclusion of measures of performance and symptom validity in the evaluation of adults (Bush et al., 2005; Heilbronner, Sweet, Morgan, Larrabee, & Millis, 2009). More recent research has also suggested that the same guideline should apply to pediatric evaluations (Donders et al., in press). It is important to appreciate that failure of a performance or symptom validity test does not automatically imply "malingering." However, the potential relevance of such findings to the interpretability of the numeric test findings must be considered prior to preparing the clinical neuropsychological report.

Eventually, it is the *integration* of all the above-mentioned variables that should drive the message of the written neuropsychological report. That means that the report should be clearly organized in the mind of the neuropsychologist, prior to its initiation (Williams & Boll, 2000). First, it can be helpful to think about the referral question and to determine how to answer that question in the clearest and most evidence-based, succinct manner. The next step is to decide what else the reader should know and what the follow-up plan should be. This is where a report can have incremental value, as opposed to just regurgitating what is already available in other records. We have found it helpful to think about what we would really want to include if we had to leave a voice mail for the referring agent, and we had a 60-second time limit for it or, in the case of an e-mail, a 250-word limit. Arranging the available information in some logical order, prior to doing any writing or dictating, is advisable. For interview data, this may mean making an outline to assist in organizing the information into sections. The specific organization of those sections may vary from case to case but will be more readable if it is generally divided into distinct paragraphs. The following outline presents an example of how this could be done:

- Current symptoms
  - Cognitive
  - Emotional/psychological
  - Physical
- Functional status
  - Basic activities of daily living (if applicable)
  - Instrumental activities of daily living (if applicable)
  - Work/school performance
- History
  - Medical/neurological
  - Psychosocial
  - Developmental

Only the information that is *pertinent* to the condition of interest should be detailed. For example, one would not typically need to report on basic activities of daily living in a case of learning disability but would in a case of moderate dementia.

For the test results sections, it is useful to make a summary sheet of the test data and to place all documents in the file in the same order, to avoid having to thumb through it several times to find things. Another helpful heuristic can be to draw a diagram with the key message(s) of the report at the center and then decide what key elements of the history, test results, or other variables must be emphasized to provide the supporting foundation for that message. "Those "building blocks" can be drawn on one side of the key message(s), and the conclusions that logically flow from that on the other side. Figure 1.1 exemplifies this approach.

TECHNICAL ASPECTS OF REPORT PREPARATION

An effective neuropsychological report communicates relevant information in an evidence-based, orderly, and clear manner that is appropriate for the target audience. Of course, one can never predict who else might end up reading the report, so striving toward professional objectivity and accountability is always a good idea. We also value parsimony, but the length of a report can vary with the complexity of the case and/or the practice setting. Regardless of length, the report must address the referral question and present novel ideas and recommendations in a logical sequence, with smooth transitions between topics and wording that is easy to understand—even to

---

Supporting Arguments
1. There is mild left neglect and some but incomplete deficit awareness.
2. Does well on Wisconsin Cards, suggesting that he is able to learn new strategies.
3. Increased anxiety alone would not cause selective fine motor impairment of the left side of the body.

↓

Key Messages
He had premorbid problems with anxiety but now has additional cognitive and motor problems as the result of his stroke. He can benefit from outpatient rehabilitation.

↓

Main Recommendations
1. Stay on BuSpar but add outpatient psychotherapy as anxiety has worsened in reaction to stroke.
2. Occupational therapy to work on motor impairment, awareness of left side, and activities of daily living.
3. No driving at this time; may need driver evaluation down the line.

FIGURE 1.1. Sample diagram for neuropsychological report organization prior to its initiation.

a non-neuropsychologist. Lichtenberger, Mather, Kaufman, and Kaufman (2004) provide detailed examples of technical aspects such as sentence length and paragraph organization, as well as the basics of grammar, punctuation, and capitalization that are all worthy of consideration. In general, it is advisable to:

- Write short but complete sentences.
- Present one main idea per paragraph, with a few supporting sentences.
- Use the last sentence of the paragraph to transition into the next one.
- Avoid passive voice.
- Refrain from switching back and forth between past and present tense.
- Integrate findings from an earlier section of the report into a later one, but not to do it vice versa.

Specific to clinical neuropsychological reports, a few issues deserve further attention. Many such reports go into minute detail about information that may not be relevant or necessary. Concise but accurate communication is often more persuasive and less prone to misinterpretation. For example, instead of belaboring every single developmental milestone, from initial Apgar score to potty training success, it may sometimes be more appropriate to say:

```
John's early developmental history had been entirely unre-
markable until he had the bout of bacterial meningitis at
the age of 30 months.
```

Neuropsychologists also tend to use jargon in reports that they would most likely never use in their daily life. There is no reason to talk about suicidal "ideation" where the term "thoughts" would clearly suffice. Similarly, why does anybody have to refer to the patient's right arm as the "dominant upper extremity"? Admittedly, sometimes it can be helpful or even necessary to use certain technical terms to address a specific issue, but then it would behoove the clinician to include either a brief explanation or an example that also refers to the implication of the finding. For example, rather than just stating that the "patient had many perseverations on the Wisconsin Card Sorting Test," it might be helpful to elaborate by saying:

```
This means that he kept making the same mistake over and
over again, even when given feedback that he was doing it
wrong. This reflects that he has problems with adjusting
to changing task demands, and that he is not likely to
learn independently from his mistakes.
```

Another common mistake is making extensive use of ambiguous terms or qualifiers. Wording such as "It appears possible" or "I believe that it could" convey hesitancy or uncertainty. In addition, vague descriptions of behaviors or test results such as "a little bit" or subjective statements such as "pretty intelligent" do not convey a clear message. In medicolegal depositions, one is often asked whether something can be stated with "a reasonable degree of scientific certainty." It is typically a good idea to write factual statements and diagnostic impressions with that framework in mind, even in a clinical context. That does not mean that the neuropsychologist has to go above and beyond his or her comfort level. It is perfectly legitimate to acknowledge that the data do not allow for a specific conclusion about a particular topic. However, it is not legitimate to ignore the issue, let alone to fail to make a clear attempt at addressing the referral question.

ETHICAL AND PROFESSIONAL ISSUES

The content of any clinical neuropsychological report needs to be evidence-based. The APA ethics code, specifically standards 2.04 and 9.01a, prohibits clinicians from including in such a report conclusions or recommendations that cannot be substantiated by the information obtained during the course of the evaluation and/or by the current state of the scientific knowledge base. Thus, a report that does not clearly identify any deficits in academic achievement or other cognitive domains should not result in a recommendation for special education support under the learning disability qualification. Evidence-based practice requires not only the use of assessment instruments that are appropriate for the presenting problem and that (whenever possible) have known reliability and validity for use with that particular patient population, but also appreciation of research findings regarding the utility or obsolescence of those instruments, as detailed in standard 9.02a–c of the APA ethics code. Thus, a clinician who is still making in the report detailed interpretations of the "semantic clustering" score of the original California Verbal Learning Test in the evaluation of a person with TBI is likely on very shaky ground. Such practice would ignore the significant changes that were made to that test, and to that variable in particular, during the revision process (Stricker, Brown, Wixted, Baldo, & Delis, 2002) and the knowledge base that has accumulated about the validity of that revision in persons with TBI since then (DeJong & Donders, 2009; Jacobs & Donders, 2007).

It is important that the content of a report maintain a professional and respectful tone. This requirement is particularly important in the case of independent educational or medicolegal evaluations, where it is not unusual to have been retained by one "side" in a dispute. The written report is not the place to get into a shouting match with another professional.

Disagreements about procedures or diagnoses should be described in objective terms, supported by facts, and, as much as possible, devoid of grandstanding or other emotional overtones.

The content of a report must also minimize intrusions on privacy, consistent with both standard 4.04 of the APA ethics code and the Health Insurance Portability and Accountability Act (HIPAA). Thus, with an examinee who is HIV positive but completely asymptomatic, the clinician will need to consider if inclusion in the report of this kind of sensitive information is warranted. This also gets back to the issues of informed consent that were discussed previously. In addition, clinicians need to be aware of state laws that may be relevant in this regard. Sometimes, it can also be advisable for a report to refer to a private issue that reflects that the clinician has taken it into account, without going into unnecessary detail. For example, instead of belaboring all the who, how, and when of a patient's past experience of sexual abuse, it may be more appropriate to mention in the report something like:

Ms. Doe has a remote history of personal trauma, of which the details will not be disclosed here, but the potential relevance was considered in the context of the diagnostic conclusions.

The issue of whether or not to include specific test scores in a clinical neuropsychological report has been debated in the field for decades. On the one hand, it is important to maintain test security, consistent with standard 9.11 of the APA ethics code. Thus, giving detailed descriptions of the cutoff scores for a performance validity test or quoting multiple items from an intelligence test verbatim is ill advised. On the other hand, failure to provide sufficient information may make the report less useful to the consumer, as in the case of a report concerning an evaluation of a child with a learning disability that does not include any achievement test scores. A reasonable compromise may be to append a summary of the most important standardized scores, along with a caution that those scores should never be interpreted without consideration of the complete narrative report. Regardless of whether or not the clinician prefers to include scores in the report, it needs to be realized that, under HIPAA as well as the APA ethics code (specifically, standard 9.04a–b), patients or their guardians have a right to access their data or to formally release them to a third person. The only exceptions would be in the case of forensic and related procedures. In addition, some states have more restrictive laws about to whom raw test data can be released. Attix and colleagues (2007) provide more guidelines about the release of raw test data.

Finally, it is important that clinicians maintain, transfer, and (when appropriate) dispose of records in a manner that protects the confidentiality of the patient, consistent with standard 6.02a–c of the APA ethics code. The APA recordkeeping guidelines also suggest that clinicians retain records on their examinees for 7 years after the last date of service delivery for adults, or until 3 years after a minor reaches the age of majority, whichever is later (APA, 2007).

ABCN PRACTICE SAMPLE CRITERIA

The ABCN has specific criteria for reviewing neuropsychological reports that are part of practice samples during the process of board certification in clinical neuropsychology. These criteria can be downloaded from the ABCN website (*www.theabcn.org*). The ABCN periodically reviews and revises those criteria, so it is important to check the website for the most current version. However, a listing of the criteria that were current as of this writing and that are relevant to report content is offered here as they establish common and well-established guidelines for clinical neuropsychological reports. In general, the ABCN expects that the report:

- Identifies the referral source.
- Includes a reasonable presentation of the history of the present illness that captures the context of the symptoms, illness, or dysfunction, with some coverage of relevant past history and background as appropriate.
- Is based on an assessment that reflects a reasonably comprehensive approach that is sufficient to address the diagnostic and management issues inherent in the case, with adequate coverage of all relevant cognitive and psychological domains.
- Includes data from correctly administered and scored tests that are accurately reported and clearly presented.
- Offers interpretations of test data that are based on a reference group that is a reasonable match between the patient and the normative sample.
- Demonstrates knowledge and integration of brain–behavior relationships in a way that addresses the clinical question and meets the needs of the identified consumer.
- Results in conclusions that are supported by the data and reflect current standards of neuropsychological practice.
- Identifies relevant historical and medical risk factors that inform the diagnostic formulation and recommendations.
- Offers reasonable treatment recommendations that may include suggestions for further diagnostic work-up, therapeutic interventions, psychosocial adaptations, and other follow-up.

- Provides sufficient detail to foster implementation of recommendations.
- Incorporates emotional and psychopathological factors.
- Reflects that any relevant individual and cultural diversity issues were taken into account in test selection, normative references group used, and case formulation.
- Identifies any legal/ethical issues raised in the evaluation, along with appropriate documentation of their management.
- Documents any appropriate consultations with other professionals, as well as recommended referrals for other consults.
- Is written, in its entirety, in a clear, professional style that is tailored to the background and needs of the identified primary consumer.

The ABCN does not specify how applicants for board certification should address these issues. The guidelines just indicate that they should be attentive to all of them and, if relevant, address them in some responsible and professional way in the report.

We would like to make a few additional comments of our own with regard to these ABCN guidelines. We offer these observations with the intent of further amplification. However, it should be clear that the following recommendations are our own and not necessarily those of the ABCN.

Every report should identify the referral source. The reader needs to know if the referral came from a physician, an attorney, or another person. This also means that the reason for the referral, and any specific questions that the referring agent had, should be made explicit. There is no need to regurgitate the entire cover letter that may have accompanied the referral, but the key element(s) should be specified. For example, "Differentiate between normal aging, depression and early dementia" would make the purpose of the evaluation very clear.

The degree of detail included in the report with regard to the history of the present illness, the relevant past medical and psychosocial history, and any risk factors for suboptimal outcomes may vary with the complexity of the case as well as the age of the examinee. For example, if there is a question about differential diagnosis in a dementia work-up, with consideration of Lewy body pathology, then some discussion of hallmark symptoms such as fluctuating cognition, parkinsonism, rapid-eye-movement (REM) sleep behavior disorder, and visual hallucinations would be appropriate, along with a discussion of the time of onset and progression of both motor and cognitive symptoms. In contrast, not all of these issues would be expected to be reported routinely in a case of acute left hemisphere stroke with resultant global aphasia and right hemiparesis. As another example, a brief but sufficiently detailed review of prenatal, perinatal, and early developmental history would be expected in the case of the evaluation of a preschooler with a history of cerebral palsy, but this would not typically be the case with a middle-aged adult with recent onset of vasculitis.

There is no single "correct" answer to what tests or batteries should be included in a neuropsychological evaluation. In addition, their choice does not have to be elaborated in the report, unless there are specific reasons for deviating from accepted standards in the field. For example, consensus guidelines have been developed (Benedict et al., 2002) and validated (Benedict et al., 2006) for the evaluation of patients with multiple sclerosis. If the examiner deviated very significantly from those guidelines, it might be helpful to document in the report why he or she did that. Similarly, in an evaluation of a child with severe TBI where the Wechsler Intelligence Scale for Children—Fourth Edition (WISC-IV) was administered, one would typically expect to see documentation of the Processing Speed index because that happens to be the one that is most sensitive to such injury (Donders & Janke, 2008). However, if the neuropsychologist explained in the report that subtests comprising that index were omitted because of a comminuted fracture of the forearm used for writing, that would clarify things for the reader. Whatever battery of tests is eventually chosen, the report must show that the assessment was sufficiently comprehensive, with adequate coverage of various cognitive, behavioral, and emotional issues, to address the referral question and the associated diagnostic and follow-up issues.

Neuropsychologists differ significantly in their presentation of test results. Regardless of stylistic differences, the test interpretation should be readable, integrating the findings in a well-organized fashion, as opposed to simply listing test descriptions and scores. Some clinicians prefer to divide the test results into sections according to neurocognitive domain (e.g., separate headings for "Attention," "Language skills," etc.). Others may organize the report according to the most salient findings, given the condition that is being assessed. For example, when ruling out mild cognitive impairment, the neuropsychologist might want to focus on findings that are most relevant to that condition, including memory and executive test results, as well as information about the instrumental activities of daily living. Regardless of the manner in which the test results are presented, we encourage description of the patient's relative strengths and assets, not just weaknesses or deficits. This assists in the development of recommendations and of compensatory rehabilitation strategies.

Neuropsychological reports must include a diagnostic formulation. The report should present a section in which the practitioner succinctly "ties the data together" and makes differential diagnoses. The neuropsychologist should not just regurgitate the details of the more extended prior test results section, but should instead summarize and highlight the most relevant interview and test findings supporting the suspected diagnosis and the associated recommendations for managing the condition or guiding rehabilitation.

The nature, purpose, and outcomes of consultations with other professionals should also be documented in the report. These may include not only referrals for other consults but also explanations of the involvement of a technician or trainee, as well as interactions with other providers that may have shaped the decision-making process. For example, on one occasion, we had to see a patient who was congenitally deaf and then in midadulthood experienced a stroke that affected her ability to use her hands for sign language. We were able to find a local provider who was fluent in sign language but did not feel comfortable dealing with the impact of a neurological disorder, particularly because it was not clear if the patient also had lost some of her ability to read lips. We then consulted with a neuropsychologist out of state who had considerable experience with this population. This made a significant impact on our test selection and interpretation. All of these issues were clearly documented in the report, along with a caution that the unusual complexity of the case necessitated a conservative interpretation of the findings.

Some reports may necessitate the documentation of specific diversity, ethical, and/or legal issues. For example, there is general consensus in the field that it is preferable for patients to be evaluated by a neuropsychologist who is fluent in their language and knows their culture. However, such a person cannot always be found locally. If the neuropsychologist used an interpreter in such a case, it would be expected that the report documented the competency of the interpreter as well as any limitations use of an interpreter placed on the data interpretation. This would also be consistent with standards 2.05 and 9.03a–c of the APA ethics code.

Ethical issues can range from sharing raw data with nonpsychologists to concerns about incompetence about another provider of neuropsychological services. Legal issues may range from concern about the validity of a patient's request to amend his or her records to the mandated reporting in a case of suspected child abuse. If any such issues came up during the evaluation, prior to report preparation, the neuropsychologist's report must state factually what decision was made and why, without necessarily disclosing all the minute details. When in doubt, consultation of legal counsel may be advisable.

LIFESPAN ISSUES

The content of a report on a young child is likely to differ in some important ways from a report on an older person. For sake of convenience, this section uses TBI as a common example.

The age of the examinee affects documentation of the interview and observations. For example, there is no point in asking a traumatically injured toddler about his or her prior alcohol abuse, but that child might have been exposed to substances *in utero*. With children, this issue can be addressed through a combination of records review and parent/guardian interview. In contrast, information about prenatal history might not be reliably obtainable in a geriatric population. The flattened philtrum that can be suggestive of a fetal alcohol spectrum disorder would also be more easily observed in a young child than in an adult with abundant facial hair. At the same time, documentation of the examinee's self-reported substance use history would be important in the evaluation of an adult because such abuse can be both a risk factor for TBI and a symptom of poor adjustment afterward (Horner et al., 2005).

The most common comorbidities that must be considered in the report will also vary across the lifespan. For example, when evaluating a school-age child with mild TBI, learning disability and attention-deficit/hyperactivity disorder are some of the most common premorbid complicating factors (which highlights the necessity of documenting a review of academic records). In contrast, when evaluating an older adult, there are more worries about issues such as diabetes mellitus, hypertension, and/or polypharmacy (Donders, 2010). In some special populations, such as veterans of the wars in Iraq or Afghanistan, careful consideration of posttraumatic stress disorder needs to be documented (Vanderploeg, Belanger, & Brenner, 2013). Failure to address potentially confounding premorbid or comorbid factors will lessen the value of many a clinical neuropsychological report.

Lifespan issues also affect how a report addresses the impact of a specific event or condition. For example, in the case of a severe TBI in a high school senior, the clinician will likely need to address in the report issues such as eligibility for special education services and/or the potential need for a legal guardian when the examinee turns 18. In contrast, in the case of an older person who is developing dementia at a relatively early age, the clinician should document whether the examinee ever had a severe TBI; such an injury could have contributed to the earlier or accelerated development of the dementia in a predisposed individual (Starkstein & Jorge, 2005).

Finally, lifespan considerations also affect statements in the report about prognostic issues. For example, much is known about the nature and trajectory of recovery of cognition after moderate to severe TBI during the first year after injury in adults (Christensen et al., 2008), but less information is available about trajectories of specific cognitive functions after that. The situation is more complicated with pediatrics, where there is not only an immature brain to consider but also the strong influence of family environment (Ryan et al., 2014). In general, the clinician must be careful in the report to make only prognostic statements that can actually be supported by the available data, and not engage in speculation. In addition, clinicians need to be aware that risk factors are always relative, based on group data, and do not necessarily apply to each and every individual. For example, incurring severe TBI during earlier phases of childhood is associated with a relatively lower likelihood of driving independently and of functioning as one's own legal guardian during early adulthood (Donders & Warschausky, 2007). However, that does not mean that every preschooler with a severe TBI will need a guardian and third-party transportation after turning 18. Thus, when evaluating that child at the age of 6 years, the clinician should avoid statements in the report such as that the patient will "never" be able to function independently. It would be more appropriate to stress the need for long-term follow-up.

PSYCHOMETRIC AND INTERPRETIVE ISSUES

In analyzing a large set of test results, it is important that the clinician have a good understanding of psychometric variables and how they affect interpretation of test results (for thorough reviews, see Adams & Waldron-Perrine, 2014; Brooks & Iverson, 2012; Donders, 2012; Schoenberg, Scott, Rinehardt, & Mattingly, 2014). Yet, many clinical neuropsychological reports do not clearly reflect awareness and integration of such variables. We discuss here some of the most common errors that we have encountered over the years in this regard.

Clinicians need to pay careful attention to how they define impairment or what constitutes a low score. Setting the bar relatively stringent (e.g., more than two standard deviations below the mean) will reduce false positives but increase false negatives. Using a more liberal criterion (e.g., one standard deviation below the mean) will have the opposite effect. Whatever standard the clinician uses, it is important that this choice be made with consideration of whether it is more important to avoid a false negative or a false-positive error, and that decision will not be uniform across practice settings. For example, in a conventional neurological practice, most clinicians will want to avoid missing any emerging impairment in a person with a family of Huntington's disease. In contrast, in a criminal forensic setting, the neuropsychologist will want to avoid making an error that might help convict an innocent person. Whatever the standard that the clinician uses for impairment, it is important that he or she apply that standard consistently when dealing with similar cases. For example, in a personal injury context, it would not be proper to use a more stringent criterion when evaluating a person for the defense attorney than for the plaintiff's attorney.

One of the most common mistakes that we have encountered across neuropsychological reports pertains to overinterpretation of minor and common fluctuations in the data. Examples include equating a "statistically significant" ($p < .05$) discrepancy between two individual standard scores on the Wechsler Adult Intelligence Scale—Fourth Edition (WAIS-IV) with clinical significance, or the assumption that even a single subtest score that is more than a standard deviation below the mean is unusual. Despite common lore, scatter or variability is *not* an indication of brain damage. Test score variability and having at least one or more "low" scores are normal in healthy individuals, both with children (Brooks, Iverson, Sherman, & Holdnack, 2009; Brooks, Sherman, & Iverson, 2010) and adults (Binder, Iverson, & Brooks, 2009; Schretlen, Testa, Winicki, Pearlson, & Gordon (2008). The more tests one administers and the more individual comparisons one makes between test scores, the more likely that at least one of them will appear indicative of a problem, where none may exist. A multivariate approach that takes into account base rates of low scores and contrasts is strongly recommended. An example is the algorithm developed by John Crawford for interpretation of score discrepancies on the WISC-IV, which is freely accessible on the Internet (*http://homepages.abdn.ac.uk/j.crawford/pages/dept/psychom.htm*).

Another common mistake pertains to superficial equation of isolated test scores with a specific syndrome. Just because a sixth grader with a recent uncomplicated mild TBI has a poor score on a test of written arithmetic does not necessarily mean that this child now has a nonverbal learning disability. However, if that child also has an unusually low standard score on Perceptual Reasoning, in combination with selective fine motor impairment with the left hand and deficits in interpersonal pragmatics on standardized rating scales from several independent sources, that would lend more credence to such a diagnosis. Review of school records that reflect a precarious drop in math achievement during the fourth and fifth grades would also suggest that this condition was longstanding and not caused by the uncomplicated mild TBI. This reflects the importance of describing in the report how various findings converge to support a specific diagnostic conclusion.

A related mistake is the tendency to take reported symptoms for granted and assume that they reflect a particular condition. For example, many persons who have recently sustained a mild TBI may report headaches, but that does not mean that they necessarily have significant, let alone permanent, cerebral dysfunction. An important consideration is that headache has a considerable base rate in the general population (Smitherman, Burch, Sheikh, & Loder, 2013). Similarly, although it may be tempting in light of sensationalized media coverage to attribute a suicide attempt to presumed chronic traumatic encephalopathy after a history of uncomplicated mild TBI, the current state of the scientific literature does not clearly support such an interpretation (Iverson, 2014; Wortzel, Shura, & Brenner, 2013). It is important for neuropsychological reports to be soundly grounded in empirical evidence, with proper consideration of base rates and other psychometric issues, and a demonstrated awareness of the current state of the literature on the condition of interest.

CASE EXAMPLE

To illustrate some of the less and more desirable ways of presenting information in a report, let us consider the case of Jane, a 9-year-old, right-handed, Caucasian girl who is living with her biological parents and two younger brothers. She had a surgical resection of a left frontal arteriovenous malformation 6 weeks earlier, which was initially discovered during a work-up for a single tonic–clonic seizure that she had experienced 10 days prior to that. Her postoperative course has been unremarkable. At 1-month postsurgery, there was no seizure activity on electroencephalogram (EEG) and no residual edema on magnetic resonance imagery (MRI). She has completed outpatient rehabilitation therapies. The current evaluation was requested to assist with school reentry. The psychometric data are presented in Table 1.1. We first contrast different ways of presenting parts of the history, observations, test results, and recommendations. Finally, we show how the more desirable descriptions can be integrated into a complete report.

Example 1: Interview

LESS DESIRABLE: DOCTOR A

Jane was born at approximately 7 pounds after a pregnancy during which mother remained fairly active, did not smoke, and did not consume alcohol. There was no respiratory distress during or after birth, and she never had febrile seizures. She sat up by 6 months, demonstrated mild stranger anxiety by 9 months, walked on her own by 10 months, said her first recognizable words before she was 12 months old, and was putting words together in sentences when she was 18 months old. Jane has never had a surgery or other serious neurological injury before. She has also never been exposed to any personal trauma and does not have a history of behavioral problems. Jane has had no more tonic–clonic seizures since her surgery, even though the mother has not been giving her the antiseizure medication anymore because Jane complained that it always gave her a very unpleasant taste in her mouth. She has had that taste experience only a few times since the medication was discontinued.

MORE DESIRABLE: DOCTOR B

The mother described a fairly unremarkable pregnancy, delivery, and neonatal period with Jane. She attained all

TABLE 1.1. Neuropsychological Test Scores for Jane

Test variable	Test result
Test of Memory Malingering Trial 1, raw score	50 (100% correct)
WISC-IV[a]	
Verbal Comprehension	79
Perceptual Reasoning	96
Working Memory	90
Processing Speed	84
KTEA-II[a]	
Reading Comprehension	94
Math Computation	92
WCST-64[a]	
Perseverative Errors	94
Nonperseverative Errors	90
Categories Completed, raw score	3 (> 16th %ile)
CPT-II[b]	
Omissions	66
Commissions	42
Reaction Time	60
Variability	68
WRAML-II[c]	
Story Memory, immediate recall	9
Story Memory, delayed recall	8
Story Memory, delayed recognition	8
Picture Memory, immediate recall	10
Picture Memory, delayed recognition	11
NEPSY-II[c]	
Comprehension of Instructions	10
Speeded Naming	6
Affect Recognition	11
Geometric Puzzles	11
Trail Making Test, Part A[d]	31 sec, $z = -1.06$
Trail Making Test, Part B[d]	93 sec, $z = -2.21$
Grooved Pegboard	
Right hand[d]	98 sec, $z = -1.60$
Left hand[d]	82 sec, $z = -0.13$
CBC[b]	
Internalizing	54
Externalizing	42

Note. WISC-IV, Wechsler Intelligence Scale for Children—Fourth Edition; KTEA-II, Kaufman Test of Educational Achievement—Second Edition; WCST-64, Wisconsin Card Sorting Test (one-deck version); CPT-II, Conners' Continuous Performance Test—Second Edition; WRAML-II, Wide Range Assessment of Memory and Learning—Second Edition; NEPSY-II, NEPSY—Second Edition; CBC, Child Behavior Checklist.
[a]Standard score ($M = 100$, $SD = 15$; higher scores reflect better performance).
[b]T-score ($M = 50$, $SD = 10$; higher scores reflect worse performance).
[c]Scaled score ($M = 10$, $SD = 3$; higher scores reflect better performance).
[d]Higher raw scores and lower z-scores ($M = 0$, $SD = 1$) reflect worse performance.

developmental milestones at normal intervals. Essentially, her medical and psychosocial histories were unremarkable until she had her seizure. The mother discontinued Jane's medication (Dilantin) 10 days ago because Jane was complaining that it gave her a bad taste in her mouth. However, the mother has *not* discussed this with the neurologist. I should also note that Jane reported that she had two more episodes within the past week of about 10 to 20 seconds of a vomit-like taste in her mouth. This raises concerns about continued epileptiform activity.

Comment on Interview

Dr. A's narrative is technically correct but problematic because it goes into minute details of the patient's premorbid history but gives short shrift to some crucial information. Instead, Dr. B sums up the history much more succinctly and informs the reader of the fact that the mother has not cleared the medication cessation with the prescribing neurologist. Furthermore, Dr. B's documentation appropriately reflects the likelihood that this child may still be experiencing auras or other seizure phenomena instead of merely reporting what was said.

Example 2: Observations

LESS DESIRABLE: DOCTOR A

Jane was dressed in jeans and a sweatshirt, wearing a headband around her head and sneakers on her feet. She was friendly and appeared to have a good sense of humor. Her interactions with her mother appeared to show a good mutual bond. In her spontaneous verbal expressions, she seemed to have some difficulties coming up with the right words. She did not demonstrate phonemic or semantic paraphasias or neologisms or circumlocutions. Prosody was not impaired, and the associated affect was not incongruent. She was able to follow two- and three-step verbal commands without apparent difficulty. Neglect of the right side of space was not observed. Symptoms of right hemiparesis were also not observed. It appeared that she was doing her best during the evaluation.

MORE DESIRABLE: DOCTOR B

Jane was appropriately dressed and groomed. Her affect and demeanor were appropriate to the situation. She spoke coherently at all times, but some subtle word-finding difficulties were noted. Nevertheless, she was able to express a wide range of ideas, and there were no problems with her comprehension. I did not note any clearly unusual sensory or motor signs on general observation. I also did not observe any seizure activity during this evaluation. Jane's effort was good on all tasks that were presented to her, yielding valid results.

Comment on Observations

Dr. A may be technically correct about the description of Jane's language. However, in a report on a school-age child that will likely be read by school professionals, it is not very helpful to only use a plethora of technical terms. Instead, Dr. B simply describes the verbal expression issues in a language that most readers will be able to understand. Dr. A's frequent use of phrases like "seemed" and "appeared" also does not convey as clear a message as Dr. B's factual statements. Similarly, Dr. A's tendency to state things in negative terms (e.g., "not incongruent") may confuse the reader, whereas the active phrasing of Dr. B is more useful.

Example 3: Results

LESS DESIRABLE: DOCTOR A

Jane's levels of psychometric intelligence range from borderline to average on the WISC-IV, in a pattern that fits with the left-hemisphere location of her arteriovenous malformation. This is reflected in the fact that the Perceptual Reasoning index is more than a standard deviation better than her Verbal Comprehension index, which is a statistically significant difference ($p < 05$). Her academic achievement in the areas of reading comprehension and written arithmetic on the KTEA-II is within normal limits. The fact that comprehension is good suggests that posterior left-hemisphere regions have been spared. She demonstrates intact executive skills on the WCST-64, which is remarkable in light of her frontal lobe injury. She is inattentive on the CPT-II. Memory is intact on the WRAML-II. The NEPSY-II shows problems with language but not with visual perception. This is an important strength. Trail Making A is mildly impaired, and Trail Making B, which is the most sensitive to brain damage, is moderately impaired. The Grooved Pegboard confirms that she is doing worse with her right hand. This is the result of left frontal involvement as the result of her brain lesion. Thus, there is no doubt that Jane has brain damage.

MORE DESIRABLE: DOCTOR B

Jane demonstrates mild impairment (i.e., doing worse than 90% of her peers) in two areas: verbal expression and complex attention. She has difficulty on tasks where she has to provide elaborate verbal answers (WISC-IV Verbal Comprehension) or when she has to talk under time pressure (NEPSY-II Speeded Naming). This difficulty is also associated with selective impairment of fine motor coordination with the right hand (GPEG), all of which fits with her known left anterior brain lesion. In contrast, she does well on tests where she can work with visual or tangible materials. In fact, when she does not have to use language, she can consider different approaches to a task and adjust to changing task demands (WCST-64).

　　Jane also has difficulties with complex attention. When she has to stay focused for an extended period of time, her attention starts to wax and wane, and she starts missing things (CPT-II). In addition, she has difficulties with shifting and dividing her attention when she has to keep more than one thing in mind at the same time (TMT, part B).

Comment on Results

On the one hand, Dr. A makes the common mistake of making the report a "laundry list" of individual test findings, without any clear integration of the different components. Dr. B, on the other hand, starts off with identifying two distinct problems, discusses those separately, and pulls information from various tests together to make a concerted point. In addition, Dr. B explains more clearly how this girl functions relatively best, as opposed to focusing primarily on the deficits. Finally, Dr. B briefly mentions the fact that the findings "fit" with what is already known about the cerebral lesion, whereas Dr. A spends too much time talking about the lesion in a way that really does not tell the reader much that is new.

Example 4: Recommendations

LESS DESIRABLE: DOCTOR A

　　1. Jane needs special education support because of her brain injury. Visual support materials need to be used extensively.

　　2. Jane has problems with attention, but her mother is worried about the use of stimulant medication in light of her seizure history. It might be best to focus instead on

environmental modifications (e.g., quiet study environment) instead of treating this with medication.

MORE DESIRABLE: DOCTOR B

1. Several strategies can be used in the classroom
to facilitate Jane's learning. As much as possible, tasks
should be made interactive, with frequent review and
feedback. In addition, a hands-on approach with visual or
tangible materials, preferably with a clear and concrete
model, is helpful.

2. A trial of pharmacological intervention with regard
to managing the difficulties with attention may be considered. However, it needs to be kept in mind that the
mother (a) already discontinued Jane's Dilantin and (b)
has concerns about lowering seizure threshold with traditional stimulant medications. Thus, she really needs to
talk to the neurologist about all this.

Comment about Recommendations

Dr. A's recommendation to use visual support materials is too vague,
whereas Dr. B uses more of the assessment information to give specific
suggestions about how this girl learns relatively best. Dr. A inappropriately
takes at face value the mother's concern about seizure risk, whereas Dr. B
makes it clear that decisions about medication are up to the physician, and
that those decisions should also take into account that this child has been
going for more than a week without her prescribed antiseizure agent.

As the rest of this volume will reflect, there is no single "right" way to
prepare a clinical neuropsychological report that will work with all cases
and in all practice settings. However, for illustrative purposes, Dr. B's entire
report is included in Appendix 1.1 (pp. 26–29). The next chapters discuss
the unique demands, challenges, and opportunities pertaining to clinical
neuropsychological report preparation in different settings and with various clientele.

REFERENCES

Adams, K. M., & Waldron-Perrine, B. (2014). Psychometrics, test design, and
    essential statistics. In K. J. Stucky, M. W. Kirkwood, & J. Donders (Eds.),
    Neuropsychology study guide and board review (pp. 79–96). New York:
    Oxford University Press.
American Psychological Association. (2002). Ethical principles of psychologists
    and code of conduct. *American Psychologist, 57,* 1060–1073.

American Psychological Association. (2007). Record keeping guidelines. *American Psychologist, 62*, 993–1004.

Attix, D. K., Donders, J., Johnson-Greene, D., Grote, C. L., Harris, J. G., & Bauer, R. M. (2007). Disclosure of neuropsychological test data: Official position of Division 40 (Clinical Neuropsychology) of the American Psychological Association, Association of Postdoctoral Programs in Clinical Neuropsychology, and American Academy of Clinical Neuropsychology. *The Clinical Neuropsychologist, 21*, 232–238.

Axelrod, B. N. (2000). Neuropsychological report writing. In R. D. Vanderploeg (Ed.), *Clinician's guide to neuropsychological assessment* (2nd ed., pp. 245–273). Mahwah, NJ: Erlbaum.

Baron, I. S. (2004). *Neuropsychological evaluation of the child*. New York: Oxford University Press.

Benedict, R. H. B., Cookfair, D., Gavett, R., Gunther, M., Munschauer, F., Garg, N., et al. (2006). Validity of the minimal assessment of cognitive function in multiple sclerosis (MACFIMS). *Journal of the International Neuropsychological Society, 12*, 549–558.

Benedict, R. H. B., Fischer, J. S., Archibald, C. J., Arnett, P. A., Beatty, W. W., Bobholz, J., et al (2002). Minimal neuropsychological assessment of MS patients: A consensus approach. *The Clinical Neuropsychologist, 16*, 381–397.

Binder, L. M., Iverson, G. L., & Brooks, B. L. (2009). To err is human: "Abnormal" neuropsychological scores and variability are common in healthy adults. *Archives of Clinical Neuropsychology, 24*, 31–46.

Boone, K. B., Victor, T. L., Wen, J., Razani, J., & Pontón, M. (2007). The association between neuropsychological scores and ethnicity, language, and acculturation variables in a large patient population. *Archives of Clinical Neuropsychology, 22*, 355–365.

Brooks, B. L., & Iverson, G. L. (2012). Improving accuracy when identifying cognitive impairment in pediatric neuropsychological assessments. In E. M. S. Sherman & B. L. Brooks (Eds.), *Pediatric forensic neuropsychology* (pp. 66–88). New York: Oxford University Press.

Brooks, B. L., Iverson, G. L., Sherman, E. M. S., & Holdnack, J. A. (2009). Healthy children and adolescents obtain some low scores across a battery of memory tests. *Journal of the International Neuropsychological Society, 15*, 613–617.

Brooks, B. L., Sherman, E. M. S., & Iverson, G. L. (2010). Healthy children get some low scores too: Prevalence of low scores on the NEPSY-II in preschoolers, children, and adolescents. *Archives of Clinical Neuropsychology, 25*, 182–190.

Bush, S. S., Ruff, R. M., Tröster, A. I., Barth, J. T., Koffler, S. P., Pliskin, N. H., et al. (2005). Symptom validity assessment: Practice issues and medical necessity NAN policy and planning committee. *Archives of Clinical Neuropsychology, 20*, 419–426.

Christensen, B. K., Collella, B., Inness, E., Hebert, D., Monette, G., Bayley, M., et al. (2008). Recovery of cognitive function after traumatic brain injury: A multilevel modeling analysis of Canadian outcomes. *Archives of Physical Medicine and Rehabilitation, 89*, S3–S15.

DeJong, J., & Donders, J. (2009). A confirmatory factor analysis of the California

Verbal Learning Test—Second Edition (CVLT-II) in a traumatic brain injury sample. *Assessment, 16*, 328–336.

Donders, J. (2001a). A survey of report writing by neuropsychologists: I. General characteristics and content. *The Clinical Neuropsychologist, 15*, 137–149.

Donders, J. (2001b). A survey of report writing by neuropsychologists: II. Test data, report format, and document length. *The Clinical Neuropsychologist, 15*, 150–161.

Donders, J. (2005). The clinical interview. In S. S. Bush & T. A. Martin (Eds.), *Geriatric neuropsychology: Practice essentials* (pp. 11–20). New York: Taylor & Francis.

Donders, J. (2010). Traumatic brain injury across the lifespan: A long-term developmental perspective. In J. Donders & S. J. Hunter (Eds.), *Principles and practice of lifespan developmental neuropsychology* (pp. 357–358). Cambridge, UK: University Press.

Donders, J. (2012). Interpretive confounds in the independent pediatric neuropsychological evaluation. In E. M. S. Sherman & B. L. Brooks (Eds.), *Pediatric forensic neuropsychology* (pp. 182–201). New York: Oxford University Press.

Donders, J., Brooks, B. L., Sherman, E. M. S., & Kirkwood, M. W. (in press). Pediatric forensic neuropsychology. In J. E. Morgan & J. H. Ricker (Eds.), *Textbook of clinical neuropsychology* (2nd ed.). New York: Taylor & Francis.

Donders, J., & Janke, K. (2008). Criterion validity of the Wechsler Intelligence Scale for Children—Fourth Edition after pediatric traumatic brain injury. *Journal of the International Neuropsychological Society, 14*, 651–655.

Donders, J., & Warschausky, S. (2007). Neurobehavioral outcomes after early versus late childhood traumatic brain injury. *Journal of Head Trauma Rehabilitation, 22*, 296–302.

Glymour, M. M., & Manly, J. J. (2008). Lifecourse social conditions and racial and ethnic patterns of cognitive aging. *Neuropsychology Review, 18*, 223–254.

Hannay, J., Bieliauskas, L., Crosson, B., Hammeke, T., Hamsher, K., & Koffler, S. (1998). Proceedings of the Houston Conference on specialty education and training in clinical neuropsychology. *Archives of Clinical Neuropsychology, 13*, 157–250.

Heilbronner, R. L., Sweet, J. J., Morgan, J. E., Larrabee, G. J., & Millis, S. R. (2009). American Academy of Clinical Neuropsychology consensus conference statement on the neuropsychological assessment of effort, response bias, and malingering. *The Clinical Neuropsychologist, 23*, 1093–1129.

Horner, M. D., Ferguson, P. L., Selassie, A. W., Labbate, L. A., Kniele, K., & Corrigan, J. D. (2005). Patterns of alcohol use 1 year after traumatic brain injury: A population-based epidemiological study. *Journal of the International Neuropsychological Society, 11*, 322–330.

Iverson, G. L. (2014). Chronic traumatic encephalopathy and risk of suicide in former athletes. *British Journal of Sports Medicine, 48*, 162–165.

Jacobs, M. L., & Donders, J. (2007). Criterion validity of the California Verbal Learning Test–Second Edition (CVLT-II) after traumatic brain injury. *Archives of Clinical Neuropsychology, 22*, 143–149.

Jasper, L. G., & Capuco, J. T. (2001). Gathering background data. In C. A. Armengol, E. Kaplan, & E. J. Moes (Eds.), *The consumer-oriented neuropsychological report* (pp. 83–94). Lutz, FL: Psychological Assessment Resources.

Lichtenberger, E. O., Mather, N., Kaufman, N. L., & Kaufman, A. S. (2004). *Essentials of assessment report writing.* New York: Wiley.

Loring, D. W., & Bauer, R. M. (2010). Testing the limits: Cautions and concerns regarding the new Wechsler IQ and memory scales. *Neurology, 74*, 685–690.

Ryan, N. P., Anderson, V., Godfrey, C., Beauchamp, M. H., Coleman, L., Eren, S., et al. (2014). Predictors of very-long-term sociocognitive function after pediatric traumatic brain injury: Evidence for the vulnerability of the immature "social brain." *Journal of Neurotrauma, 31*, 649–657.

Sbordone, R. J. (2000). The assessment interview in clinical neuropsychology. In G. Groth-Marnat (Ed.), *Neuropsychological assessment in clinical practice: A guide to test interpretation and integration* (pp. 94–128). New York: Wiley.

Schoenberg, M. R., Scott, J. G., Rinehardt, E., & Mattingly, M. (2014). Test administration, interpretation, and issues in assessment. In K. J. Stucky, M. W. Kirkwood, & J. Donders (Eds.), *Neuropsychology study guide and board review* (pp. 97–114). New York: Oxford University Press.

Schretlen, D. J., Testa, S. M., Winicki, J. M., Pearlson, G. D., & Gordon, B. (2008). Frequency and bases of abnormal performance by healthy adults on neuropsychological testing. *Journal of the International Neuropsychological Society, 14*, 436–445.

Smitherman, T. A., Burch, R., Sheikh, H., & Loder, E. (2013). The prevalence, impact, and treatment of migraine and severe headaches in the United States: A review of statistics from national surveillance studies. *Headache, 53*, 427–436.

Starkstein, S. E., & Jorge, R. (2005). Dementia after traumatic brain injury. *International Psychogeriatrics, 17*, S93–S107.

Stricker, J. L., Brown, G. G., Wixted, J., Baldo, J. F., & Delis, D. C. (2002). New semantic and serial clustering indices for the California Verbal Learning Test—Second Edition: Background, rationale, and formulae. *Journal of the International Neuropsychological Society, 8*, 425–435.

Vanderploeg, R. D. (2000). Interview and testing: The data collection phase of neuropsychological evaluations. In R. D. Vanderploeg (Ed.), *Clinician's guide to clinical neuropsychological assessment* (2nd ed., pp. 3–38). Mahwah, NJ: Erlbaum.

Vanderploeg, R. D., Belanger, H. G., & Brenner, L. A. (2013). Blast injuries and PTSD: Lessons learned from the Iraqi and Afghanistan conflicts. In S. Koffler, J. Morgan, I. S. Baron, & M. F. Greiffenstein (Eds.), *Neuropsychology: Science and practice I* (pp. 114–148). New York: Oxford University Press.

Williams, M. A., & Boll, T. J. (2000). Report writing in clinical neuropsychology. In G. Groth-Marnat (Ed.), *Neuropsychological assessment in clinical practice: A guide to test interpretation and integration* (pp. 575–602). New York: Wiley.

Wortzel, H. S., Shura, R. D., & Brenner, L. A. (2013). Chronic traumatic encephalopathy and suicide: A systematic review. *BioMed Research International, 2013*, 424280. Retrieved February 28, 2014, from *http://dx.doi.org/10.1155/2013/424280.*

Sample Complete Neuropsychological Report for Jane

Date of evaluation: 12/30/2014

Referred by: John Doe, MD (neurology)

Referral question: Evaluate for sequelae of arteriovenous malformation.

Background Information

This is a 9-year-old, right-handed, Caucasian girl who is currently living with her biological parents and two younger brothers. She had a surgical resection of a left frontal arteriovenous malformation (AVM) 6 weeks ago, which was initially discovered during a work-up for a single tonic–clonic seizure that she had experienced 10 days prior to that. The surgery was without complications, and her postoperative course has been unremarkable. EEG at 1-month postsurgery did not reveal any epileptiform activity, whereas her presurgery EEG had shown two brief episodes of spike–wave activity. MRI at the time of follow-up showed complete resolution of the mild edema that was initially noted, immediately postsurgery. She has completed a brief course of outpatient physical and speech rehabilitation therapies. The current evaluation was requested to assist with school reentry, as the next semester is about to start in 2 weeks. Academic records from elementary school showed that Jane was performing in the average range on standardized achievement tests prior to her seizure, and did not identify any behavioral or other concerns.

I personally completed the records review, interview, test selection, data integration, feedback, and report preparation components of this evaluation (CPT Code 96118; two units). The majority of the face-to-face tests were administered and scored by my assistant (Jill Smith, MA), who is appropriately licensed to do so under my direction and supervision (CPT Code 96119; four units). There was no duplication of services or charges in this regard.

Interview

Jane was brought to the evaluation by her mother, who provided informed consent for the assessment to proceed. Jane assented to it. She completed the formal testing in the absence of any third persons, consistent with standardization guidelines.

Jane was in the third grade at the time of her seizure. She expressed eagerness to return to school. She denied pain, sleep disturbance, cognitive difficulties, or emotional distress. She was able to identify several close friends who have stayed in contact with her.

The mother described a fairly unremarkable pregnancy, delivery, and neonatal period with Jane. She attained all developmental milestones at normal intervals. Essentially, her medical and psychosocial histories were unremarkable until she had her seizure. The mother discontinued Jane's medication (Dilantin) 10 days ago because Jane was complaining that it gave her a bad taste in her mouth. However, the mother has *not* discussed this with the neurologist. I should also note that Jane reported that she had two more episodes within the past week of about 10 to 20 seconds of a vomit-like taste in her mouth. This raises concerns about continued epileptiform activity.

The mother did not have current behavioral or cognitive concerns about Jane. There have also been no recent unrelated psychosocial stressors. Family medical history is significant for hypertension on the maternal side and for diabetes mellitus on the paternal side.

Behavioral Observations

Jane was appropriately dressed and groomed. Her affect and demeanor were appropriate to the situation. She spoke coherently at all times, but some subtle word-finding difficulties were noted. Nevertheless, she was able to express a wide range of ideas, and there were no problems with her comprehension. I did not note any clearly unusual sensory or motor signs on general observation. I also did not observe any seizure activity during this evaluation. Jane's effort was good on all tasks that were presented to her, yielding valid results.

Test Results

A summary of the formal psychometric data is attached. Rather than reviewing every single test or score in isolation, let me highlight the most significant findings.

Academic skills that Jane had mastered prior to the surgery have been well preserved, with regard to both reading and math (KTEA-II). However, Jane demonstrates mild impairment (i.e., doing worse than 90% of her peers) in two areas: verbal expression and complex attention. She has difficulty on tasks where she has to provide elaborate verbal answers (WISC–IV Verbal Comprehension) or when she has to talk under time pressure (NEPSY-II Speeded Naming). This is also associated with selective impairment of fine motor coordination with the right hand (GPEG), all of which fits with her known left anterior brain lesion. In contrast, she does well on tests where she can work with visual or tangible materials. In fact, when she does not have to use language, she can consider different approaches to a task and adjust to changing task demands (WCST-64).

Jane also has difficulties with complex attention. When she has to stay focused for an extended period of time, her attention starts to wax and wane, and she starts missing things (CPT-II). In addition, she has difficulties with shifting and dividing her attention when she has to keep more than one thing in mind at the same time (TMT, part B). Despite all this, she is still able to learn and remember new information when working one on one and with no distractions around (WRAML-II). I would have more significant concerns about her ability to do so in a larger and busier classroom. It should also be noted that the above-mentioned WCST-64, on which she did so well, is very interactive in nature, with frequent feedback and redirection. I anticipate that the problems with complex attention would affect Jane more when she has to independently keep track of her work over an extended period of time.

Finally, the results from a standardized rating scale (CBC) that I had the mother complete with regard to Jane's day-to-day functioning are not suggestive of a child who has pervasive internalized distress or who is just oppositional or defiant in nature. This fits with Jane's self-report and her demeanor during the formal testing.

Impression/Recommendations

This is a mildly but clinically significantly abnormal set of neuropsychological test results, with some findings that correlate with the known left frontal involvement. Jane has mild word-finding difficulties and some fine motor impairment on the right side of the body. I am relatively most concerned about her difficulties with divided and sustained attention. In this context, it is important that there was nothing in the school records to suggest premorbid difficulties with attention. Thus, these problems have clearly resulted from her recent neurological history. For this reason, I suggest that she be considered for eligibility for special education support under the qualification of Other Health Impairment. I do not see evidence for a complicating mood or adjustment disorder. With regard to her further care, I offer the following suggestions.

1. Several strategies can be used in the classroom to facilitate Jane's learning. Avs much as possible, tasks should be made interactive, with frequent review and feedback. In addition, a hands-on approach with visual or tangible materials, preferably with a clear and concrete model, is helpful.

2. A trial of pharmacological intervention with regard to managing the difficulties with attention may be considered. However, it needs to be kept in mind that the mother (a) already discontinued Jane's Dilantin and (b) has concerns about lowering seizure threshold with traditional stimulant medications. Thus, she really needs to talk to the neurologist about all this. I prefer that such a discussion take place first, particularly in light of the fact that Jane may continue to have aura experiences. Second, although it is my understanding that the balance of the literature clearly suggests that agents such as Ritalin and Adderall are safe in children with a one-time symptomatic seizure, such a consideration is a medical decision and up to her attending physician.

3. Jane can also be encouraged to develop some self-monitoring techniques, especially for use with more prolonged tasks, to help compensate for the difficulties with complex attention. An example would be to "stop, look and think" at periodic intervals to make sure she is still on track. Again, the availability of a model or outline to follow would be helpful in this regard. In addition, she should be encouraged and reminded to routinely recheck her work for mistakes after completion.

4. Jane has already completed a course of outpatient speech therapy, but I would still caution against putting pressure on her to speak quickly, and instead give her ample time to express herself. In addition, it needs to be realized that she still has some fine motor impairment with her right hand, so she may need extended time for assignments that involve a lot of writing.

Follow-Up

I have discussed these findings and recommendations with Jane's mother in a preliminary manner. I would suggest a repeat comprehensive neuropsychological evaluation only on a PRN basis. A more limited reevaluation of attention skills (e.g., CPT-II combined with standardized rating forms from parents and teacher) could be considered a few weeks after the start of school and after initiation of treatment for the attention problems, if the treatment ends up being initiated. For any further questions, please do not hesitate to contact my office directly.

CHAPTER 2

Neuropsychological Reports
for School-Age Children

Kira Armstrong
Shannon M. Lundy

The value of writing a "school-friendly" neuropsychological report may be obvious in outpatient clinical settings, especially in private practices that specialize in developmental and learning disorders. However, every pediatric neuropsychologist who evaluates a school-age child should recognize that, more often than not, their report will be presented to the child's school for consideration. This is true regardless of the setting in which one practices, or whether the report is written primarily to answer specific medical questions. Although school-related issues may not be overtly evident in the referral question, the educational consequences of a child's medical disorder and/or associated treatment are often a critical matter that should be addressed (Loring, Hermann, & Cohen, 2010). Indeed, as children increasingly survive complex neurological and medical conditions, and as health care limitations further reduce rehabilitation interventions, even those children seen in medical settings with clear neuropathology will ultimately require academic services as part of their intervention planning (Ernst, Pelletier, & Simpson, 2008). With this in mind, this chapter is designed to provide clinicians with information regarding how to best write reports that support a child's educational needs. Readers are encouraged to incorporate the components that best fit into their clinical practice model.

DEVELOPMENTAL NEUROPSYCHOLOGICAL CONSIDERATIONS AND THE ASSESSMENT PROCESS

Pediatric neuropsychology evaluations occur in a wide range of settings and with an equally variable number of referral sources and questions. In some settings, a child may be referred to document neurocognitive functioning so as to direct medical interventions and services. In other settings, the neuropsychologist may be the first person consulted to document and explain a child's cognitive, learning, social–emotional, and/or behavioral difficulties. Finally, children may be referred for second opinions when prior medical and/or psychological consultations did not offer clear explanations for concerning behavior (Baron, 2004). To best serve this role, a pediatric neuropsychologist must integrate neurocognitive data, behavioral observations, and psychological processes, with an awareness of the developing brain and underlying etiology as well as the child's unique *context* (i.e., his or her social, familial, cultural, developmental, and emotional history) (Bernstein, 2000). The neuropsychological report then becomes a vehicle for communicating diagnostic formulations, predictions of future outcomes, and recommendations to all interested parties. For this reason, the report is most useful when clinicians are cognizant of the many potential readers (e.g., medical specialists, psychologists, parents, educators) who will ultimately review the report.

In order to meet these expectations, the assessment process and report should include a thorough review of the child's family/genetic history, as well as his or her developmental, medical, educational, and psychological history. This information should be collected through direct interviews and questionnaires, as well as through a review of relevant documents. Although original medical documents are not always available (especially for outpatient clinicians), they can be critical to confirm and/or clarify reports of prior diagnoses and medical interventions. Whether or not medical records are available, it is incumbent on the clinician to ascertain a clear medical history, without deferring to undocumented claims of previous diagnoses. This is especially important when children are referred due to a history of mild traumatic brain injury (mTBI) and/or concussion, as these diagnoses are often inaccurately given based solely on self- or parent report and then perpetuated in future medical assessments (Carone, 2013).

It is also important to be knowledgeable about the child's current and/or premorbid academic functioning. When collecting this information clinicians should be cognizant of the potential conflict between the beliefs of parents and school personnel regarding a child's eligibility for special education services as well as any interventions or accommodations the child has received to date. Consequently, reasonable attempts should be made to obtain outside information, including teacher report (through informal and/or standardized inventories), report cards, and (when possible) classroom observations (Hurewitz & Kerr, 2011). Additionally, clinicians should routinely request documentation regarding previous school or "Team" assessments, Individualized Education Plans (IEPs), and/or 504 accommodation plans. Collecting information from the school as well as the family allows the clinician to directly advocate for the *child's needs* rather than inadvertently being placed in a position to "take sides." Finally, interviews with the child and his or her parent (rather than only one or the other) further provide more comprehensive information about the child's presenting challenges. Obtaining relevant information from all three sources gives the evaluator a sense as to whether the child, parent(s), and/ or school personnel are seeing a similar or disparate set of challenges. This helps set the stage for how results should be presented during the feedback session and in the report.

The specific cognitive areas assessed through an evaluation will vary to some degree depending on the clinical setting and referral question. In some instances, a targeted assessment and limited battery may adequately answer the child's medically related questions. However, when more comprehensive assessments are administered, the battery should include measures that evaluate the child's overall cognitive ability (IQ); expressive and receptive language skills; visual spatial skills; memory; attention; motor/ visual–motor; and executive functions (e.g., planning, problem solving, cognitive flexibility, organization, inhibition, and working memory). Documentation of the child's adaptive functioning (when relevant), psychological adjustment, and social–emotional functioning are also critical components of pediatric neuropsychological assessments and can be completed through both formal measures and comprehensive diagnostic interviews. Finally, the neuropsychological community is increasingly asserting that testing batteries should include some form of embedded and/or separate performance validity tests (PVTs) and when relevant, symptom validity tests (SVTs) (Bush et al., 2005; Donders & Kirkwood, 2013; Blaskewitz, Merten, & Kathmann, 2008; Heilbronner et al., 2009).

Although testing these domains will provide a solid understanding of the child's cognitive abilities, documenting a child's academic strengths and weaknesses is also critical for creating thoughtful recommendations that translate into the academic setting (Ernst et al., 2008). This is especially important for children whose medical conditions place them at known risk for learning delays and associated disabilities. Test selection should be designed not only to document academic-based deficits or relevant weaknesses, but also to allow the clinician to clearly *explain the source* of the child's problems so as to best direct intervention services. This often requires an error analysis of the child's performance rather than a strict interpretation of the scores alone. For example, a child whose math fluency score is impaired because he or she made a high number of impulsive/

inattentive errors would require different intervention than a child who completed every item correctly but worked at an especially slow pace.

UNDERSTANDING SPECIAL EDUCATION LAW AND ELIGIBILITY CRITERIA

In our clinical practice, we have seen many reports in which neuropsychologists have made recommendations (and even demands) that reflect a limited understanding of special education law and eligibility criteria. This deficit can lead to unnecessary conflict between the school, the child's parents, and other service providers. It also reduces the likelihood that a neuropsychologist's recommendations will be integrated into a child's educational program. To avoid this situation, it is incumbent on the clinician to have a solid understanding of school administrative procedures, policies, and guidelines, as well as federal and state laws that govern special education services. It is equally important to understand the range of accommodations, modifications, and support that public schools are mandated to provide (Ernst et al., 2008), as well as what the schools do *not* need to offer.

All children between the ages of 3 and 21 are entitled to a "free and appropriate public education" (FAPE) in the least restrictive environment (LRE) that allows them to *access the curriculum* and to make *effective progress*. There are two federal laws that document the rights of children with disabilities in an academic setting. The first of these is the Individuals with Disabilities Education Act (IDEA: Public Law 94-142). IDEA was written in 1975 and expanded upon in 1977 to ensure that all children with disabilities are (1) identified by a multidisciplinary school team and (2) provided with individually designed instruction in the LRE. IDEA includes 13 disability categories for special education services with defining criteria that can vary from state to state. IDEA was reauthorized in 2004 and is now referred to as the Individuals with Disabilities Education Improvement Act (IDEIA). The most relevant changes in IDEIA pertain to the determination of special education eligibility for specific learning disabilities (SLDs). With the implementation of this law, schools can no longer base SLD determinations *solely* on a severe discrepancy between intellectual ability and achievement (Fletcher, Coulter, Reschly, & Vaughn, 2004). The law does continue to allow for the use of a discrepancy model, but it also provides alternative qualification methods and encourages schools to consider the underlying psychological processing deficits contributing to an SLD.

The federal laws associated with IDEA/IDEIA were designed as guiding principles establishing the "floor" of rights for students with special needs. Each state has varying interpretations of the law including what should not fall below that "floor," as well as associated differences in the methodology and criteria to determine eligibility for an SLD. Additionally, even within a state, school districts may interpret and implement state laws very differently. As a result, policies across the country can vary significantly, and some of the qualification methods are not always intuitive for neuropsychologists. For example, to qualify for an SLD designation in Maine, a child must (among other criteria) "score ≥ 1.5 standard deviations below the mean in one area of *psychological processing* or ≥ 1 standard deviations below the mean in two areas of psychological processing (i.e., measures of memory, processing speed, or phonological processing)" (Ahearn, 2008, p. 6, emphasis added). Notably, counter to current neuropsychological constructs and research regarding learning disorders, this law does not mandate or even allow for a child's performance on specific academic achievement tests (aside from measures of phonological processing) to determine eligibility.

IDEIA also includes policy relating to response to intervention (RTI). RTI mandates the provision of tiered research-based interventions to improve a child's skills in deficit areas (Fletcher et al., 2004; Ernst et al., 2008). A full review of RTI is beyond the scope of this chapter. However, it should be acknowledged that some school districts determine eligibility for SLD services based on the child's performance in these increasing levels of interventions (or RTI) in addition to and/or instead of a child's performance on standardized testing. This further demonstrates how imperative it is for clinicians to be aware of how these laws are applied within each state, so as to write reports that map onto relevant eligibility criteria.

Finally, Section 504 of the Rehabilitation Act (1973) is the second federal law that defines services for students with disabilities. This law outlines a broader definition of the term *disability* and focuses on determining whether an individual's disability substantially limits one or more major life activities. The law precludes recipients of federal funds from discriminating against qualified handicapped individuals. As most public schools receive federal funds, they are subject to withdrawal of this money if they engage in discriminatory practices against qualified handicapped individuals. The law, therefore, ensures that a child with a disability has equal access to a public education through the provision of accommodations and modifications. Children who are eligible for accommodations under this law are provided with a 504 Plan, whereas children who are eligible for specialized instruction and services under IDEA/IDEIA are provided with an IEP, which includes associated goals and special education interventions.

DETERMINING ELIGIBILITY FOR SPECIAL EDUCATION SERVICES: THE DISTINCTION BETWEEN "DISORDER" AND "DISABILITY"

Public schools are mandated to provide children with documented disabilities an education that ensures effective progress. However, a medical diagnosis is not sufficient to determine eligibility for special education services, even if the diagnosis is an SLD. Pediatric neuropsychologists should be aware of the distinction between the words "disorder" and "disability." A "disorder" is a diagnosis made by a medical or behavioral health professional, whereas a "disability" is a legal term indicating that a child's disorder is significantly limiting his or her ability to access the general education curriculum and make effective progress. Eligibility is determined by a student's school "Team," which includes multidisciplinary school personnel, parents, and any outside professionals attending the meeting. The school Team is expected to make decisions regarding eligibility and programming based on the child's performance on testing (both within the school and on outside evaluations), as well as his or her daily academic performance. School Teams are mandated to *consider* any outside or "independent" evaluation, including neuropsychological assessments, but they are *not required* to accept the findings (including test results, diagnoses, and predictions for a child's academic challenges); nor are they required to implement the recommendations. Consequently, a child can meet the criteria for a medical disorder, but still be found ineligible for accommodations through a 504 Plan or special education services through an IEP if the Team believes the disorder is not limiting the child's ability to access the curriculum and make effective educational progress.

When evaluating a child whose medical disorder and/or diagnoses are contributing to a significant disability, the report should clearly detail how the child's cognitive profile will have an adverse impact on his or her academic development and performance. This documentation will be most meaningful if it is written in a way that maps onto specific state laws regarding disability designations and eligibility. This again requires an understanding of how the child's disorder and associated disability is defined in a clinician's region. For example, in some states and school districts an acquired brain injury (ABI) is subsumed under the "Other Health Impairment" (OHI) designation, whereas in other settings, children with ABIs receive services under a TBI designation.

WRITING FOR AND COLLABORATING
WITH SCHOOL PROFESSIONALS

In order to best understand how a neuropsychological report can support a child in the educational setting, it is first important to highlight how medically based evaluations differ from school-based Team assessments. Each approach brings its own advantages and disadvantages. For example, although there are some exceptions, most pediatric neuropsychologists do not observe children in the classroom. Clinicians must therefore rely on secondary sources to build a comprehensive impression of the child's day-to-day presentation, whereas school psychologists have the advantage of conducting classroom observations and/or directly consulting with the child's educators over multiple conversations. At the same time, neuropsychological evaluations are better positioned to provide a more objective evaluative process. When school-based clinicians evaluate children for special education purposes, there is an unavoidable dual relationship that can potentially prevent schools from accessing essential information. For instance, parents may feel uncomfortable sharing personal information about the child and/or family system that can be critical for understanding the child in his or her context. Although school assessments do not typically lead to *diagnoses*, this information still can drastically change impressions regarding the source of a child's difficulties, which in turn informs intervention planning.

When a child is being considered for special education eligibility, he or she participates in a multidisciplinary school assessment. Schools are required to evaluate all areas of *suspected* disability. As such, the domains assessed can vary widely based on the child's presentation and the school's determination of need for testing; whereas some assessments may be quite thorough, others may be relatively brief and targeted. It is important to remember that a school's role in these circumstances is to determine whether a child has a *disability*. For some children, this emphasis can inadvertently limit the scope of an evaluation as well as the Team's ability to document a child's vulnerabilities, especially when the interpretation of the data focuses primarily (or solely) on whether a child has a *learning disability*. This is particularly true for children with medical conditions whose deficits are not easily captured by targeted testing and especially by standardized academic assessments. In these instances, the child may be at risk for being found ineligible for special education services even when his or her daily academic performance is clearly limited by an underlying medical condition. Similar outcomes can arise for younger children with dyslexia (e.g., in grades 1–3) who are able to compensate for decoding deficits by memorizing a finite number of sight words; these children may perform well on targeted academic testing, especially if their fundamental reading skills (i.e., phonological awareness, nonword reading/decoding, and reading fluency) are not assessed. In contrast, neuropsychological evaluations are uniquely positioned to delve more deeply into the child's cognitive and academic abilities so as to provide an understanding of (1) how the child's medical and/or developmental issues affect brain–behavior relationships; and (2) how related impairments are adversely impacting the child's educational performance (Ernst et al., 2008).

Neuropsychological evaluations are also designed to understand the totality of test results through a single lens focused on the whole child. In contrast, most Team evaluations are conducted by a number of specialists (e.g., speech–language therapist, occupational therapist, psychologist, educational specialist), who each summarize and formulate their impressions separately. For children who have clear and consistent cognitive profiles, this approach can effectively document a child's disability and associated needs. However, when children present with variable cognitive performances, especially in the context of executive dysfunction (a common finding in children with brain-related disorders), his or her performance across a large test battery can be inconsistent. In a school assessment model, this can lead to a number of different conceptualizations and impressions regarding the child's needs, much akin to the idea of the six blind men and the elephant (where each man feels a different part of the animal and comes up with disparate hypotheses as to what they are feeling). When these seemingly incongruent results are not interpreted through an integrative, brain-based lens, the child's cognitive profile and associated vulnerabilities can be minimized, misunderstood, or overlooked entirely. For some children, this may lead to a decision of ineligibility; for other children, these interpretations can lead to well-meaning, but misdirected and/ or inefficient interventions.

In contrast, the pediatric neuropsychologist's appreciation of brain–behavior relationships and the application of this knowledge across the entire neurocognitive profile can better support a more integrative interpretation of the findings. Of course, this means that the report should not only document the child's cognitive strengths and weaknesses, but also provide an *explanation* for the child's cognitive profile in the context of relevant etiologies, associated risks, and recommendations. The report should be written as a stand-alone document that (1) answers specific referral questions; (2) educates the child's parents, medical providers, and school Team; and (3) provides recommendations designed to facilitate the child's adaptation (Bernstein, 2000).

TECHNICAL ASPECTS OF REPORT PREPARATION

The length of a pediatric neuropsychological report will vary widely from setting to setting, depending on the primary focus and goals for the evaluation as well as the clinician's style. There is no "right or wrong" way to write a report as long as the important features are addressed and the referral questions answered. However, when writing a report to best support the child's educational needs, the following features should be considered.

Tone

The report should be written with an authoritative, but *respectful* and collaborative tone. This becomes especially important when discussing recommendations but is equally important when highlighting a child's educational history. This area is one in which clinicians can vacillate between being too forceful and demanding (e.g., "The school must provide this child with a 24-hour one-on-one aide to support his educational needs") or too deferential (e.g., "The Team may want to provide Johnny with physical therapy at school, as it might be really helpful in supporting his recovery from his recent TBI"). A pediatric neuropsychological report should find a balance between these extremes. In other words, it should simultaneously reflect the clinician's *expertise* and deference to the team process. Therefore, recommendations should be written clearly and without equivocation (i.e., "the child *will need* these services" rather than "the child *might benefit* from services"). However, whenever possible, it is equally important to acknowledge the positive work that school personnel have already provided. For example, the following was written in the case of a child who had been receiving special education services for reading for many years. Notice that the text highlights the school's efforts while still respectfully indicating that the child needs more intensive services than the school can provide:

> Before discussing Johnny's other academic risks, it should be acknowledged and emphasized that his school has committed a great deal of resources to supporting his academic development. Despite these supports, Johnny continues to exhibit very marked deficits in reading accuracy and fluency, as well as severe deficits in encoding/spelling and written expression. In fact, the gap between Johnny's abilities and those of his same-age peers has increased over time, rather than decreasing, indicating that while he has made some gains, he is not making effective progress. Again, this point is not being made to disparage Johnny's school, as his teachers are very clearly committed to his educational development and have been working intensively to support him to the best of their abilities. Johnny is simply one of those students whose needs are so intense that he is unable to make effective gains within a public school setting, even when provided in his substantially separate, language-based program.

Summary of Relevant History

The amount of history included in a report will vary from setting to setting. However, any details that are relevant in making diagnostic conclusions or recommendations should be highlighted so as to provide the reader with a "road map" to follow the clinician's thinking process. This can be especially important for reports that are presented in a school setting, as diagnostic conclusions and even interpretation of the data may be reviewed by others who at times will come up with alternate conclusions, especially if the neuropsychologist does not attend the school meeting (either in person or by phone).

Summary of Test Results

There is no uniformly agreed upon approach to providing test scores in a pediatric neuropsychological report. Some neuropsychologists append a full table of scores to the end of the report (with or without percentiles and descriptive labels), whereas others integrate some or all of the scores into the body of the report. In either case, it is essential to provide an *interpretation* of the scores based on the child's approach to the data as well as how the scores relate to the child's overall cognitive profile. When relevant, reports should clearly explain how the child's performance on various measures was hampered by deficits in seemingly unrelated cognitive domains. For example, the Wechsler Coding and Symbol Search subtests are ostensibly designed to measure processing speed. However, when children earn low scores on these measures due to an elevated number of impulsive errors and/or a decreased ability to remain focused on the task, these behaviors critically change the interpretation of the data, diagnostic impressions, and recommendations for intervention. It is not enough for a clinician to *understand* these concepts; the information needs to be written into the report so as to ensure that the document speaks accurately for itself and without ambiguity.

When relevant, reports should also explain why a child may have presented differently during the neuropsychological assessment relative to his or her day-to-day school presentation and/or previous testing. For example, some children with attentional difficulties can work very hard to sit still in class, even though it takes a great deal of effort to do so. These same children may also be relatively well regulated during school assessments, in part because these assessments often occur over much shorter testing sessions. Consequently, it is not uncommon for children to be more overtly dysregulated during a neuropsychological assessment than he or she is at school. In contrast, there are other children who may be more dysregulated in a classroom than he or she is during individualized, one-on-one testing sessions. Although each of these circumstances are a reflection of the child's *environment* and associated expectations, if the difference is not directly addressed within a report, school personnel may discount the findings of the neuropsychologist because the report does not appear to capture the student they see on a regular basis. This discussion also provides a perfect segue to explain the child's needs for movement breaks and other accommodations that may not have been apparent due to the child's attempts to hide his or her difficulties at school, or to explain how an increase in external structure can support a child's ability to better attend in class. Finally, interpretive comparisons regarding academic performance should be made relative to previous testing results. This should include a discussion as to whether the child's performance reflects meaningful growth, ineffective growth (i.e., he or she has made some progress but not enough to close the gap between his or her peers), or regression (i.e., a loss of skills).

Diagnostic Conclusions

The report should clearly and unambiguously state the child's medical and/ or psychological diagnoses. It is equally important to rule out diagnoses that others may make if they look only at the test data. Similarly, if the child meets criteria for multiple disorders, it is important to distinguish how these diagnoses are distinct. For example, if a child has *both* ADHD and dyslexia, it can be critical to clarify that they are in fact distinct diagnoses. For example:

> Although Mary's ADHD is likely exacerbating her reading difficulties, she also meets criteria for dyslexia, independent of her ADHD (i.e., her ADHD is not *causing* her dyslexia and associated disability).

When an evaluation has been requested as a second opinion, it is important to explain why resulting diagnoses may seem contradictory to what others have suggested. This can be especially important if current findings now confirm diagnoses that have previously been ruled out. For example:

> Diagnostically, Mary's psychosocial history, academic history, teacher report, and neuropsychological profile are all consistent with ADHD, primarily inattentive presentation (often informally referred to as "ADD"). Importantly, the impact of her executive dysfunction was evident across both verbal and visual spatial skills, and therefore, it is clearly *not* secondary to her language difficulties. The reason an ADHD diagnosis has not been made in the past is likely because many of her difficulties were attributed solely to her previously documented language disorder rather than recognizing how her comorbid ADHD contributes to her clinical presentation.

Finally, although the school Team determines whether a child meets the criteria for special education services, when a neuropsychologist believes the results are consistent with a disability, this position should be clearly stated. For example, a report should include comments such as:

Mary's dyslexia is significantly hampering her ability to read grade-level material and contributes to her ongoing delays in spelling and written expression. In academic terms, these findings are best summarized through a language-based learning disability or a specific learning disability (affecting reading, spelling, and writing).

Psychosocial/Educational Risks and Strengths

A medically diagnosed *disorder* is not sufficient to demonstrate a child's disability, but clearly tying a child's academic challenges to that medical disorder can often provide the necessary evidence to do so. Therefore, reports should include statements that specifically address how the child's medical condition and associated cognitive profile will limit his or her academic progress without appropriate intervention. For example:

Following Johnny's gross total resection of the brain tumor, he received both radiation and chemotherapy that subsequently led to bilateral sensorineural hearing loss for which he now wears hearing aids. Johnny's hearing loss and complex medical history will continue to have a negative effect on his language skills, other cognitive processes, and academic achievement, as well as his alertness to stimuli in the educational environment and social development. Johnny was also right-handed premorbidly; however, following his surgery, he has been using his left hand, which has now become his preferred, more dominant hand. Unfortunately, his fine motor dexterity and speed are quite slow, and his handwriting, although legible, is not neat and becomes laborious over time. Consequently, he will have significant difficulties in his ability to keep up with the writing/copying of directions, notes, assignments, etc., particularly as he advances in grade.

It is equally important to describe the child's strengths, resources, and areas of resilience, as these issues will serve to direct intervention as much as the child's areas of weakness and impairments.

Recommendations

Recommendations should be written to reflect what services the child needs to be a successful learner, or to make effective progress, in the LRE. They should be tailored specifically to the child and not written as a generic, extensive list of interventions for any student with the same diagnosis/diagnoses. They should also reflect a realistic appreciation of what the school can and should provide. Reports that advocate for "everything including the kitchen sink" will not be looked upon favorably and may lead the Team to assume that the neuropsychologist does not understand special education laws or the "realities" of a classroom. Additionally, when reports advocate for services that are in excess of the child's needs, or otherwise reach beyond the neuropsychological findings, they unnecessarily set up (or perpetuate) unproductive and contentious interactions between the child's parents and school personnel. In contrast, clinicians should not avoid detailing specific recommendations for accommodations and interventions that a child may need even when a school does not currently have the capacity to provide these services; schools are mandated to meet a child's educational needs, even when that means hiring qualified staff to provide those services (e.g., to provide a child with a one-on-one aide for medical needs or to provide a child with a specialized reading program with a certified specialist).

Finally, in addition to documenting a child's needs for services and accommodations, an IEP will also specify a child's placement. This can range from full inclusion in a regular education setting (with pull-out services), to a substantially separate setting or outside placement. When warranted, reports should provide specific recommendations regarding the child's need for placement. Such reports should be written respectfully, but again in a manner that reflects the expertise and authority of the clinician. Recommendations for placement must also be realistically based on the child's clinical needs and educational history and should include specific reasons that support the clinician's opinion. For example:

> Johnny's acquired bilateral sensorineural hearing loss will markedly limit his ability to process teacher's instructions and lesson plans, as well as his ability to participate in classroom discussions, even with the support of his hearing aids. Consequently, it is this clinician's opinion that he will need to be placed in a language-based classroom setting for children with language and hearing impairments.

Setting the Stage

Schools are expected to serve a diverse population of children, many of whom may have extensive educational needs. They are mandated to provide specialized services for these students, often without sufficient funding to do so. This climate can lead to contentious interactions between schools and parents even when both "sides" genuinely have the child's best interest in mind. It also means that despite a clinician's best efforts, a child may be found ineligible for special education services, or a Team may choose to accept only part of the findings and associated recommendations in the neuropsychological report. When this is considered a viable possibility, reports can be written to "set the stage" to support the parent's ability to advocate for the child's future needs. For example:

> Although Mary has previously been found ineligible for an IEP, she exhibits significant encoding and decoding deficits that will increasingly limit her ability to successfully and efficiently decode grade-level text. Indeed, although Mary has been able to get by to date, she has done so through her exceptionally well-developed verbal skills and memorization. She has also done so at a level that is markedly below her otherwise above-average cognitive abilities. If Mary is not immediately provided with intensive and appropriate services in the next year, she will be at risk for a life-long disability.

COMMON MISTAKES

There are a number of important issues clinicians should avoid when writing pediatric neuropsychological reports. Some of these are detailed below.

Confirmation Bias

One of the most common errors we have seen while reviewing other neuropsychological reports is associated with a tendency to assume test results are "consistent with" a child's medical history (whether it is a seizure disorder, concussion, new medication, etc.). In these instances, the clinician has failed to review the child's history so as to (1) confirm that the medical diagnoses are in fact accurate and/or (2) determine whether another, comorbid etiology is the better explanation for the child's presentation. An effective neuropsychological report does not merely document a child's cognitive strengths and weaknesses and map it onto the reason for referral. Rather, it is the neuropsychologist's role to sort through the psychosocial, emotional, academic, medical, and developmental histories to provide clear and accurate explanations for the source of the child's profile.

Reports Written with Too Much "Jargon"

Although the accurate inclusion of medical and neuropsychological terminology is important to conveying a child's history and presentation, this should not be done at the expense of creating a *readable* document that can be understood and implemented by a child's parents, school Team, and outside (nonmedical) providers.

Reports That Do Not Clearly State (or Make) Diagnoses

Surprisingly, we have read a number of neuropsychological reports that never make diagnostic conclusions. In other cases, diagnoses are implied but not clearly stated (e.g., "the results appear to be consistent with X disorder"). This approach can still support a child's educational needs when he or she is being evaluated for a documented medical condition and when the child's profile can be attributed accurately to that diagnosis. However, in outpatient settings the role of a neuropsychological evaluation is to specifically assist with differential diagnosis. Therefore, a diagnosis should either be clearly stated or, when appropriate, ruled out.

Reports That Include Pages of Recommendations That Are Not Meaningful or Specific to the Child

Recommendations should be written specifically for the child based on his or her history, cognitive profile, and current needs. Although neuropsychologists can certainly rely on a "bank" of recommendations, only those that speak to the child's specific needs should be included in the report. The recommendations should also be modified to reflect the unique characteristics of each patient as appropriate. Failing to do so not only reduces the utility of a neuropsychological report, but can also reduce the neuropsychologist's *credibility*, especially for cases that become involved in the special education legal process (as it gives the appearance that the clinician did not write the report based specifically on that child's needs). Of equal importance, recommendations that are overly broad or general leave the child's Team, parents, and other professionals in the position of having to interpret the neuropsychological recommendations rather than implementing them.

In summary, in order for neuropsychological assessments to be effective within the school setting, reports must reflect an understanding of disability criteria, as well as the rights and limits of the public school setting. For example, the school needs to provide services to allow children to make effective progress, but it is not required to provide the best possible interventions available. Effective and useful reports are concise and accurate, and avoid unexplained medical jargon. The impact of a child's medical condition and cognitive profile on his or her educational performance should be clearly documented in a manner that justifies the need for special education services (if warranted). Finally, recommendations should be concrete, implementable, and clearly tied to the child's needs without being overly inclusive, excessive or unrealistic. They should also be written with an authoritative but respectful tone and should be specific enough to translate into measurable goals and objectives for the child's IEP (if relevant) or clear enough to implement as accommodations in a 504 Plan.

FINAL THOUGHTS REGARDING REPORT WRITING FOR SCHOOL-AGE CHILDREN

For many pediatric neuropsychologists, report writing styles, content, and emphasis will evolve over the course of their careers. One of the best ways to ensure that reports are useful within an academic setting is to participate in Team meetings. These interactions can help to identify what kinds of test results and report writing styles can be inadvertently misinterpreted. This experience can then be used to reevaluate how such information is communicated in future reports. Collaborating with multidisciplinary school professionals as well as child advocates and special education attorneys can further improve one's ability to write reports that are meaningful and useful within a school setting. Some clinicians can become very defensive when asked to include certain phrases or recommendations in their reports during these kinds of interactions. Although it would be unethical and inappropriate to make any changes that the results do not clinically substantiate, it is equally important to realize that clinical language does not always interface with terminology used in legal and educational settings. As the lens of the reader can change the interpretation of one's findings, it is critical to use the correct language to ensure that your results and intentions are accurately understood by all readers. Additionally, pediatric neuropsychologists are not always aware of the many educational options and interventions that may not only be *available* to the child, but that would be warranted to meet his or her needs. These kinds of interactions can, therefore, be an important learning opportunity to better serve one's patients.

For clinicians who are relatively new to writing reports that emphasize academic issues a number of additional useful resources are available. For example, many states have advocacy and educational groups that provide information regarding the special education process (e.g., the Federation for Children with Special needs in Massachusetts: *www.fcsn.org*). In addition, a number of recent publications and websites specifically emphasize the interface of neuropsychology and the school (e.g., Ernst et al., 2008; Hurewitz & Kerr, 2011; *www.wrightslaw.com*).

CASE EXAMPLES

In order to address a wider range of issues for consideration, these case examples do not all come from the same patient. When necessary, relevant background history is provided to orient readers to the case content.

Example 1: Summary and Interpretation of Academic Data (Part 1)

Interpreting the results of academic data involves more than simply summarizing a child's *scores*. This is demonstrated by Annie's scores on the Gray Oral Reading Tests—Fifth Edition (GORT-5), reported in the following table; Annie was 14 years old at the time and in ninth grade.

GORT-5 Test Scores for Annie

	Scaled score	Percentile
Reading Rate	14	91
Reading Accuracy	5	5
Reading Fluency	9	37
Reading Comprehension	10	50

LESS DESIRABLE: DOCTOR A

Annie's reading rate was above average on the GORT-5, and her reading fluency and comprehension were average. However, she exhibited a significant weakness in her reading accuracy, which was below average. Children whose accuracy scores are this low often exhibit significant applied reading deficits that limit their ability to successfully access the curriculum. Although she did perform reasonably well on the comprehension subtest, this only reflects her ability to understand the *context* of the passage despite her many reading errors.

MORE DESIRABLE: DOCTOR B

Annie's performance on the GORT-5 documents an above-average reading rate in the context of below-average reading accuracy. Nevertheless, these results should be interpreted cautiously as her reduced accuracy was secondary to her very quick, impulsive, and inattentive reading style. Notably, when told she should read the passages as quickly but as *well* as she could, Annie anxiously responded, "If I read too fast I don't remember it." However, she then proceeded to sacrifice accuracy for speed. In fact, Annie made a very high number of inattentive/impulsive word substitutions, deletions, and additions (e.g., for words like *and, she, we, you, but, it*). She also skipped small phrases and more meaningful words (e.g., *with it, were, extreme, north*) that limited her ability to

answer many comprehension questions. In contrast, Annie
did not exhibit any actual decoding difficulties and in
fact was able to read many, more complex words (e.g., *synopsis, reveries, tranquility, inoperative*, and *exemption*).

Comment on Academic Data Summary and Interpretation (Part 1)

Dr. A's narrative is technically correct but problematic as it reflects an interpretation of her *scores* without considering the nature of Annie's misreads. This interpretation would likely lead to the recommendation for intensive reading services that she does not require. It could also lead to an unnecessary conflict between Annie's parents and school personnel if the Team determines that she does not qualify for special education services because she is accessing the curriculum successfully.

Example 1: Summary and Interpretation of Academic Data (Part 2)

Now, consider the alternative scenario. In this case, the scores of Mary, a rising fifth-grade student, are within normal limits, but the qualitative interpretation documents more concerning findings. Examples of her reading errors and her reading test results are summarized in the following two tables.

Examples of Mary's Reading Errors

Target word	Read as	Target word	Read as	Nonword	Read as
distance	"distace"	*frequently*	"fregratly"	*clurt*	"curlert"
budge	"bugged"	*provided*	"provoided"	*lirst*	"ilir/liser"
ruin	"rune"	*disguises*	"disgusting"	*smaut*	"smat"
poise	"pose"	*diseases*	"disenses"	*tellitry*	"telli-try"
choir	"chore"	*perilous*	"perligous"	*mudger*	"mud-ger"

Reading Test Scores for Mary

Test/subtest	Standard/scaled score	Percentile
GORT-5—Form A		
Rate	8	25
Accuracy	8	25
Fluency	7	16
Comprehension	9	37
TOWRE-2—Form A		
Sight Word Reading	96	39
Pseudoword Decoding Efficiency	99	47

LESS DESIRABLE: DOCTOR A

Mary's results on standardized testing document low average to average reading skills in all domains assessed. More specifically, her sight word and nonword fluency were both average on the Test of Word Reading Efficiency—Second Edition (TOWRE-2). Mary's reading rate, accuracy, and fluency were in the low average range on the GORT-5, and her reading comprehension was average. These scores also reflect significant gains since her previous assessment.

MORE DESIRABLE: DOCTOR B

Mary has made significant gains in reading since her previous assessment. Indeed, her scores are now within the low average to average range across all areas assessed. However, her error pattern when misreading words and nonwords documents ongoing and concerning difficulties with a number of reading patterns including diphthongs (e.g., *oi, au*) and blends (e.g., *dg*).

Mary also exhibited notable difficulties when reading connected text. For example, she misread words based on context (e.g., she read *it's* instead of *this*) and exhibited additional decoding difficulties with more challenging passages. As the passages became more complex, she also had to work harder to decode words, further limiting her understanding of the story. For instance, although Mary was able to decode some complex words such as *chattered, poisons*, and *chemicals*, it took so much work for her to do so that she was unable to attend to the content of the later (more challenging) passages administered to her.

Comment on Academic Summary and Interpretation (Part 2)

Once again, Dr. A's interpretation of the scores is accurate, but it fails to reflect the full constellation of Mary's performance and associated needs. In this case, a strict interpretation of the scores limits the clinician and the child's school Team from recognizing her ongoing reading challenges that are in fact consistent with dyslexia. This presentation is not uncommon in younger children with partially remediated reading disorders and is therefore important for the neuropsychologist to both recognize and highlight to ensure the child receives the appropriate services for his or her associated disability.

Example 2: Summarizing Data

Pediatric neuropsychologists make diagnoses based on an integrated interpretation of the child's comprehensive history, testing results, and *behavioral* approach to the assessment process. At times, this leads to diagnostic conclusions that may not be overtly evident to readers who skip the text and look only at the summary of test scores. This example demonstrates how to provide an unambiguous interpretation of data when results reflect a discrepancy between verbal and nonverbal/visual–spatial skills:

LESS DESIRABLE: DOCTOR A

Mike's overall cognitive ability is in the average to high average range. However, testing results also reflect a discrepancy between his average to high average performance on language-based tasks and his low average to average performance on visual-based tasks. Mike also exhibited clear difficulties with executive dysfunction, including sustained mental effort, attention, impulsivity, organization, and distractibility.

MORE DESIRABLE: DOCTOR B

In summary, Mike's overall cognitive ability is in the average to high average range, as are language-based skills. His performance on visual-based tasks is *relatively* weaker, falling primarily in the low average to average range. However, this variability was very clearly secondary to Mike's significant difficulties with executive functions. That is, despite his well-developed cognitive abilities, Mike has difficulties exhibiting his full cognitive abilities on a daily basis owing to his significant impairments in sustained mental effort, attention, impulsivity, organization, and distractibility. Consequently, the apparent split between his language and visual spatial domains is secondary to his executive dysfunction rather than a nonverbal learning disorder (NVLD). Notably, Mike's strong capacity to understand non-verbal social cues and empathize with others is also not consistent with this diagnosis.

Comment on Summarizing Data

Dr. A's interpretation of the data is again *technically* correct. However, even if Dr. A has ruled out an NVLD in his or her mind, without explicitly doing so in the report other readers may assume that Dr. A failed to recognize what is otherwise an "obvious" diagnosis. This could lead to a significant misunderstanding regarding the child's needs as well as unnecessary and even inappropriate school interventions. For example, Mike might be placed in a social skills group to support his capacity to understand nonverbal social cues even though this is already a strength of his.

Example 3: Recommendations for Placement

LESS DESIRABLE: DOCTOR A

Joe's test results document a severe language-based learning disability that is significantly limiting his ability to access the curriculum. Although he has been provided with special education services, they have clearly been insufficient in supporting his needs. Consequently, Joe should be placed at the XX School without delay. As such, his parents have been encouraged to share this report with his school Team to discuss these findings and associated recommendations as soon as possible.

MORE DESIRABLE: DOCTOR B

Given the combined impact of Joe's multiple disabilities, his Team will need to consider his academic placement very carefully. Although he is capable of understanding, following, and learning most grade-level content, he will continue to need considerably more scaffolding, support, and organizational structure than is typically provided in a regular classroom setting. Without ongoing and specialized support services, Joe will exhibit increasing difficulties in successfully accessing the curriculum, and the gap between him and his same-age peers will continue to grow. Although he is already attending a substantially separate program, it is unclear from his IEP whether his pull-out services are being provided in a language-based program. If they are not, it is recommended that Joe be placed in a language-based program that is capable of supporting his disabilities in all academic courses while still teaching to his otherwise intact cognitive abilities. This classroom should have a high teacher: student ratio (e.g., no less than one teacher for every four to five students) to allow for the frequent repetition, reframing, and supportive education that Joe needs to learn and automatize new concepts. Given Joe's anxiety, it will be especially important that he not be placed with children who are exhibiting behavioral difficulties within the classroom, as their acting-out behaviors and/ or the necessary interventions and redirections to keep them on task will almost certainly exacerbate Joe's own anxiety symptomatology. Notably, if Joe has already been attending a language-based program, these results suggest rather robustly that this program is not meeting his needs. Consequently, consideration for an alternative and/ or outside placement (such as the XX or YY School) would be warranted.

Comment on Recommendations for Placement

Dr. A's recommendation for placement contains many errors, including a lack of appreciation or awareness of what Joe has received to date (per Dr. B's added commentary). This will almost certainly reduce Dr. A's credibility in the eyes of the school Team, which will further reduce the likelihood that his findings and/or recommendations will be accepted. Dr. A's authoritarian recommendation also fails to reflect his awareness of the Team process and the fact that an outside evaluator is not in a position to independently make placement decisions (i.e., he fails to maintain a balance between respectful deference and clinical authority). Demanding a specific placement rather than a description of Joe's programming needs may further alienate school personnel, and may also inadvertently limit the child's options if there are other appropriate settings for his needs. This approach can also unnecessarily increase tension between Joe's parents and school if the Team disagrees with Dr. A's assertions. In contrast, Dr. B acknowledges that Joe's needs still might be met by his school *if* he has not already been placed in a language-based program as described in the report. No specific schools are mandated for placement, although several are recommended, and more importantly a description of his specific needs is provided. This would allow the school Team to agree upon Joe's academic needs and the setting even if they believe that XX School is not the correct placement for him.

ABRIDGED SAMPLE NEUROPSYCHOLOGICAL REPORT

The sample report in Appendix 2.1 (pp. 54–61) summarizes the neuropsychological assessment of Joe Bruin, a 7-year, 8-month-old boy with a history of articulation delays, attentional difficulties, and anxiety. Joe was referred for this neuropsychological assessment by his pediatrician, Community Doctor, MD, to document his neurocognitive strengths and weaknesses, assist with differential diagnoses, and provide recommendations for intervention. This is an abridged report, which includes the summary of test results, diagnostic considerations, and summary of the child's academic and social risks. It also includes *some*, but not all, of the academic recommendations that might be included in a typical report. Notably, a separate section relating to interventions outside of school, including his emotional adjustment, is not included here but would be in an actual report. This report illustrates many of the technical aspects described above, including those relating to data interpretation, differential diagnoses, recommendations, and tone.

REFERENCES

Ahearn, E. M. (2008). State eligibility requirements for special education. National Association of State Directors of Special Education. Retrieved November 15, 2014, from *www.nasdse.org*.

Baron, I. S. (2004). *Neuropsychological evaluation of the child*. New York: Oxford University Press.

Bernstein, J. A. (2000). Developmental neuropsychological assessment. In K. O. Yeates, M. D. Ris, & H. G. Taylor (Eds.), *Pediatric neuropsychology: Research, theory, and practice* (pp. 405–438). New York: Guilford Press.

Blaskewitz, N., Merten, T., & Kathmann, N. (2008). Performance of children on symptom validity tests: TOMM, MSVT, and FIT. *Archives of Clinical Neuropsychology, 23*, 379–391.

Bush, S. S., Ruff, R. M., Troster, A. I., Barth, J. T., Koffler, S. P., Pliskin, N. H., et al. (2005). Symptom validity assessment: Practice issues and medical necessity NAN policy and planning committee. *Archives of Clinical Neuropsychology, 20*, 419–426.

Carone, D. (2013). Mild traumatic brain injury diagnosis: Principles and pitfalls. *NAN Bulletin, 27*, 11–15.

Donders, J., & Kirkwood, M. W. (2013). Symptom validity assessment with special populations. In D. A. Carone & S. S. Bush (Eds.), In *Mild traumatic brain injury: System validity assessment and malingering* (pp. 399–410). New York: Springer.

Ernst, W. J., Pelletier, S. L. F., & Simpson, G. (2008). Neuropsychological consultation with school personnel: What clinical neuropsychologists need to know. *The Clinical Neuropsychologist, 22*, 953–976.

Fletcher, J. M., Coulter, W. A., Reschly, D. J., & Vaughn, S. (2004). Alternative approaches to the definition and identification of learning disabilities: Some questions and answers. *Annals of Dyslexia, 54*, 304–331.

Heilbronner, R. L., Sweet, J. J., Morgan, J. E., Larrabee, G. J., Millis, S. R., & Conference Participants. (2009). American academy of clinical neuropsychology consensus conference statement on the neuropsychological assessment of effort, response bias, and malingering. *The Clinical Neuropsychologist, 23,* 1093–1129.

Hurewitz, F., & Kerr, S. (2011). The role of the independent neuropsychologist in special education. *The Clinical Neuropsychologist, 25,* 1058–1074.

Individuals with Disabilities Education Act (PL No. 101-476), § 20 U.S.C. Chapter 33. Amended by PL No. 105-17 in June 1997. Regulations appear at 34 C.F.R. Part 300. Retrieved November 15, 2014, from *www.gpo.gov/fdsys/granule/STATUTE-111/STATUTE-111-Pg37/content-detail.html.*

Individuals with Disabilities Education Improvement Act. (2004). United States Department of Education. Retrieved from *http://idea.ed.gov/explore/view/p/%2Croot%2Cstatute%2C.*

Loring, D. W., Hermann, B. P., & Cohen, M. Y. (2010). Neuropsychological advocacy and epilepsy. *The Clinical Neuropsychologist, 24,* 417–428.

Rehabilitation Act of 1973, 29 U.S.C. § 794. Retrieved November 15, 2014, from *www2.ed.gov/policy/speced/reg/narrative.html.*

Abridged Sample Neuropsychological Report for Joe Bruin

Impressions and Recommendations

Joe's overall cognitive ability is in the average to above average range. However, his ability to demonstrate these skills is limited by his executive dysfunction (e.g., difficulties with attention, sustained mental effort, working memory, and cognitive impulsivity). Joe also exhibits clear difficulties with behavioral regulation. Within this context, language and nonverbal/visual-spatial skills were equally developed, falling in the average to above average range; relative weaknesses across tests from both domains were secondary to his executive dysfunction rather than actual cognitive difficulties. Learning and memory were also very clearly vulnerable to difficulties with sustained attention as well as relative weakness with organization. Joe learns best when information is intrinsically organized for him (e.g., for stories) and when it is not presented in a way that taxes his attentional abilities. Finally, parent report, teacher report, and psychosocial history all highlight significant anxiety associated with performance-based fears, and a need for predictability, consistency, and a reliance on routines. Additionally, Joe acknowledged a tendency to worry about the safety of things he loves.

Academically, mathematic computation is vulnerable to inattentive/impulsive errors but still falls in the high end of the average range. Reading, spelling, and written expression are more variable, with performances falling in the below average to low average range. Notably, even Joe's low average scores reflect performances that are well below cognitive expectations. Additionally, a qualitative review of Joe's errors suggests greater difficulties than his scores might otherwise indicate. More specifically, reading errors were secondary to (1) ongoing difficulties with decoding, including an inability to accurately and/or consistently read consonant blends or vowel teams, or to decode using any strategy beyond slavishly sounding out each letter; (2) difficulties correctly blending letter sounds even when he did decode them accurately; (3) ongoing letter confusion (e.g., for b/p/d); (4) a tendency to impulsively guess words based on their initial few letters or the context of the passage; and (5) a vulnerability for making inattentive/impulsive insertions/deletions and substitutions of smaller words and suffixes, especially when reading easier text. Joe's reading fluency was also slow and labored despite his vulnerability for impulsive errors, and his spelling reflects a lack of awareness of many common rules, as well as letter confusion (e.g., v/w). Not surprisingly, written expression was also markedly limited by spelling challenges.

Diagnostically, Joe's psychosocial and academic history is consistent with attention-deficit/hyperactivity disorder (ADHD). His behavioral presentation and neuropsychological profile are also consistent with this diagnosis, as testing variability was primarily related to his deficits in executive functioning, and Joe was especially behaviorally dysregulated throughout this assessment. Test results are also consistent with dyslexia (i.e., a specific learning disorder with impairment in reading). Joe is unable to decode novel words (and nonwords) quickly or accurately, and he continues to present with a below-average naming speed (a skill set that is tightly correlated with reading ability). He also exhibits clear difficulties with encoding (i.e., spelling) and written expression that are best captured through a specific learning disorder with impairment in written expression. The challenges associated with both learning disorders area are best described from an academic perspective through a language-based learning disability or a specific learning disability (affecting reading, spelling, and written expression) that will warrant ongoing specialized services.

However, Joe's ADHD and learning disorders/disabilities are not sufficient to explain his full presentation. He also presents with anxiety symptoms relating to safety and performance-based fears, as well as a strong need for order, routine, and predictability. These symptoms are best captured through the comorbid presentation of generalized anxiety disorder and social anxiety disorder. Joe also presents with obsessive-compulsive traits, but they do not currently meet the threshold for formal diagnosis. Although seemingly counterintuitive, in some ways, his anxiety has actually contributed to clear *strengths*. For example, *when he is attentive*, Joe can be very perceptive about how others are thinking or feeling, which helps him to connect with his friends and maintain these relationships. Because it is so important for Joe to be seen as a "good kid," he also exerts a great deal of effort to hide his challenges from others, at least when he can. His anxiety also helps to drive him to succeed, even though it requires a considerably higher amount of effort than might be expected for others. Nonetheless, his anxiety also contributes to his inability to tolerate frustration or transitions easily, as well as his reliance on routines. Additionally, Joe is likely experiencing some degree of anxiety at all times, especially when he is at school, given the inherent evaluative process in an academic setting. Joe's current teachers appear to have a solid understanding of how he can struggle in this domain. However, it is important to note for future teachers that Joe is not being "oppositional" if he repeatedly engages in unwanted behaviors even after redirection; teachers will need to understand that this is due to his difficulties with behavioral dysregulation, attention, and sustained mental effort (which are not entirely under his control). Thinking about Joe as an oppositional child will inadvertently lead teachers to implement behavioral plans that will actually exacerbate rather than support his emotional and behavioral difficulties.

Educational Risks

When children have both ADHD and an anxiety disorder, the presentation of their symptoms can be confusing, and even misleading. For this reason, it is helpful to further explore how these two characteristics may present. For example, although Joe does have perfectionistic tendencies, he will often work quickly, inattentively, and impulsively when faced with tasks he feels are well within his ability level. However, when task complexity increases, he has greater difficulties remaining on task. At other times, Joe may be very quick to give up on tasks if he is feeling uncertain of his ability to perform "well" and when his difficulties with sustained mental effort make it too challenging for him to exert himself to find the answer. Because of his ADHD, Joe can also find it challenging to attend to, understand, and retain orally presented information, which in turn limits his ability to efficiently encode new information and to access it when he needs to share his knowledge with others.

Joe's performance-based anxiety and associated cautious approach to tasks can exacerbate these difficulties and further reduce his output. For example, it places him at risk for decreased "comprehension skills," as Joe may be prone to taking a more concrete and even rigid approach to interpreting directions. Similarly, his anxiety may limit him from accurately drawing inferences, especially when he has no way of confirming that his answers are correct. This ambiguity can be especially distressing for children like Joe and contributes to his reluctance to answer questions or initiate tasks even when he is more than capable of providing accurate responses. As he progresses in school, Joe will also be at risk for overthinking problems and ruminating on possible options, which can further slow down his output. However, on other occasions he will be at risk for reading directions too quickly or skipping them altogether, further reducing his ability to follow written instructions accurately. In other words, he will be at risk for misreading directions (or text), reading directions too quickly, and/or putting too much emphasis on being "exactly right," which may lead him to overinterpret their meaning. Consequently, he might find himself answering the "wrong" questions and/or requiring extra time in order to demonstrate his range of knowledge.

More generally, Joe's difficulties with sustained mental effort and attention are limiting his ability to follow multiple step directions and to complete tasks within an expected time frame. He may be prone to giving up on tasks even when they are well within his cognitive ability because it takes so much *work* (or mental effort) for him to finish them. Joe will also have greater difficulties learning through "listening" rather than "doing." In other words, unless lessons have an applied hands-on component and he is given some degree of individualized assistance, he will find himself unable to consistently attend to, understand, and automatize new skills.

Before discussing his other academic risks, it should be acknowledged and emphasized that Joe's school recognized his language-based learning disability at a very young age and has been providing an increasing level of services over the past two years. However, despite these supports, Joe continues to exhibit very concerning deficits in reading accuracy and fluency, as well as deficits in encoding/spelling and written expression. Although he has been making some progress, the gap between his abilities and those of his same-aged peers has increased over time (i.e., his progress has not followed the same rate as that of his classmates). Consequently, as he prepares to enter third grade, these deficits will increasingly limit his ability to successfully and independently read and write at his grade level and/or cognitive ability. Consequently, these results indicate that Joe requires an increase in the intensity and frequency of his language-based intervention. Without such services, his disabilities will significantly limit him from demonstrating his knowledge through written expression because of difficulties he has in *reading his own responses* so as to edit, correct, and improve upon his work. His disabilities will also significantly limit his ability to adequately and efficiently understand written directions, let alone read or learn from textbooks or other written resources. He will also be at similar risk for difficulties even when completing "nonverbal" tasks such as math or science when there is an emphasis on word problems or novel vocabulary.

Strengths and Recommendations

Strengths

Fortunately, Joe has *many* factors working in his favor. In particular, most of his cognitive abilities are well within the average to above-average range. He is also a very sweet and endearing boy who is motivated to please others, and he can work tenaciously when he is able to sustain his attention and mental effort and/or when he is not feeling emotionally over-whelmed. His teachers should be able to draw on these resources to promote his school progress. Joe's psychosocial adjustment will also continue to be fostered by the ongoing support of his family, teachers, and health care providers.

Ironically, it is because of these strengths that Joe may confuse some people in an academic setting. In particular, teachers and other caretakers should realize that his eager-ness to please others will often mask his cognitive weaknesses, and he will actively attempt to hide his anxiety and learn-ing difficulties whenever he can (as it is his goal to look as "normal" as possible). On some occasions (and as his teachers have already recognized), he may have difficulties completing work because he is feeling emotionally overwhelmed. However, at other times his challenges may be due to his difficulties with attention and sustained mental effort. At other times, he may be having difficulties understanding how to approach and/or organize the task at hand. Thus, in those instances when he appears to not be performing up to his potential, teachers will want to carefully consider the *source* of his problems and determine whether he is having problems because of his (1) ADHD and executive dysfunction (2) reduced tolerance for frustration and associated tendency to become emotionally overwhelmed; or (3) compulsive need to manage his environment before he can follow directions or classroom expectations.

Recommendations

The combined impact of Joe's ADHD, anxiety disorders, and language-based learning disability contributes to a *signifi-cant disparity* in his ability to independently access the cur-riculum, make effective progress, and perform to his potential given his otherwise strong cognitive skills. He should continue to qualify for services under his current specific learning disability, as well as through the Health Impairment (ADHD), and Emotional Impairment (anxiety) designations. Notably, research shows that children who do not receive appropriate *remediation* for reading by fourth grade are likely to exhibit some degree of reading disability throughout their lifetime. Consequently, the next two years will be critical in ensuring that Joe receives the education he needs to succeed. Although it is possible that he can make the necessary gains in his current setting, with an increase in targeted services, his school Team will need to monitor his progress closely. If he does not begin to close the gap between himself and his peers in the next year, he will require placement in a substantially separate, specialized language-based program that can support Joe's language-based disability while simultaneously allowing him to access grade-level curriculum. This placement should include a high teacher:student ratio that focuses on his reading and writing skills in all academic classes and that is designed to serve children with similar cognitive profiles (i.e., children with average to above-average cognitive abilities) and "typical" social skills, but who also have language-based learning disabilities. Given these concerns, I encourage Joe's parents to share this report with his school and recommend that his Team incorporate the following recommendations into his IEP:

1. Ongoing, specialized reading intervention is clearly warranted, as is associated support in encoding/spelling and written expression. This intervention should be provided daily and include at least 60 minutes of specialized instructional time with no more than three children *who are in need of the same level of instruction*. If it is not already, this intervention should be based on an empirically based, multisensory reading program (such as Wilson or Orton-Gillingham) that is provided by an instructor who is fully certified in the program being implemented. Notably, he should <u>not</u> be taught using an intervention program that encourages (and/or requires) "guessing" at words based on context or pictures, as he is already attempting to do this and it is leading to significant misreads. Benchmark goals should be updated to specifically indicate the sounds that he will be expected to master (which should be developed based on the reading program materials). He will also require reading fluency goals that specify his reading rate (in words correct per minute) based on a specifically stated text level so as to clearly monitor his progress.

2. Joe's spelling goals and intervention will need to be more systematically spelled out in his IEP. Specific sound patterns that he is expected to learn should be outlined and should map onto the reading interventions he is receiving (i.e., he should be working on similar sounds in both reading and spelling interventions whenever possible).

3. Joe experiences significant difficulties with attention and sustained mental effort. He is also easily distracted by both his own thoughts and external stimuli. Therefore, he should continue to be provided with preferential seating as a means of helping him focus better in the classroom setting. In particular, he should sit in a part of the room that will limit distractions (either from friends, windows, or other "engaging" interests) and increase the likelihood that he will attend to the instructor. Care should also be taken to ensure that he is

not sitting near other children who will distract him through their own behavioral dysregulation.

4. Even more than other children his age, Joe will also require the use of "hands-on" activities that promote active participation. When he does work independently, he will need close monitoring and frequent, discrete prompting to ensure that he is staying on task.

5. Joe will not always attend to, remember, and therefore understand and/or follow, classroom instructions. At times, he may be reluctant to admit his confusion to his teacher or to ask for clarification because he does not want to look "bad" or open himself up for possible criticism. Consequently, his teacher should repeat directions and/or provide written instructions (at his reading level) for his reference. Joe will also be more likely to remember information if it is presented with direct ties to already familiar material.

6. Teachers should continue to allow Joe to take short breaks to address attentional difficulties. This may need to be done both *during* and between activities. For example, they could allow him to collect papers or pass out handouts, or engage in other activities that allow him to move around in class while working on academic tasks. Some schools have developed "gas stations" where children are able to engage in motor tasks to improve their focus. Ongoing consultation with his school's OT may be useful to create such a station in his classroom if this is possible. However, care should be taken to ensure that any use of fidget toys does not inadvertently lead to further distraction.

7. Joe requires the physical, emotional, and cognitive release provided by recess and gym classes even more than most of his peers. These opportunities to have free time and to burn off extra energy should *never* be removed as part of a behavior plan or intervention (e.g., if he forgets to complete homework). To my knowledge, this has not yet happened to him, but it is worth highlighting given his significant need to have downtime built into his day.

8. As academic demands increase, Joe's ADHD and associated executive dysfunction will place him at increasing risk for difficulties with written output, which will be exacerbated by his language-based learning disability. For example, he will find it challenging to develop the content of his stories while simultaneously focusing on rules for spelling, punctuation, and struggling with his word-finding difficulties. Joe's difficulties with organized verbal output will also impact his ability to write at a level that is otherwise commensurate with his level of verbal knowledge. Consequently, Joe should be taught a

"process" approach to writing whereby he learns to brainstorm ideas on a topic, organizes these ideas in an outline, writes an initial draft using this outline, and then performs multiple edits (e.g., initially for organization and content, then for spelling, then grammar, etc.). While these skills are generally taught in elementary school settings, it will be especially important for Joe to *automatize* the process so that he has more cognitive "energy" left to help him compensate for his executive dysfunction. This will require specialized instruction and associated IEP goals to monitor his progress.

9. Joe's *ability* to make inferences is often better than his actual performance on such tasks. This is related, at least in part, to his anxiety especially around ambiguous or open ended questions and tasks and putting himself "on the line." Consequently, he should be taught specific strategies to pull out relevant information out of readings and lectures and to summarize the material *in his own words*. This will also help him to gain more confidence in his ability to accurately make inferences from texts and will improve his overall reading comprehension skills.

CHAPTER 3

Neuropsychological Evaluation of the Medically Complex Child

Marsha Vasserman
Ida Sue Baron

Children with medically complex conditions present unique challenges to the many professionals who provide them direct and personalized care. The challenges encountered in their treatment regimen often extend well beyond the acute stages of illness to long-term effects related to psychosocial development, cognitive development, educational accomplishment, and ultimately occupational attainment. At each stage across varied settings, pediatric neuropsychologists have specific opportunities to evaluate and treat children and adolescents experiencing a complex medical course. However, optimal consultation in service of the child, family, and treatment team is dependent on the specific medical event and context in which consultation is requested. Medical care and technological advances have also had an impact on the current landscape of care, and lifesaving treatments and procedures are in continuous development. Medical and psychological research substantially increased rates of survival for several conditions that once were terminal and others that were so severe as to not warrant concern about future outcome. Yet, these advances have also resulted in greater disease burden and an increased focus on promoting optimal quality of life and functional outcomes. Furthermore, as the probability of mortality lessens and the likelihood of morbidity increases for a longer lifespan, the role of pediatric neuropsychologists has also shifted to include transition planning from childhood to adolescence and young adulthood (i.e., to a lifespan model), as well as rehabilitative and cognitive therapies.

In this chapter we highlight the importance of the context in which the assessment takes place (e.g., inpatient vs. outpatient; intensive care unit [ICU] vs. standard room) and focus on the targeted recipients of the results of a neuropsychological evaluation. These circumstances guide the assessment methods selected, as well as content and form of an intended thorough, yet succinct and pragmatic, evaluation report. Our discussion is specific to the evaluation of children with medically complex conditions, with additional focus on the implications of such a dire circumstance as an acute, perhaps life-threatening, illness or sudden severe injury with long-term implications for the family and caregivers. We have three main aims. First, in advance of any discussion of evaluation and report preparation for children with medically complex needs, it is useful to review what is meant by medical complexity. Second, we review specific assessment, family and long-term prognostic issues that are typically encountered in serving this special population. Third, we conclude with principal considerations and suggestions when generating written reports regarding the patient's neuro-psychological status, providing examples of how to effectively communicate evaluation results in writing for those caring for the medically complex patient.

COMPLEX MEDICAL CONDITIONS

Definitions of medical complexity have been inconsistent. To address this problem, Cohen et al. (2011) proposed a definition of medical complexity that identified four components. First, children with a medically complex condition have substantial needs that can include medical care, specialized therapeutic services, and special education needs. Together, these needs exert important influences on the family, resources, and time. Second, children with a medically complex condition have chronic conditions that are severe and/or result in medical fragility. Third, children with a medically complex condition experience functional limitations that require assistance from a wide range of professionals. Lastly, these cases inevitably involve high health care utilization.

Acceptance of this four-part definition omits many chronic conditions from consideration as medically complex. For example, a child born with a ventricular septal defect that is now asymptomatic, or well-managed, would not have a medically complex condition under this definition, even though the medical condition may become life threatening or at some future time require chronic medical care. In contrast, a teenager with longstanding, uncontrolled insulin-dependent diabetes mellitus who has peripheral neuropathy and vision loss would meet this definition of medical complexity. Thus, it is important to consider current and predicted associated functional limitations and health care impact, and not just the condition and its chronicity. Although Cohen et al. (2011) provide a comprehensive and inclusive definition, other definitions have also been proposed. In fact, because of the multiple methods of defining medical complexity and chronicity of disease, prevalence research in these populations has often been inconsistent. Some definitions have focused on the chronicity of illness, whereas others have emphasized the functional impact of the medical condition (Van der Lee, Mokkink, Grootenhuis, Heymans, & Offringa, 2007).

In this chapter, we apply the term "medically complex" to children whose illnesses are chronic, persistent, or predicted to last longer than one year, (Stein, Bauman, Westbrook, Coupey, & Ireys, 1993); result in limitation of function; and, require that treatment providers provide acute or long-term medical care and interventions. A common, important, but limiting issue that often arises when evaluating children with medically complex conditions is that there is often an initial lack of clarity regarding the symptom presentation and appropriate treatment course. Symptoms may result from multiple alternative etiologies and the treatment course may differ depending on which clinician is conducting the evaluation and recommending treatment strategies. Thus, it often becomes the responsibility of the neuropsychologist to obtain comprehensive records and integrate this diverse information from multiple sources, with the intent that this thorough review will disambiguate the commonly contradictory information that is perplexing to the child and family. The neuropsychologist's ability to formulate a cohesive and meaningful summation based on disparate sources of information is a critical role in these complex circumstances.

Another important issue is that available treatments for medically complex illnesses may place a heavy cognitive burden on the child, which in a context of concerns about medical management is often not fully appreciated by either the medical team or family. This burden is often not given its due significance by the medical community in the circumstances of a life-threatening condition when survival is the primary treatment goal. The neuropsychologist then has an important responsibility to identify and highlight the combined effects of these many variables on the child's current functioning. Ideally, the neuropsychologist will be able to anticipate and prognosticate for the medical team and family about the expected immediate developmental course, as well as any long-term effects that might persist beyond the acute period, absent appropriate intervention. Identifying cognitive deficits that may interfere with one's ability to follow medical regimens (e.g., memory deficits that may lead to missed medication doses) is also necessary in order to develop proper strategies to increase treatment compliance.

The family faces enormous hurdles when a child has a medically complex condition. First and foremost, family members must begin the process of understanding myriad facts about a disease and its treatment regimen with which they have little familiarity. Simultaneously, they experience the enormity of what it means to have a critically ill child and the accompanying range of emotions that may adversely affect their ability to make the best decisions in service of their child's health and welfare. Moreover, parents and the ill child's siblings often differ in how they cope with and manage stress (Goldbeck, 2001; Knafl & Zoeller, 2000). Family functioning can be expected to be responsive to these individual coping strategies, the short- and long-term effects of prolonged treatment regimens, and the ill child's resultant health and psychological outcomes (Shudy et al., 2006).

Second, an added family burden is how to understand the information provided by multiple specialists encountered in the course of disease diagnosis and treatment. Families struggle when inconsistent prognoses are conveyed by the diverse providers caring for their child (Aitken, Mele, & Barrett, 2004). These conflicting messages have the potential to cause confusion and decrease trust in the clinical team. A major source of parental stress relates to the effort to ensure informational continuity between providers and systems. In essence, parents find they have to become a conduit of informational exchange, even though they may have limited understanding of the information they are relaying (Miller et al., 2009). A major source of sibling stress may relate to perceived ineffectiveness in making their sibling healthy again, guilt that they somehow contributed to the unfortunate circumstance, or even jealousy over parental attention being directed toward the ill sibling for an extended time. Provider continuity across disciplines is a particularly important supportive measure for patients and families. Furthermore, the potential for a breakdown in informational continuity is not solely confined to the medical setting but is also common in the communications between medical and educational personnel (Lash & Scarpino, 1993; Miller et al., 2009).

Third, families with medically complex children often experience a significant financial burden. Financial obligations added to an already heightened emotional state can be both draining and devastating, weakening the family's coping abilities while also absorbing carefully saved resources. Further, effective and approved treatments for an illness may be in limited supply, expensive, and not covered by insurance, or exclusively experimental and not accessible except with compassionate care dispensation by a pharmaceutical firm. A risk of relapse and of a need for further treatment following initial treatment is a further burden.

Finally, for certain conditions, the impact of the illness on quality of life and cognitive functioning is so great that parents must rethink their personal expectations for their child's future functioning. For others, the entire family structure must grasp the hard realities of end-of-life care. Thus, the role of the neuropsychologist extends beyond that of assessment to a more nuanced role in recommendations related to the child's treatment, psychotherapeutic and educational needs, and for the multiplicity of family issues that ensue.

ASSESSMENT ISSUES

In pediatric neuropsychology, it is essential to have a developmental framework that is responsive to salient maturational factors. For a child with a medically complex illness, this framework should consider the child's chronological age, current acquisition of developmental milestones, the expected future trajectory consequent to the medical insult, the chronological age at onset of the disorder, and the presence of psychological consequences (Baron, 2004; Spevack, 2011). Cultural factors, educational experience, as well as family dynamics and influential sociodemographic factors, also must be considered. However, several additional confounds arise for children with medically complex conditions owing to their different experiences and environmental exposures compared with their typically developing peers. For example, a child undergoing an extended treatment protocol for acute lymphocytic leukemia is likely to spend prolonged periods in the hospital, which directly impacts the child's educational experiences and opportunities (a cognitive and educational impact) (Barrera, Shaw, Speechley, Maunsell, & Pogany, 2005) and results in fewer adaptive social experiences (Schultz et al., 2007).

Concerns about test reliability and validity in the assessment of a child with a complex medical condition arise across both inpatient and outpatient settings. As described by Baron (2004), inpatient test sessions often have inherent obstacles that interfere with the aim of assessment of optimal performance across multiple domains of function. In contrast with assessments conducted with a scheduled outpatient visit, an assessment of a hospitalized child may have to be conducted in an environment inconsistent with recommendations for standardized testing. The hospital room may be noisy or nonprivate and therefore subject to distractions related to the care of others, and there is a high likelihood of interruptions by medical staff for scheduled routine care of the patient. A brief screening in a limited number of domains, rather than comprehensive testing across all domains, may be all that can be completed at any one time. Thus, testing may require multiple brief sessions, each presenting confounds to valid assessment.

Because the inpatient setting may provide limited access to family members, and because parents must adjust their hospital visits around their work schedule and family responsibilities, an opportunity for parental interview may not be possible on the assessment day. Moreover, patient history may still be incompletely noted in medical records, limiting a full understanding of all relevant circumstances. In the outpatient setting, the examiner has greater control over the environment and an enhanced ability to establish rapport and to sample a wider variety of cognitive functions. However, even in the outpatient testing environment, the clinical needs of a medically complex child may interrupt testing (e.g., for catheterization, nutritional breaks, or emptying of a colostomy bag).

Further obstacles to valid assessment include complications that occur during an assessment, such as an epileptic seizure, which may delay test completion or necessitate discontinuation of testing. Additionally, in either an inpatient or outpatient setting, the child's internal states, such as the experience of fatigue, anxiety, fear, or pain, may further complicate the evaluative process. Effects of polymedication (e.g., steroids, narcotics, psychiatric medications), can also interfere with performance on cognitive tasks (Heyer et al., 2000; Waber et al., 2000; Warrington & Bostwick, 2006). Together, these many confounds to reliable and valid assessment must be understood, recognized, and adjusted to by a flexible and sensitive examiner.

Flexibility in test selection, based on behavioral observations, guided by the child's emotional and physical state, and with knowledge of the likeliest functions that could be affected by the disorder, is imperative (Bellinger & Newburger, 2013). Although obtaining valid information in the absence of standardized procedures may be necessitated, the integrity of the process through use of standardized test procedures is not diminished. For example, when a child has a sensorineural (e.g., vision or hearing) impairment and/or physical disability (e.g., cerebral palsy diagnosis) tests must often be adapted so that the child's true functional abilities can be understood (Warschausky, Kaufman, & Felix, 2013). Use of nonstandardized tests or of adapted methods of course comes with the added obligation to recognize that their use becomes a threat to validity, and these adjustments should be acknowledged in the prepared report.

Finally, parents familiar with the roles of multiple providers involved in their child's care may not be familiar with the special role of the neuropsychologist or with the potential benefits of a neuropsychological evaluation. Families already overwhelmed by multiple caretakers may resist yet another professional's involvement, especially if they are uncertain as to the purpose and aims of the assessment (Stark et al., 2014). For example, if a family of a child with a chronic heart condition has had the same treatment team of surgeons and cardiologists for many years before a neuropsychological consultation is requested, the family may not understand the reason for referral or how a chronic heart condition may affect cognitive functioning (Marino et al., 2012). For such families, cognitive function may not be a priority. Thus, a recommendation to obtain such consultation may not be pursued until the goals of the evaluation are explained. Parents who were once told that their child may not survive may minimize or overlook their child's cognitive deficits. In such cases, it may be helpful to consult with the treatment team to identify a team member most trusted by the family who can provide education about how the assessment may improve care and outcome. Validating the family's experience, concerns, and misgivings, in conjunction with psychoeducation about the assessment process, can also help gain family trust and agreement.

FAMILY ISSUES

It is well established that a child's illness can exacerbate underlying family dysfunction. A chronically ill child places great strain on familial relationships, and while some individuals demonstrate resilience and good coping skills, others do not have, or cannot access, the same psychological resources (Heiman, 2002; Raina et al., 2005). Social support, access to helpful resources and interventions, as well as the temperament and personality of the child, have been shown to have an impact on family functioning (Goldbeck, 2001; Heiman, 2002; Raina et al., 2005). Parents may be expected to have different reactions to their child's illness, or they may express similar feelings through contrasting methods of dealing with personal stress. It is also well established that a child's complex medical illness or injury will often lead to parental conflict, and even increase the likelihood of separation and divorce (Goldbeck, 2001), putting further strains on an already damaged family structure. In addition, family functioning has been shown to correlate with treatment compliance more generally. As mentioned above, parents of a child with a life-threatening illness may be less likely to value cognitive assessment, and parental resistance may result in noncompliance with referral, poor or inconsistent follow-up, or dismissal of findings as irrelevant.

Because parents are often unaware of available resources and educational options, they rely on the treatment team to help guide their decisions about their child's medical care and also about other aspects of their now-changed lives. Even when they are aware of potential resources, their ability to access these services may be perceived as overwhelming or of limited utility. In such cases, the neuropsychologist has an opportunity to provide a bridge for families to access required resources. It is important to work with the case manager and others involved in the child's care to help connect families to such appropriate resources and professionals. For example, many children with medically complex illness are entitled to financial support, although families may be unaware of the availability of this support. Similarly, children are entitled to public education until age 21, yet this critical information is unknown to many families.

MANAGING LONG-TERM PROGNOSTIC ISSUES

Neuropsychologists consider current neurocognitive deficits and the likely long-term impact of such impairments on functioning as the child matures. Thus, there are long-term prognostic issues to be addressed, along with managing parental expectations. A particular challenge arises with very young children. That is, their parents and providers may not be aware of the full extent of the existing cognitive difficulties since they are not overtly demonstrated in daily life experiences. A young child's relatively limited demands on now dysfunctional brain systems may not be fully appreciated until older age when these abilities are challenged. For example, a neuropsychologist evaluating a 7-year-old who has executive function deficits may have to help the parent understand how such deficits might become more evident at older age. Nonetheless, neuropsychological data enable prediction. For example, requirements for independent task initiation, planning, and organization may be especially difficult for this child by middle school. Thus, the neuropsychological report is an opportunity to address the likely developmental trajectory and provide recommendations to intervene early and to address such difficulty should predicted behaviors arise.

Although long-term prognostic determinations and recommendations are particularly difficult for children who demonstrate significant functional or intellectual impairments, it is an effort worth undertaking when the data are clear. Early identification leads to early intervention, and early intervention often results in a more optimal outcome than might otherwise be expected (Baron & Anderson, 2012). The neuropsychologist may have to discuss recommendations for assisted living or guardianship, which many parents find particularly difficult to accept. Similarly, a focus on educational interventions to further encourage development of functional adaptive skills (e.g., use of money and navigating the community instead of a focus on college as an outcome) may also be in the purview of the neuropsychologist.

GENERAL REPORT-WRITING CONSIDERATIONS

Report writing is an art that is increasingly refined and perfected over time. Stylistic differences and alternative formats adjusted to the practitioner's patient characteristics and setting are expected. The novice–experienced practitioner effect becomes evident in a comparison of a report written by a neuropsychologist-in-training with that produced by a more experienced neuropsychologist. Less experienced practitioners are more likely to write:

- Long-winded narratives that are wordy rather than focused on the message to be conveyed and providing the major conclusions concisely and clearly. The reader must then extract the key points, embedded in extraneous text.
- Jargon that assumes every reader understands professional terminology and concepts, which often has the effect of overwhelming the reader.
- Rule-bound interpretations that lead to misattribution when "textbook" lessons are applied to real-world results; for example, that a low Block Design score indicates right-hemisphere dysfunction.

Experienced professionals recognize that some lowered scores are within normal variability and should not be construed as indicative of impairment, particularly if other test results provide no back-up confirmation.

- Using inconsistent descriptors (e.g., low average, below average) for similar levels of performance, misinforming the reader about the patterning of strengths and weaknesses.
- Inadequate, overly broad recommendations that may have wide-spread applicability but little direct correlation for the individual child; that is, the "cookie-cutter" approach to report writing.
- Conclusions that misjudge the reason for referral and goal of assessment. For example, if the goal is to identify language lateralization prior to epilepsy surgery, then educational recommendations are not yet relevant. However, if the goal of the assessment is to determine cognitive strengths and weaknesses prior to hospital discharge, recommendations for school placement and academic interventions are expected.

With greater experience, reports better reflect a maturing confidence in one's professional opinions about brain–behavior relationships and an ability to integrate the data in a clear and concise manner that will be universally understood.

WRITING FOR MEDICAL PERSONNEL

Knowledge of the above-mentioned factors (i.e., family, assessment, and prognostic issues) in relation to a child with a complex medical condition is central to fulfilling the role of neuropsychologist in these circumstances. As part of the basic assessment responsibilities, a written report will diverge in several ways from that provided following an outpatient evaluation of a child not as seriously ill. The report format, content, and recommendations are influenced by child-specific considerations and the reason for referral, and are written to be useful to the many readers caring for the child. That said, reports for an inpatient often differ from those written for an outpatient, those requiring transition planning, or those who require educational recommendations. For example, a presurgical report for a child who has intractable epilepsy must address language lateralization and offer an opinion about the potential for cognitive decline following surgery. This information is crucial for the surgical team's immediate decisions, and the report has limited usefulness if it fails to address this issue. However, interventions that could ensure more appropriate self-management are timely if the evaluation is of a child with spina bifida and hydrocephalus who is found to have, for example, executive dysfunction. Thus, reports written for inpatients principally contribute to immediate medical decisions and enhance understanding of a child's cognitive course in the acute period, whereas reports prepared for an outpatient are better able to comment on a wider range of functioning and address with more accuracy the potential long-term impact of the medical condition.

Inpatient Report Writing

Preparation of a report for an inpatient presents special challenges. First, the evaluation findings are often time-sensitive and only the most relevant details need be conveyed to the physician. A multipage report is inconsistent with attending physician preference for a concise summary rather than a detailed descriptive test results section (Hilsabeck, Hietpas, & McCoy, 2014).

Second, the report will be available to many readers (e.g., other attending physicians, social workers, therapists, parents, and/or academic personnel), each with a varying degree of medical and neuropsychological sophistication. Generally, a single written report is prepared for hospitalized patients. Inpatient reports prepared within a larger electronic medical record may reflect bulleted points of interest, while discharge reports and outpatient reports may read more like a narrative. Alternative report styles have to be individually developed by neuropsychologists to best suit the circumstances. For example, highlighting the key features and summary of domain-specific performance on the first page of the report may best serve the purpose of the evaluation. Or, as one of us (ISB) prefers, a summation in a consistent one-page template that captures critical information has shown wider acceptance by medical staff than lengthier reports for an inpatient and may be included later with a longer report. An example is provided in Figure 3.1.

Although such a summary template may be all that is needed by medical staff, a report written for parents requires succinct summarization of the test results, perhaps clarified with consistent descriptive ranges (e.g., below average, above average). Writing that guides parents from domain to domain while highlighting strengths and weaknesses within each category provides a strong basis for a medically unsophisticated reader to understand conclusions and recommendations. Overly lengthy or complex reports serve no reader well and will not best inform the reader about brain–behavior relationships and targeted recommendations. Clear statements with practical significance, as well as specific recommendations that can be readily implemented, are highly desirable (Cheung, Wakefield, Ellis, Hons, & Mandalis, 2014; Farmer & Brazeal, 1998; Stark et al., 2014). A report for a medically complex pediatric case is challenging, as it must convey a substantial amount of information simply but not simplistically. Opinions vary about report length and content based on training and

Intelligence	Average (IQ range: 90–109).
Executive function	Moderate cognitive inflexibility, left upper extremity motor organizational deficit.
Effort	Good motivation and cooperation.
Attention	Good auditory span, inconsistent visual attention.
Language	Intact receptive and expressive language; intact verbal fluency.
Nonverbal	Perceptual errors, left upper extremity sensory–perceptual errors.
Motor	Bilateral motor slowness, tremor using pencil with right hand.
Visual–motor	Below average.
Learning/memory	Poor learning and poor immediate and delayed recall of nonverbal stimuli, not helped by recognition cues.
Processing speed	Slowed information processing.
Behavior	Cooperative, alert, motivated, not clinically depressed, mood euthymic.
Focal signs	Left upper extremity speed and dexterity worse than right.

Neuropsychological impression: Results provide a valid baseline assessment prior to initial V-P shunt placement for hydrocephalus. Maximal involvement of right cerebral regions indicated by motor, visual–motor, perceptual deficits; poor nonverbal learning and memory; nonverbal reasoning deficit. Deficits are mildly reduced from prior testing, consistent with right lateral ventricular volume increase shown on MRI. Verbal and left-hemisphere functioning relatively unchanged.

Recommendations: Reevaluation at 3 months s/p shunt placement. Full evaluation required to detail recommendations for school to follow. Occupational therapy for fine motor deficit should continue. IEP may require adjustment.

FIGURE 3.1. Completed template of inpatient neuropsychological test results for a child with hydrocephalus. Courtesy of Ida Sue Baron.

mentorship. However, children with chronic complex medical illnesses are accompanied by a large volume of historical data that must be reviewed and summarized in the acute stages of an injury or illness. Lastly, written reports for inpatients become part of the medical record. The expectation for clarity is essential to the child's immediate care. Extraneous details that encumber the reader should be avoided.

Outpatient Report Writing

Although reports for an inpatient principally contribute to immediate medical decisions and enhance understanding of a child's cognitive course in the acute period, reports prepared when the child is in the outpatient setting describe functioning more broadly and also obtain additional information that help address the potential long-term impact of the current medical condition. Children with medically complex conditions presenting as outpatients are accompanied by many medical and educational records that have to be distilled carefully and considered with respect to the most optimal intervention strategies once a complete diagnostic formulation is developed. This relates to evidence of functional as well as dysfunctional abilities to support their recovery. A clear timeline with prominent findings specified becomes a helpful preliminary step. In addition, the neuropsychologist may find it necessary to explain conflicting findings between various consultants, as well as any declines in functioning, and to frame previous results within a grounded neuropsychological framework. Thus, the neuropsychologist compiles an integrated history that conveys essential data in a cohesive formulation. Medical records inevitably contain errors, given the occurrence of so many consultations. The neuropsychologist must avoid further transferring such errors and must take the opportunity to correct misstatements in prior consultations by identifying and highlighting these inaccuracies for the record going forward.

OTHER CONSIDERATIONS

Forensic considerations are salient even if the neuropsychologist does not accept forensic work. This is particularly true for cases in which the child has sustained a traumatic brain injury, in the event that a medical malpractice complaint is filed at a future time, or when the child's academic progress is poor and academic programming is thought to be inadequate in preparing the child according to federal regulations. Any written report at any time subsequent to its release has the potential to be scrutinized by either plaintiff or defense expert witnesses in future legal matters. Thus, an accurate summary of the medical records that identifies inconsistencies or inaccuracies in the acquired historical data is useful. In addition, test interpretation and each aspect of report preparation are expected to be consistent with best practices and potentially subject to confirmatory scrutiny in a future legal venue, with the neuropsychologist called upon in the role of a treating provider. In cases where there are high levels of family discord, the neuropsychologists may find themselves the subject of a civil action, that is, a personal malpractice claim. Thus, cautious attention to each aspect of one's entries in the medical records is essential. The information that is provided should be factual and not hearsay; that is, data that are not confirmed should not be given the weight of fact. Conclusions reached by others involved in the child's care may be referred to but should not be reinterpreted as to alternative meaning without substantial basis. The report remains one's own product and not just an opportunity to contest the opinions of others.

Data are interpreted principally for the attending physicians in the inpatient setting and for the referring physician and parents in the outpatient setting. These different venues also have a temporal significance. Parents may not see the neuropsychologist's inpatient note but will nonetheless be informed about its content. Yet, the non-neuropsychologist conveying results might not have knowledge of neuropsychological principles or how data may be variable based on experience and the specific features of the child's performance. In this instance, the report should be succinct and free of jargon. For outpatient evaluation, the parent may have preexisting understanding of information collected in the inpatient setting, or a more distorted or incomplete recollection of results in the acute period owing to the emotional toll associated with this stage. These must now be integrated and adjusted based on the new evidence of performance strengths and weaknesses obtained weeks or months after the acute episode. This is a critical time to clarify that constructs and test results are understood as to their implications about cognitive, social, and emotional responding. Errors in interpretation should be corrected, and the data interpreted in a highly personal way and with real substance as to how this particular child will manage daily activities and responsibilities. It is not a question of what range a child falls in as much as how that child will respond to the specific day-to-day encounters in personal, social, and academic venues. Parents who taught or disciplined one way prior to the insult may well need to make substantial adjustments that are not yet habitual or may not fully appreciate why these changes must occur to ensure their child's progress. The interpretive session of the outpatient evaluation is a key time to convey this new knowledge.

CASE EXAMPLE

All data pertaining to the case example are presented in Table 3.1.

Reason for Referral

Juan was referred because he was not making sufficient progress in academic skills, with concern expressed that perhaps he was not just stabilizing but declining. His primary care physician wondered whether there was evidence of loss of neuropsychological competencies.

TABLE 3.1. Test Data for Juan

Test variable	Test result
Intellectual functioning	
WISC-IV	Standard scores
Full Scale IQ	74
Verbal Comprehension	81
Perceptual Reasoning	81
Working Memory	80
Processing Speed	68
Language functioning	
Boston Naming Test	$z = -0.5$
CELF-4	Scaled scores
Recalling Sentences	7
Understanding Paragraphs	5
D-KEFS	
Letter Fluency	7
Semantic Fluency	6
Learning and memory	
CVLT-C	(Raw)/z
Total Trials 1–5	$T = 31$
Trial 1	(5) $z = -1.5$
Short Delay Free Recall	(8) $z = -1.5$
Long Delay Free Recall	(9) $z = -1$
Learning Slope	$z = 0$
Recognition	$z = 0$
False Positives	$z = 5$
Sematic Clustering	$z = -1.5$
Serial Clustering	$z = 1$
RCFT	T-scores
Immediate Recall	<20
Delayed Recall	22
Recognition Total	30
Attention/executive functions	
CPT-II	T-scores
Omissions	44
Commissions	63
Reaction Time	55
Variability	60
Perseverations	71

(continued)

TABLE 3.1. *(continued)*

Test variable	Test result
Stroop Color Word Test	*T*-scores
Word Score	19
Color Score	26
Color Word	34
Interference	50
Symbol Digit Modalities Test (Oral)	$z = -2.1$
Auditory Consonant Trigrams	$z = -2.7$
TOL-2	Standard scores
Total Correct	92
Total Moves	80
Total Time	<60
TrailMaking Test	z-scores
Part A	−7.4
Part B	−3.3
BRIEF	
Parent Report	No elevations
Self-Report	No elevations
Conners' Adult ADHD Rating Scale	
Parent Report	No elevations
Self-Report	No elevations
Sensorimotor	
Dean–Woodcock Sensory–Motor Battery	
Visual Confrontation Right	WNL
Visual Confrontation Left	Mild to WNL
Visual Confrontation Simultaneous	Mild to WNL
Palm Writing Right	WNL
Palm Writing Left	Moderate
Object Identification Right	WNL
Object Identification Left	Severe
Finger Identification Right	WNL
Finger Identification Left	Moderate
Grooved Pegboard	
Right Hand (Dominant)	$z = -2.88$
Left Hand	Unable to complete
Visual perceptual functions	
JOLO	$z = -2.5$
Rey Copy	$z = -3$

(continued)

TABLE 3.1. *(continued)*

Test variable	Test result
	Standard scores
Beery VMI	68
Academic functioning	
WIAT-III	
Reading Comprehension	85
Numerical Operations	83
Word Reading	70
Pseudoword Decoding	68
WJ-III	
Reading Fluency	69
Math Fluency	70
Writing Fluency	70
Adaptive and social/emotional	
Vineland	
Adaptive Behavior Composite	80
Communication Domain	96
Daily Living Skills	74
Socialization Domain	80
BASC-2 Parent Report	At risk somatization scale
Self-Report	At risk somatization scale

Relevant Background Information

Juan, a 14-year-old, Hispanic, right-handed, boy was developing well until age 7 when he presented with headaches, vomiting, double vision, and left-sided weakness. A right frontotemporal oligodendroglioma was resected. The postsurgical course was uncomplicated, and radiotherapy followed. Tumor recurrence at age 10 in the right parietal region necessitated a second resection, with pathology now indicating an ependymoma, and there was no radiotherapy or chemotherapy recommended. He was subsequently hospitalized and given high-dose steroids for pancreatitis, myocarditis, and Crohn's disease. Multiple psychiatric symptoms (e.g., hallucinations, physical aggressiveness) resolved with discontinuation of steroid medication. Recently, at the age of 14, Juan was hospitalized in a confusional state. Further evaluation revealed high blood sugar values, and a diagnosis of insulin-dependent diabetes mellitus was made.

Juan's academic history was notable for difficulties in learning the alphabet and acquiring a sight word vocabulary. He was placed in special education following his second tumor resection, and then a self-contained classroom with counseling services, as well as provided with classroom and testing accommodations (extended time, extra breaks, separate testing location, directions read aloud). Previous evaluations documented Juan's low average reasoning skills and relative weaknesses in focusing his attention on what he had heard and in responding quickly. Age-appropriate single-word vocabulary contrasted with weaknesses when words had to be combined to form sentences; when he had to follow multistep oral directions; and when he tried to understand the meaning of a read paragraph or an oral lecture. Juan lived with his family in Puerto Rico until age 8 and now resides with his mother and three siblings in the United States. Family history is significant for paternal substance abuse, physical aggression, and dyslexia. Juan is currently struggling academically, is forgetful, and requires extra support in order to manage daily activities.

Rule 1: Summarize history succinctly; avoid overdocumentation of medical encounters

LESS DESIRABLE

Juan presents with a complicated medical history. He came to medical attention at age 7 following complaints of headaches, accompanied by vomiting, double vision, and left-sided weakness. He underwent a neurological evaluation and neuroimaging, which identified a frontotemporal tumor. Histopathology identified the tumor as an oligodendroglioma. Juan underwent surgical resection, which was followed with radiotherapy. Juan was seen for an ophthalmological evaluation at age 8 due to complaints of poor visual acuity, but that evaluation did not reveal any concerns. He was seen in the emergency room when he was 9 due to a broken wrist. At age 10, Juan again experienced headaches and vomiting and was diagnosed with recurrence of brain tumor. Histopathological assessment noted that the tumor was an ependymoma. Another resection was completed with no other postsurgical treatment.

Juan was hospitalized in 2011, 2012, and 2014 due to complaints of severe stomach pains. His mother also reported frequent diarrhea and vomiting. Juan was diagnosed with Crohn's disease in 2012. During his most recent hospitalization, Juan was diagnosed with pancreatitis and myocarditis. He was started on high-dose steroids, which were effective at reducing the gastrointestinal symptoms. However, Juan developed multiple concerning symptoms, including becoming physically aggressive. Further, he reported multiple visual and auditory hallucinations and was reported to be quite paranoid in school and at home. At that time, steroid medications were discontinued, and these psychiatric symptoms resolved. In the summer of 2014, Juan was observed to become very confused during a camp field trip. He was taken to the hospital where his blood sugar was noted to be 457. Following monitoring and further assessment, he was diagnosed with insulin-dependent diabetes mellitus.

MORE DESIRABLE

Juan, a 14-year-old Hispanic, right-handed boy, was developing well until age 7 when he presented with headaches, vomiting, double vision, and left-sided weakness. A right frontotemporal oligodendroglioma was resected. Postsurgical course was uncomplicated, and radiotherapy followed. Tumor recurrence (now diagnosed as ependymoma) at age 10 in the right parietal region necessitated a second resection, but no radiotherapy or chemotherapy. He was subsequently hospitalized and given high-dose steroids for pancreatitis, myocarditis, and Crohn's disease. Multiple psychiatric symptoms (e.g., hallucinations, physical aggressiveness) resolved with discontinuation of steroid medication. At age 14, Juan was hospitalized in a confusional state. Evaluation revealed high blood sugar values and a diagnosis of insulin-dependent diabetes mellitus was made.

Comment on Rule 1

This case presents a common challenge, notably reconciling inconsistencies within the medical record. In this instance, Juan's tumor was initially identified as an oligodendroglioma, whereas the second tumor pathology results noted it to be an ependymoma. Although the neuropsychologist is unable to make a determination as to the accuracy of histopathological findings, understanding the difference between these tumor types, as well as their quite differing prognostic impressions, is important, as is ensuring that the information is presented clearly.

   The information provided in both examples is largely the same, but in the first example, the information is not integrated and follows a confusing chronological course. With a complex medical history, information irrelevant to the child's current medical course (e.g., negative ophthalmological evaluation, broken wrist) only encumbers the reader. The second example integrates the medical history's key points in a clear, cohesive, and concise manner.

Rule 2: Summarize past evaluations; integrate data and make key points once; avoid repetitive descriptions; do not simply report scores

LESS DESIRABLE

Previous evaluations conducted by the board of education in 2011 and 2013 administered measures of intellectual functioning and language skills. In 2011, Juan was administered the WISC-IV, and his performance was low average (Full Scale IQ Standard Score = 82). His verbal comprehension was low average, as was his perceptual reasoning (Verbal Comprehension Index Standard Score = 88; Perceptual Reasoning Index Standard Score = 86). Working memory and processing speed were borderline (Working Memory Index Standard Score = 79; Processing Speed Index Standard Score = 78). Language testing revealed average vocabulary but borderline ability to formulate sentences. Following directions was borderline, and repetition was low average. In 2013, Juan was again administered the WISC-IV, which showed below-average verbal comprehension and perceptual reasoning abilities. Working memory and processing speed were low average. The 2014 language evaluation again noted that his vocabulary was average. Listening to paragraphs was below average, and his ability to formulate sentences was borderline.

MORE DESIRABLE

Previous evaluations documented Juan's low average reasoning skills and relative weaknesses focusing attention on what is heard and responding quickly. Age-appropriate single-word vocabulary contrasted with weaknesses when words had to be combined to form sentences, when he had to follow multistep oral directions, and when he tried to understand the meaning of a paragraph or oral lecture. This pattern of reduced intellectual skills, poor focused attention, slow information processing, and difficulty with complex language is often observed in children with neurological insults.

Comment on Rule 2

A common responsibility of the pediatric neuropsychologist is reviewing previous evaluation records. This information is then used to help frame the current data and identify any changes from previous assessments. As such, information gathered from previous evaluations is often helpful to include in the pediatric neuropsychological report, as it provides a framework for understanding the child's pattern of strengths and weaknesses. In such cases, there may be multiple evaluations that have never been integrated prior to the current assessment. For example, several speech, occupational therapy, and psychoeducational assessments may be completed without anyone assimilating the information gathered from these assessments or explaining how these additional data explain the child's neurological and medical course. Simply repeating obtained test results, without relating the import of past and current assessments, is not helpful to the reader.

Although the information provided in both scenarios is essentially identical, the first example presents previous assessments in a loosely integrated way and tasks the reader to independently make sense of the presented material. The second example considers and integrates the previous evaluations, and distills it into a pattern of strengths and weaknesses that should be understandable to a non-neuropsychologist.

Behavioral Observations

Juan was evaluated over the course of two sessions. He was well groomed and quickly established a good rapport with the examiner. Juan's gait was notable for a limp, and he demonstrated weakness in his left arm and hand. He often used made-up words in conversation. He pronounced many words inaccurately, for example, saying "excalator" for escalator. Such errors may follow neurological insult and are thus meaningful. He often relied on hand movements as a communication aid because word retrieval was difficult. His handwriting resulted in poorly formed but correctly sequenced letters, and irregular-sized words with poor spacing. Juan appeared engaged during the current evaluation, but fluctuations in attention were observed. Additionally, he tired easily and required several rest breaks. Overall, Juan worked slowly across tasks. He was also observed to take longer in daily tasks, such as eating a snack. Juan responded well to encouragement and reassurance and completed all tasks presented to him. His effort and motivation appeared adequate.

Rule 3: Use simple language; avoid jargon

LESS DESIRABLE

Juan's language was notable for neologisms and literal paraphasias, and he gesticulated frequently. He had a left-sided hemiparesis, and dysgraphia was evident.

MORE DESIRABLE

Juan's gait was notable for a limp, and he demonstrated weakness in his left arm and hand. He often used made-up words in conversation. He pronounced many words inaccurately, for example, saying "excalator" for escalator. He often relied on hand movements as a communication aid since word retrieval was difficult. His handwriting resulted in poorly formed but correctly sequenced letters and irregular-sized words with poor spacing.

Comment on Rule 3

Although the first example is shorter and seemingly more concise, the use of jargon makes it difficult for non-neuropsychologists to understand. For example, paraphasia, dysgraphia, and hemiparesis are terms familiar to neuropsychologists and neurologists but less well understood by non-neuroscience professionals.

Language Functioning[1]

Juan's functional communications skills appeared adequate. He required some clarification of directions and questions. He was soft-spoken, but prosody and articulation were normal. The word-finding difficulties he reported in his day-to-day conversations since his second surgery were also observed during the current assessment. Formal language assessment revealed verbal skills to be mostly below average, with repetition, verbal initiation, and verbal reasoning skills all falling in the below-average range. Juan had greater difficulty understanding lengthier and more complex language such as short stories.

Rule 4: Use consistent descriptors; avoid variable descriptive labels for the same level of performance

LESS DESIRABLE

Juan's repetition skills were within low average limits . . . his verbal initiation was within low limits . . . verbal reasoning skills were below average.

MORE DESIRABLE

Formal language assessment revealed verbal skills to be mostly below average, with repetition, verbal initiation and verbal reasoning skills also falling in the below-average range.

---

[1] See "Language Functioning" section of Table 3.1.

Comment on Rule 4

Consistency in terminology use when describing levels of performance is crucial, as those unfamiliar with tests and measurements and statistical methods may not understand similarities and difference in terms and scores. Thus, using terms such as below average, low, and low average is confusing to the reader.

Learning and Memory[2]

Impairments in acquisition of information were noted. Juan encoded less information initially, impacting his overall learning, but he benefited from repetition. Despite difficulties encoding new information, once learned, he retained information over time. Juan demonstrated inefficient learning strategies that would benefit from instruction in rehearsal and repetition, as well as chunking of stimuli. He had greater difficulty with visual material, and his learning and recall of visual information was severely impaired, with minimal benefit from a recognition format.

Rule 5: Interpret based on actual data; avoid overstatements

LESS DESIRABLE

Juan demonstrated verbal memory deficits that were in part driven by his overreliance on inefficient learning strategies. Consistent with his executive functioning weaknesses, he relied solely on learning information based on order of presentation, and this resulted in him being unable to recall information effectively. Notably, he showed much better performance over time, indicating that he requires additional time to consolidate new information.

MORE DESIRABLE

Impairments in acquisition of information were noted. Juan encoded less information initially, adversely affecting his overall learning, but he benefited from repetition. Despite difficulties encoding new information, once learned he retained information over time. Juan would benefit from such strategies as rehearsal and repetition, and pairing of verbal and visual stimuli.

---

[2]See "Learning and Memory" section of Table 3.1.

Comment on Rule 5

Neuropsychological evaluations often result in a multitude of scores, some of which are more relevant than others and some of which are not empirically supported. As the number of scores produced in a battery increases, so does the chance of error. An understanding of normal variability is crucial for accurate interpretation. Some neuropsychologists are prone to over-interpret normal variability or the influence of variables that are not well supported empirically.

The less desirable example reflects several concerns. First, the interpretation is somewhat inaccurate. Although Juan recalled less information than his peers, the interpretation does not account for his impaired encoding and overall learning, leading one to assume that the impairment is in storage rather than encoding. Second, there is an overinterpretation of a small difference between the short-delay recall score and the long-delay recall score. This difference is not statistically or clinically significant, and the interpretation of this difference is not supported. Lastly, too much focus is placed on the semantic and serial cluster scores, variables not well supported in the literature (Beebe, Ris, & Dietrich, 2000).

Rule 6: Understand and answer the referral question; avoid extraneous content[3]

LESS DESIRABLE

Juan has shown much progress in many areas, but he continues to display persistent left-sided motor weakness, indicating a recovery course that requires continued close monitoring and therapy. Concern about limited progress is warranted given these indications of only slight resolution of deficits.

MORE DESIRABLE

Juan's slowed academic progress can be attributed to the combination of his cognitive deficits subsequent to his two resections, as well as the increasing demands of academic work. While Juan has not demonstrated a decline in neurocognitive skills and has made progress relative to himself, his considerably slower progress compared with that of his peers has resulted in a widening gap between his skills and expectations for age. Additionally, Juan's multiple school absences due to his complex medical history have further contributed to slowed academic gains.

---

[3] See "Intellectual Functioning" and "Academic Functioning" sections of Table 3.1.

Comment on Rule 6

Although both scenarios above provide accurate and important information, only the second example directly answers the referral question posed by Juan's physician.

Summary and Conclusions

Juan is a 14-year-old boy who was referred for neuropsychological evaluation in the context of two right frontoparietal resections, radiotherapy, multiple autoimmune disorders, as well as a recent diagnosis of insulin-dependent diabetes mellitus. The evaluation was requested to gain a better understanding of Juan's cognitive profile and to identify what treatments and supports he currently requires. The evaluation reflected low average intellectual abilities that are believed to be a decrease from his pre-resection baseline. Simple language skills were largely intact, while more complex comprehension was borderline impaired. Impairments were observed in visual spatial skills, focusing of attention, processing speed, learning of verbal information, visual memory, as well as complex attention and planning and organization. Motor skills were also impaired with both hands, with significant left-sided extremity weakness. The currently noted deficits in visual perception, attention, planning and organizational skills, together with left-sided motor deficit, is consistent with the presentation of right frontoparietal lesions such as expected following Juan's two resections. Furthermore, noted processing speed deficits are consistent with effects of a localized lesion, but are more likely late effects of his radiation treatment. Lastly, Juan's poor reading abilities observed in context with early problems learning the alphabet, phonological errors, and a family history of reading difficulties indicate an underlying reading disability that is independent of, albeit compounded by, his neurological history.

Juan's difficulties with planning, organization, time management, and regulation of his attention require increased individual support in his high school classroom. In light of his recent diagnosis of diabetes, Juan's executive functioning deficits will need to be considered in his treatment regimen. For example, Juan may not regularly check his blood sugar or manage his injections. Developing a behavior plan with reminders, prompts, and reinforcement for checking glucose levels and preparing injections should help him manage a successful routine for his new diagnosis.

Juan also demonstrates poor daily living and self-care skills. Community-based day habilitation services could be provided to help him independently navigate the community, complete daily self-care skills, and develop more independence in his medical self-management. Furthermore, academic programming should include functional academic subjects such as money management. Vocational services should be incorporated into his academic program, and school-based vocational training should be provided.

Rule 7: Integrate medical history with findings, using all data points to formulate conclusions; avoid negating preinjury history

LESS DESIRABLE

Juan's intellectual skills have declined from his base-line due to his two resections. His previous surgeries have also resulted in significant difficulties across all domains. In particular, deficits were identified in language, visual spatial skills, attention, executive functioning, learning, and memory. Due to his brain tumor and associated treatments, Juan has been unable to acquire age-appropriate academic skills, although he performs relatively better in math.

MORE DESIRABLE

Juan's low average intellectual abilities are likely a decline from his premorbid baseline. Simple language skills were largely intact, while more complex comprehension was borderline impaired. Impairments were observed in visual spatial skills, focusing of attention, processing speed, learning of verbal information, visual memory, as well as complex attention and planning and organization. Motor skills were also impaired with both hands, with significant left-sided extremity weakness. The currently noted deficits in visual perception, attention, planning, and organizational skills, together with left-sided motor deficit, is consistent with the presentation of right frontoparietal lesions such as expected following Juan's two resections. Furthermore, noted processing speed deficits are consistent with effects of a localized lesion, but are more likely late effects of his radiation treatment. Lastly, Juan's poor reading abilities observed in context with early problems learning the alphabet, phonological errors, and a family history of reading difficulties indicate an underlying reading disability that is independent of, albeit compounded by, his neurological history.

Comment on Rule 7

The first example attributes all observed deficits to the tumors and respective treatments without integrating all available data (e.g., late effects of radiation, early developmental red flags for reading disability), whereas the second example makes associations between specific areas of deficit and the most likely root cause. This is particularly important in children with medically complex presentations, as these associations will drive interventions. For example, for those working with Juan, understanding that his overall processing speed deficits are potentially related to late effects of radiotherapy will alert the team to monitor for other late effects while also communicating to educational personnel that this is not likely to improve. Similarly, correctly identifying the source of Juan's reading difficulty as being developmental leads to more appropriate intervention targeting a reading disability, rather than accommodation of a brain injury-related academic concern.

Rule 8: Maintain focus on current functioning and address future implications; avoid overprognosticating[4]

LESS DESIRABLE

Juan demonstrated prominent executive functioning deficits which impact his daily functioning at home, as well as his ability to manage within the classroom setting. He will need additional supports to address his executive functioning weaknesses. Juan also will require interventions to target his daily living skills. In light of his poor daily living skills and significant executive impairment, it may be difficult for Juan to attend college or live independently.

MORE DESIRABLE

Juan's difficulties with planning, organization, time management, and regulation of attention would benefit from individualized supports in his high school classroom. Juan's executive functioning deficits should be considered relative to his recent diagnosis of diabetes and its treatment regimen. For example, Juan may not check his blood sugar regularly or manage his injections appropriately. Development of a behavior management schedule with reminders, prompts, and reinforcement for checking glucose levels and preparing injections should help him develop a successful routine for managing his new diagnosis.

Juan demonstrates poor daily living and self-care skills. Community-based day habilitation services could help him independently navigate the community, complete daily self-care skills, and become more independent in

---

[4]See "Attention/Executive Functions" and "Adaptive and Social/Emotional" sections of Table 3.1.

medical self-management. Academic programming inclusive of functional academics such as money management is
desirable. Vocational services should be incorporated into
his academic track, and school-based vocational training
options should be provided.

Comment on Rule 8

Although it is necessary to make prognostic comments about a child's future functioning, such statements should be based on data and tied directly to specific recommendations. For Juan, at this time, his executive impairments are more relevant to his new diagnosis of diabetes and its management rather than to discussion of independent living and college. The level of Juan's impairments definitely does not necessarily preclude him from living independently if he is provided with appropriate interventions.

Rule 9: Make practical recommendations; avoid broad ones that apply universally

LESS DESIRABLE

Juan demonstrated difficulties with reading and written
expression skills. School-based accommodations are recommended to help support him.

MORE DESIRABLE

Individualized interventions targeting phonological and
decoding skills are required to ameliorate Juan's poor
reading accuracy and verbal fluency; for example, the
Orton-Gillingham or Wilson Reading Method programs. His
parents are encouraged to share these assessment results
with his school district in order to update his individualized education program. Juan requires systematic,
intensive, multisensory intervention specific for children who have reading disabilities. In addition, extended
time, a reader for examinations, access to audiobooks, and
a scribe for standard and in-class assessments should be
useful additional accommodations.

Comment on Rule 9

This example demonstrates that parents should be informed about specific guidelines for what recommendations, interventions, and accommodations they should request for their child. A broad recommendation for school-based accommodations is not as helpful as more specific methods for addressing a child's weaknesses.

Final Comment

In addition to the apparent indications of Juan's brain dysfunction and of lateralized findings, one should be alert for transient signs of acute injury in the records or by report—for example, word-finding problems or semantic paraphasia in the early stages of recovery from a brain injury, motor weakness accompanying a brief period of expressive aphasia, or mutism associated with documented cerebellar insult. Signs or symptoms that highlight specific brain regions as dysfunctional may be especially fleeting in children, unlike in adults.

REFERENCES

Aitken, M. E., Mele, N., & Barrett, K. W. (2004). Recovery of injured children: Parent perspectives on family needs. *Archives of Physical Medicine and Rehabilitation, 85*(4), 567–573.

Baron, I. S. (2004). *Neuropsychological evaluation of the child.* New York: Oxford University Press.

Baron, I., & Anderson, P. (2012). Neuropsychological assessment of preschoolers. *Neuropsychology Review, 22*(4), 311–312.

Barrera, M., Shaw, A. K., Speechley, K. N., Maunsell, E., & Pogany, L. (2005). Educational and social late effects of childhood cancer and related clinical, personal, and familial characteristics. *Cancer, 104*(8), 1751–1760.

Beebe, D. W., Ris, M. D., & Dietrich, K. N. (2000). The relationship between CVLT-C process scores and measures of executive functioning: Lack of support among community-dwelling adolescents. *Journal of Clinical and Experimental Neuropsychology, 22*(6), 779–792.

Bellinger, D. C., & Newburger, J. W. (2013). Late neurodevelopmental outcomes in children with congenital heart disease. In I. S. Baron & C. Rey-Casserly (Eds.), *Pediatric neuropsychology: Medical advances and lifespan outcomes* (pp. 99–112). New York: Oxford University Press.

Cheung, L. L. T., Wakefield, C. E., Ellis, S. J., Hons, B. A., & Mandalis, A. (2014). Neuropsychology reports for childhood brain tumor survivors: Implementation of recommendations at home and school. *Pediatric Blood Cancer, 61,* 1080–1087.

Cohen, E., Kuo, D. Z., Agrawal, R., Berry, J. G., Bhagat, S. K. M., Simon, T. D., et al. (2011). Children with medical complexity: An emerging population for clinical and research initiatives. *Pediatrics, 127*(3), 529–538.

Farmer, J. E., & Brazeal, T. J. (1998). Parent perceptions about the process and outcomes of child neuropsychological assessment. *Applied Neuropsychology, 5*(4), 37–41.

Goldbeck, L. (2001). Parental coping with the diagnosis of childhood cancer:

Gender effects, dissimilarity within couples, and quality of life. *Psycho-Oncology, 10*(4), 325–335.

Heiman, T. (2002). Parents of children with disabilities: Resilience, coping, and future expectations. *Journal of Developmental and Physical Disabilities, 14*(2), 159–171.

Heyer, E. J., Sharma, R., Winfree, C. J., Mocco, J., McMahon, D. J., McCormick, P. A., et al. (2000). Severe pain confounds neuropsychological test performance. *Journal of Clinical and Experimental Neuropsychology, 22*(5), 633–639. Retrieved from *www.ncbi.nlm.nih.gov/pmc/articles/PMC2548406*.

Hilsabeck, R. C., Hietpas, T. L., & McCoy, K. J. M. (2014). Satisfaction of referring providers with neuropsychological services within a Veterans Administration medical center. *Archives of Clinical Neuropsychology, 29*(2), 131–140.

Knafl, K., & Zoeller, L. (2000). Childhood chronic illness: A comparison of mothers' and fathers' experiences. *Journal of Family Nursing, 6*(3), 287–302.

Lash, M., & Scarpino, C. (1993). School reintegration for children with traumatic brain injuries: Conflicts between medical and educational systems. *NeuroRehabilitation, 3*(3), 13–25.

Marino, B. S., Lipkin, P. H., Newburger, J. W., Peacock, G., Gerdes, M., Gaynor, J. W., et al. (2012). Neurodevelopmental outcomes in children with congenital heart disease: Evaluation and management. *Circulation, 126*(9), 1143–1172.

Miller, A. R., Condin, C. J., McKellin, W. H., Shaw, N., Klassen, A. F., & Sheps, S. (2009). Continuity of care for children with complex chronic health conditions: Parents' perspectives. *BMC Health Services Research, 9*, 242–253.

Raina, P., Donnell, M. O., Rosenbaum, P., Brehaut, J., Stephen, D., Russell, D., et al. (2005). The health and well-being of caregivers of children with cerebral palsy. *Pediatrics, 115*(6), 626–636.

Schultz, K. A. P., Ness, K. K., Whitton, J., Recklitis, C., Zebrack, B., Robison, L. L., et al. (2007). Behavioral and social outcomes in adolescent survivors of childhood cancer: A report from the childhood cancer survivor study. *Journal of Clinical Oncology, 25*(24), 3649–3656.

Shudy, M., Lihinie, M., Almeida, D., Ly, S., Landon, C., Groft, S., et al. (2006). Impact of pediatric critical illness and injury on families: A systematic literature review. *Pediatrics, 118*(S3), S203–S218.

Spevack, T. (2011). A developmental approach to pediatric neuropsychological intervention. In S. J. Hunter & J. Donders (Eds.), *Pediatric neuropsychological intervention: A critical review of science and practice* (pp. 6–29). New York: Cambridge University Press.

Stark, D., Thomas, S., Dawson, D., Talbot, E., Bennett, E., & Starza-Smith, A. (2014). Paediatric neuropsychological assessment: An analysis of parents' perspectives. *Social Care and Neurodisability, 5*(1), 41–50.

Stein, R. E. K., Bauman, L. J., Westbrook, L. E., Coupey, S. M., & Ireys, H. T. (1993). Framework for identifying children who have chronic conditions: The case for a new definition. *Journal of Pediatrics, 122*(3), 342–347.

Van der Lee, J. H., Mokkink, L. B., Grootenhuis, M. A., Heymans, H. S., & Offringa, M. (2007). Definitions and measurement of chronic health conditions in childhood: A systematic review. *Journal of the American Medical Association, 297*(24), 2741–2751. Retrieved from *http://dx.doi.org/10.1001/jama.297.24.2741*.

Waber, D. P., Carpentieri, S. C., Klar, N., Silverman, L. B., Schwenn, M., Hur-
witz, C. A., et al. (2000). Cognitive sequelae in children treated for acute lym-
phoblastic leukemia with dexamethasone or prednisone. *Journal of Pediatric
Hematology/Oncology, 22*(3), 206–213. Retrieved from *http://journals.lww.
com/jpho-online/Fulltext/2000/05000/Cognitive_Sequelae_in_Children_
Treated_for_Acute.4.aspx.*

Warrington, T. P., & Bostwick, J. M. (2006). Psychiatric adverse effects of cortico-
steroids. *Mayo Clinic Proceedings, 81*(10), 1361–1367.

Warschausky, S., Kaufman, N., & Felix, L. (2013). Cerebral Palsy. In I. S. Baron
& C. Rey-Casserly (Eds.), *Pediatric neuropsychology: Medical advances and
lifespan outcomes* (pp. 80–98). New York: Oxford University Press.

CHAPTER 4

Differential Diagnosis in Older Adults

Laura H. Lacritz
Heidi C. Rossetti

GENERAL GERIATRIC NEUROPSYCHOLOGICAL CONSIDERATIONS

One way to characterize your neuropsychological evaluation report is that it tells a story about the person you are assessing. Before writing your report, you might consider what story you need to tell to address the questions you are trying to answer. You will gather much more information as part of the evaluation process than you need to actually include in your report. When in doubt of what to include, step back and consider if the information is relevant to the story you want to tell. For example, remote history of birth complications in a person who otherwise developed normally and had a successful career is likely not relevant to the assessment of new memory problems in late life.

Ideally, your report will include information from multiple data sources, including medical records, family, and the patient, along with your own behavioral observations and test findings. It is not uncommon to end up with contradictory information as part of the dementia assessment process for a number of reasons, including the patient's lack of insight or forgetfulness, denial or unawareness of the caregiver in some instances, or deficits that may not be detectable on brief screening from the referring physician. In addition, information obtained through collateral sources may be censored if they are obtained in the presence of the patient, which underscores the importance of procuring information from family separate from the patient.

Because the neuropsychological evaluation is usually one part of a more comprehensive dementia assessment, a brief history is often sufficient, highlighting current symptoms, functional abilities and/or changes, and relevant medical and psychiatric history that is important for the differential diagnosis. Our training as neuropsychologists helps us to elicit relevant symptoms related to personality, mood, cognition, and behavior, which should be articulated in the report as they pertain to differential diagnosis. As such, it may be appropriate to include areas in which the patient is "not" having problems as well as what symptoms they do demonstrate. See Table 4.1 for a summary of common elements that may be expected in various cognitive disorders and could be covered in your history of an elderly person with suspected neurobehavioral changes.

Considerations for test selection when evaluating geriatric patients include battery length, patient stamina, referral question, necessity of reevaluation over time, and availability of age-appropriate norms. Battery length may vary depending on the referral question but can often be abbreviated in uncomplicated dementia assessments, which is preferable to reduce burden on the patient. In instances where reevaluation will be necessary to clarify or confirm diagnosis (e.g., intervening factors that might

TABLE 4.1. Elements to Include in Interview and Report

	Delirium	Alzheimer's disease	Lewy body disease	Frontotemporal dementia	PD dementia	Vascular dementia
Abrupt onset	+	−	−	−	−	±
Insidious onset	−	+	+	+	+	±
Early personality change	±	−	−	+	−	±
Cognitive fluctuations	+	−	+	−	−	−
Insight	−	±	±	−	+	±
Apathy	−	±	±	±	−	±
REM behavioral disorder	−	−	+	−	±	−
Psychosis	+	±*	+	−	±	±
Motor symptoms	−	−	+	±	+	±

Note. Any of these elements may be present in MCI depending on the underlying etiology. +, Expected or supportive symptom; −, not expected; *, can be seen later in the disease; PD, Parkinson's disease; REM, rapid eye movement.

resolve, such as medication effects or delirium), the battery length and test battery may be modified. For example, more detailed testing might be indicated in an individual with mild cognitive impairment (MCI) who will need retesting to assess for change over time, whereas a shorter battery is appropriate in cases of suspected delirium/drug toxicity. Including statements in your report regarding your approach to testing may be helpful to your referral source. For example:

> The test battery was shortened given the patient's hypersomnolence and trouble attending during the evaluation. Although a sufficient sample of her abilities was obtained to help answer the referral question, some aspects of the results may represent an underestimate of her true abilities.

In cases where reevaluation will be needed, test selection may be guided in part by the availability of test norms as the patient ages. For example, the Wechsler Memory Scale–IV (Wechsler, 2009) has adult (16–67 years) and older adult (65–90 years) versions. If assessing someone who is 65 years old, you would need to consider which version to administer to aid in comparison at later retesting. Although a variety of test norms have extended the age range of available normative data (Heaton, Ryan, Grant, & Matthews, 1996; Lucas et al., 2005), some measures are still subject to floor effects when assessing elderly patients and how best to report test performance may vary as a result. As one example, scaled scores (SS) for WMS-IV Visual Reproduction have a lower limit of SS = 5 for some age ranges, meaning that a patient can have complete forgetting of the figures and still have a scaled score of 5. In such instances, reporting the percent retention rather than the scaled score will better convey the patient's performance.

An older adult's ability to function independently is an important aspect to assess as part of the evaluation, in part because functional impairment is a key feature of the diagnosis of dementia and also because of the potential implications for practical considerations such as safety, living arrangement, and quality of life recommendations. Functional assessment includes basic everyday skills such as personal grooming and complex abilities such as managing finances, medications, and driving. Appropriate assessment of functional status is of particular importance in civil competency/capacity cases and forensic settings (Grisso, 2003; Moye, Marson, & Edelstein, 2013). An estimation of functional ability commonly relies on the patient's self-report or the informant report gathered during clinical interview; however, individuals with dementia typically overestimate their functional abilities, and caregivers are also prone to misestimation (Schulz et al., 2013). This discrepancy may be less of an issue in MCI (Farias, Mungas, & Jagust, 2005). Performance-based measures, such as the Texas Functional Living

Scale, provide an objective, ecologically valid way to measure the ability to execute everyday tasks (Cullum et al., 2001) and provide important data to help write your recommendations.

Your summary and recommendations section will be the most commonly read section of your report and should include a clear but brief synopsis of the results and a specific opinion regarding diagnosis and support for your opinion (e.g., in the case of differentiating between conditions). Avoid repeating back what the referral source already knows, and highlight issues that are not likely to come up in medical evaluations.

PRETEST CONSIDERATIONS

- Have a clear understanding of referral question(s). Patient or family may have different questions than the referring physician (e.g., differential diagnosis versus "can my parent still drive").

- If capacity is a concern, be sure to get consent from a family member as well as from the patient (Marson, Schmitt, Ingram, & Lindy, 1994). If the evaluation may be used for competency/guardianship purposes, make sure the patient is aware of this before starting the evaluation. In addition, be aware of what aspect of capacity you are being ask to evaluate, keeping in mind that capacity is multifaceted (e.g., a patient may have the capacity to give informed consent for a medical procedure or designate a power of attorney, but not to manage financial affairs). If a power of attorney was invoked, have a copy for your records. This will help with later release of records or conveying results back to family.

- Have access to appropriate collateral data sources. Patients with MCI or dementia may have reduced insight into their deficits or be in denial of symptoms. It is important to interview or have access to an informant who knows the patient well enough to provide accurate information about daily functioning and onset and progression of symptoms. Collateral interviews tend to yield the most accurate information when conducted apart from the patient. Some caregivers will not feel comfortable sharing examples of difficulties in front of their loved one.

- Be familiar with the spectrum of dementing disorders; diagnosing clear-cut Alzheimer's disease (AD) is fairly easy in many cases, but there are a variety of other etiologies that must be considered and ruled out in making an accurate diagnosis.

- Have access to relevant medical, imaging, and past neuropsychological test records. In some instances, patients must be followed over time to clarify the diagnosis. Knowing what has been considered and ruled out and having access to past imaging, neurological findings, and test results can be critical in piecing together a chronology of symptoms and pattern of progression.

• Ensure your battery includes the measures needed to make the differential diagnosis. Do you need to add additional measures of language, praxis, motor functioning, or executive functioning to inform your diagnosis?

• Make sure there are no sensory deficits that need to be compensated for, such as poor eyesight (it is good to have a few pairs of reading glasses or a magnifying sheet handy), decreased hearing (there are adaptive amplifying devices that could be used if necessary), tremor (minimize tasks with a motor component; have large pencils/pens to make holding easier), or fatigue (may have to prioritize battery components if patient cannot tolerate lengthy testing).

• Be an astute observer of behavior. Some qualitative aspects of behavior may not show up on formal testing. How does the patient communicate during interview? Can the patient find his or her way around the office when returning after breaks? Are there any unusual motor symptoms?

• Include formal as well as embedded measures of effort/validity.

SPECTRUM OF MCI TO DEMENTIA

As our population ages, the incidence of MCI and dementia is rising, with the annual number of new cases of dementia projected to double by 2050 (Hebert, Beckett, Scherr, & Evans, 2001), resulting in a growing number of individuals presenting for cognitive assessment. This increase is fueled in part by the 2010 Patient Protection and Affordable Care Act which requires providers to "detect any cognitive impairment" as part of the annual wellness visit for Medicare recipients (Cordell et al., 2013) and an increasingly sophisticated society that realizes extensive cognitive loss is not a routine part of normal aging. As a result, individuals are presenting for dementia assessment much earlier in the course of the disease or even prior to expression of meaningful symptoms. Consequently, individuals with subtle cognitive symptoms or isolated deficits on testing, constituting a diagnosis of MCI, are commonplace in assessment settings. Furthermore, these individuals typically require serial assessments to clarify their diagnosis. This is particularly important given that many individuals who receive an initial diagnosis of MCI may revert to normal or remain stable over time and may not eventually progress to dementia. Such estimates range from 4 to 55%, depending on the setting and length of follow-up (Koepsell & Monsell, 2012). Having a clear understanding that MCI represents a spectrum of possible disorders and that prognosis is uncertain in many cases provides a framework for how one approaches assessment and report writing in such cases. As we attempt to make diagnoses earlier and earlier, the trajectory of MCI is less certain, and report conclusions need to avoid overstating what the results can tell us. At the same time, functional problems are sometimes greater than would be expected for evaluation results, perhaps because some patients have enough cognitive reserve to perform better in a structured test setting than in real-world environments. In such instances, behavioral observations or report of functioning by the caregiver may be given greater weight in forming and articulating your conclusions than the test results per se; for example:

> Despite Mr. Smith's mostly average performances on memory testing, he could not identify any of his current medications and became turned around in the testing suite with trouble finding his way back to the office after a break. This raises concerns about his ability to independently manage his medication regimen and navigate in new environments.

Once an individual has passed the threshold from MCI to dementia, the two main issues to be included in the report are making a conclusion regarding the differential diagnosis (i.e., assist the referral source in making a diagnosis) and helping to guide functional recommendations to promote safety and quality of life.

WRITING FOR AND COLLABORATING WITH NEUROLOGISTS

Neurologists and neuropsychologists frequently collaborate in the assessment and diagnosis of dementia, with referrals in both directions depending on who sees the patient first. Physicians requesting neuropsychological evaluation are most commonly seeking assistance with establishing and confirming a diagnosis (Tremont, Westervelt, Javorsky, Podolanczuk, & Stern, 2002). As such, the evaluation summary and conclusions need to provide more than just cognitive strengths and weaknesses. The report should include as definitive an opinion as possible regarding diagnosis. It is important to avoid the pitfall of simply repeating back what you have been provided in the referral question (e.g., dementia versus depression), and you should include support for your conclusion. If your impression is based on information you received that is different from the referring source, articulate these points to help support your diagnosis. For example, if the patient and caregiver were seen together with the neurologist, important collateral information may not have been provided, whereas neuropsychologists often have more time to spend with the patient and usually interview the caregiver separately, increasing the likelihood of getting more detailed and accurate information about cognitive and functional changes. In addition, the neuropsychological evaluation affords more opportunity to observe behavior over a longer period of time than is possible during a routine visit in the physician's office. Aside from assistance with differential diagnosis, roughly a third of surveyed physicians requesting neuropsychological evaluation do so in order to obtain treatment recommendations or guidance regarding legal capacity (Temple, Carvalho, & Tremont, 2006). Therefore, providing specific recommendations on issues such as legal capacities, driving, financial management, and independent living is critical for your reports to be helpful to your referral source.

SECTIONS OF THE REPORT

- Reason for referral
- Current symptoms
  - Cognitive, emotional/psychological, physical
  - Include report from patient as well as informant; highlight contradictory reports
  - Indicate absence of key symptoms relevant for differential diagnosis
- Functional status
  - Basic activities of daily living (independent or need assistance)
  - Instrumental activities of daily living (independent or need assistance)
  - Work performance (if applicable)
  - Be sure to comment on areas that you will later address in your recommendations (e.g., report getting lost or accidents if present to support recommendations about driving)
- History
  - Medical/neurological. Be attuned to elements that could contribute to cognitive deficits (e.g., sleep disturbance/sleep apnea, medications, falls with head injury, and sensory deficits that can mimic cognitive impairment).
  - Psychological. Be sure to ask about symptoms that can be seen in certain dementias (e.g., hallucinations, delusions, obsessive–compulsive tendencies, behavior/personality change).
  - Psychosocial. This includes variables that provide the context of prior level of functioning.
  - Developmental—as needed. You can review briefly in interview but may not be relevant for report.

CASE EXAMPLE

There is no single correct way to present information in a report, but to illustrate examples of less and more desirable ways of presenting report elements a case of dementia versus depression will be reviewed. Ms. Smith is a 50-year-old Caucasian female with a 1-year history of short-term memory loss that has progressively worsened'over time. She also reported mild symptoms of depression and anxiety. Medical history was negative for neurocognitive risk factors, and head CT was read as normal. She described difficulties with recent memory, problem solving, and getting lost, which her husband minimized. She was referred for evaluation to assist with differential diagnosis of her symptoms. The psychometric data are presented in Table 4.2, and the full written report is presented in Appendix 4.1 (pp. 113–117).

Example 1: Interview

LESS DESIRABLE: DOCTOR A

Ms. Smith has heartburn and occasionally requires medication to control the symptoms. She recently sprained her ankle, which has made exercise difficult. Cognitively, she loses her train of thought when speaking, struggles to find the words she wants to use during conversation and when composing e-mails, and related multiple episodes where she was uncertain of how to get to her desired location when driving, including to a friend's house, a store she has been to before, and a soccer field where her children regularly have games. She previously paid the household bills and took care of routine paperwork, but has turned this over to her husband due to difficulty organizing and responding to items in a timely fashion. Her family also noted a variety of cognitive and functional problems, but attributed these to stress.

MORE DESIRABLE: DOCTOR B

Ms. Smith loses her train of thought, has word-finding difficulty, and gets lost when driving. She is indecisive, and her husband has taken over the finances because she was allowing bills to pile up. Additional information obtained through a phone interview with her husband indicates that she forgets conversations, is slower to complete tasks, and has trouble using her GPS, with greater functional difficulties when "stressed out." Medical

TABLE 4.2. Psychometric Data for Ms. Smith

Test	Score (raw unless specified)	z-score
WAIS-IV (scaled scores)		
Similarities	9	−0.3
Vocabulary	11	0.3
Digit Span	4	−2.0
Block Design	2	−2.7
Matrix Reasoning	4	−2.0
Coding	1	< −3.0
Test of Premorbid Functioning (standard score)	96	−0.3
Dementia Rating Scale–2	120/144	—
Wisconsin Card Sorting Test		
Perseverative Responses	54	< −3.0
Categories Completed	1	—
Set Failures	0	—
Trail Making Test, Part A	215″ (1 error)	< −3.0
Trail Making Test, Part B	>300″ (1 error)	< −3.0
Boston Naming Test	48	−1.9
Verbal Fluency (F, A, S)	34	−0.9
Animal Fluency	11	−2.7
WMS-IV (scaled scores)		
Logical Memory I	5	−1.7
Logical Memory II	5	−1.7
% Retention	64	—
Visual Reproduction I	1	< −3.0
Visual Reproduction II	2	−2.7
% Retention	13	—
California Verbal Learning Test II		
Total Learning	33	−1.8
Delayed Recall	3 (4 with cues)	−3.0
Intrusion Errors	31	< −3.0
Recognition Discriminability	15 Hits, 17 False positives	−2.0
Rey–Osterrieth Complex Figure		
Copy Trial	10	< −3.0
Immediate Recall	6	< −3.0
Delayed Recall	3	< −3.0
Finger Oscillation Test		
Right Hand (dominant)	46	−0.1
Left Hand	38.8	−0.6
Personality Assessment Inventory	No clinically significant elevations	

Note. WAIS-IV, Wechsler Adult Intelligence Scale—Fourth Edition; WMS-IV, Wechsler Memory Scale—Fourth Edition.

history appears noncontributory, and she is currently not taking any medication.

Comment on Interview

Dr. A and Dr. B both provide similar information, but Dr. A begins the section describing medical information that is essentially irrelevant to the referral question and current symptoms. In addition, Dr. A provides more detail about the cognitive symptoms than necessary to convey the problem areas, which makes the report longer and more cumbersome to read. However, Dr. A does not elaborate on information obtained from Ms. Smith's husband (or identify from whom the information was obtained), leaving the reader to wonder about what types of changes her family has noticed. In contrast, Dr. B begins with the most relevant symptoms, presented in a concise fashion, and includes several examples from the patient's husband to better understand the nature of her deficits.

Example 2: Observations

LESS DESIRABLE: DOCTOR A

Ms. Smith was 10 minutes late for the evaluation and wore slacks and a blouse. Despite her recently sprained ankle, she seemed to walk without difficulty and did not lose her balance. She had trouble understanding instructions on the WCST, Trail Making Test, and on the Coding subtest of the WAIS-IV. As a result, directions for these tasks were repeated or simplified if needed to facilitate her comprehension. She was slow in completing office paperwork, as well as on a variety of other tasks, particularly on WAIS-IV Matrix Reasoning. Even though the testing took a while to complete, her effort remained good throughout the evaluation.

MORE DESIRABLE: DOCTOR B

Ms. Smith presented as a neatly dressed female with normal speech and gait. No gross motor difficulties were observed, though slight left/right confusion was evidenced on one test. She had mild difficulty understanding test instructions, necessitating repetition and simplification of directions on some tasks. She moved slowly through the testing but appeared to put forth good effort. Therefore, these results are considered to be a valid representation of her current functioning.

Comment on Observations

Dr. A gives information in the observations that is not necessary, such as a recently sprained ankle that did not interfere with her motor functioning. In addition, Dr. A references specific tests, which is not necessary to convey that she was slow during the evaluation or had trouble understanding instructions. Dr. B provides a more concise description of her presentation. Key elements of her behavior pertaining to individual tests during the evaluation can be described in more detail in the interpretation section.

Example 3: Results

LESS DESIRABLE: DOCTOR A

Ms. Smith was administered a variety of tests that assess frontal lobe functioning. On the Wisconsin Card Sorting Test, the individual must figure out how to sort novel stimuli when provided with minimal information on how to do so, though are given corrective feedback on whether they are "right" or "wrong." Performance on this test was severely impaired. On a test of numerical sequencing that assesses processing speed and eye–hand coordination, she performed in the severely impaired range. When mental set shifting was additionally required, her performance was severely impaired. The Digit-Symbol Coding task of the WAIS-IV involves processing speed and visual–motor coordination, and is one of the most sensitive tests of brain dysfunction. Her performance on this test was severely impaired.

MORE DESIRABLE: DOCTOR B

Problem solving and concept formation were mildly to moderately impaired, as she completed only 1/6 categories on a card-sorting test, with severe perseveration and confusion on the task. She had trouble following instructions on a processing speed task involving digit-symbol substitution, completing only two items in the time allotted. Processing speed on a visual scanning and numerical sequencing test was severely impaired (< 1st percentile), and she was unable to complete a similar task that additionally involves mental set shifting, despite heavy coaching before the task was discontinued due to time constraints.

Comment on Results

Dr. A takes the approach of describing characteristics of individual tests and associating them with specific brain regions, spending much more time expounding on the test than on the patient's actual performance. This approach oversimplifies what our tests measure and provides limited useful information on the patient's strengths and weaknesses or qualitative features of their behavior. Dr. B describes the test in a limited fashion and adds useful qualitative information that conveys the severity of her difficulties on the tasks being described.

Example 4: Summary

LESS DESIRABLE: DOCTOR A

```
These results are consistent with a dementia, with severe
impairment in problem solving, processing speed, category
fluency, and visual memory, moderate impairment in atten-
tion, visuospatial abilities, and verbal memory, and mild
impairment in confrontation naming. A frontotemporal demen-
tia could be considered because of her young age and prob-
lems with executive functioning. Alzheimer's disease could
be considered because of her memory deficits, and Lewy body
disease is possible because of her pronounced visuospatial
difficulties and possible cognitive fluctuations.
```

MORE DESIRABLE: DOCTOR B

```
The overall pattern of results suggests global cognitive
dysfunction, with somewhat greater involvement of right-
hemisphere systems. These results are consistent with a
mild to moderate dementia, with the pattern most consis-
tent with early-onset Alzheimer's disease. Given more pro-
nounced visuospatial difficulty, Lewy body disease could
also be considered, and she does report some cognitive
fluctuations, though she does not have other prototypical
symptoms of Lewy body disease (e.g., parkinsonism, visual
hallucinations, REM behavioral symptoms), and it is not
unusual for early-onset cases of Alzheimer's disease to
have some atypical features.
```

Comment on Summary

Dr. A reiterates the results in more detail than is needed, whereas Dr. B provides a more concise summary of the findings as well as the pattern of performance. Dr. A does introduce a variety of possible diagnoses, with limited support for each, but does not provide a more definitive opinion about the diagnosis. In contrast, Dr. B presents the two most likely diagnoses along with some support for why Lewy body disease (LBD) was ruled out.

EXAMPLES OF CONCLUSIONS

The concluding statement in your report is often the first place your referral source will look and is likely the most important part of your report. Articulating the most relevant differential diagnosis and support for each may be particularly helpful. Below are some examples of common differential diagnoses that occur in the assessment of dementia.

Differential Diagnosis of Language-Variant Frontotemporal Dementia versus AD

History

Patient has multiple medical issues, early language impairment, and prior neuropsychological testing diagnosing the patient with a "dementia." Referred for evaluation to help differentiate between language-variant frontotemporal dementia (FTD) versus AD.

LESS DESIRABLE: DOCTOR A

These results reflect primary impairment in language, processing speed, and memory, most consistent with Alzheimer's disease or possibly a mixed (AD + vascular) etiology.

MORE DESIRABLE: DOCTOR B

These results reflect a decline in language, processing speed, and memory compared with prior testing. While his prominent and early language deficits raise concerns for a language variant of frontotemporal dementia, his global cognitive impairment and quality of language deficits (e.g., primary trouble with word retrieval, with no agrammatism or loss of word knowledge) are more consistent with a left-hemisphere presentation of Alzheimer's disease than a language-variant frontotemporal dementia. Microvascular changes noted on MRI may be contributing to his deficits but cannot account for the entirety of his symptoms.

Comment

Dr. A's conclusion is briefer and more straightforward than Dr. B's, which may be desirable in some settings, but Dr. A's conclusion does not provide a comparison with the prior testing or work through the differential diagnosis to support the conclusion. In complex neurodiagnostic cases, it is often helpful to articulate your support, or lack thereof, for relevant differential diagnoses. For the knowledgeable referring physician, this additional information can be very helpful, and for those less familiar with dementia, the information may help the referral source better understand the nuances of dementia diagnoses.

Differential Diagnosis of AD versus LBD

History

Patient has a 2-year history of cognitive decline and behavioral changes, with initial difficulties in short-term memory that have progressed and now cause functional problems. She was referred to help with differential diagnosis of her symptoms.

> **LESS DESIRABLE: DOCTOR A**
>
> Deficits were seen in IQ, executive functioning, processing speed, language, visuospatial functioning, attention, and memory, indicating global impairment. There were some features of Lewy body disease. The patient appears to have a moderate to severe dementia that could be Alzheimer's disease or Lewy body disease.

> **MORE DESIRABLE: DOCTOR B**
>
> The overall pattern of results suggests global cognitive dysfunction, with somewhat greater involvement of frontotemporal and right-hemisphere systems. These results suggest a moderate to severe dementia, with many features of Lewy body disease (or mixed Alzheimer's and Lewy body disease), including motor dysfunction, prominent visuospatial deficits, visual hallucinations, cognitive fluctuations, and REM behavior disorder.

Comment

Dr. A lists the areas of cognitive impairment but does not indicate the pattern of impairment as does Dr. B, which can be instrumental in differentiating between types of dementia. Furthermore, Dr. B also highlights symptoms indicative of a diagnosis of Lewy body disease or mixed AD + LBD, to provide support for the diagnosis. This additional information helps the referring physician and family understand how you are making the diagnosis.

Differential Diagnosis of MCI versus AD

History

Patient has a 1-year history of short-term memory loss of unclear progression. She is independent in managing medications, bill paying, and taking care of household chores, including cooking and cleaning. She was referred to help with differential diagnosis of her symptoms.

LESS DESIRABLE: DOCTOR A

The patient demonstrated memory impairment, but has no functional changes and does not meet criteria for dementia. She should return for evaluation if she notices any cognitive changes.

MORE DESIRABLE: DOCTOR B

The overall pattern of results suggests severe impairment in memory, with subtle changes in executive functioning, within an otherwise intact profile. Her pattern of memory results is consistent with what is often seen in individuals with Alzheimer's disease, though there do not appear to be any significant functional changes at this time. As such, she meets criteria for a diagnosis of amnestic mild cognitive impairment. Neuropsychological reevaluation in one year is recommended to assess for additional changes and further assist with differential diagnosis.

Comment

Dr. A's summary is technically correct, but is lacking in sufficient detail. MCI is a recognized diagnostic category and should be used when appropriate. Furthermore, Dr. A makes only a broad comment about reevaluation. In contrast, Dr. B gives more information about the pattern of results, provides a diagnosis, and articulates the utility of reevaluation as well as the time frame.

REPORT RECOMMENDATIONS

Recommendations in the context of a dementia report may cover a variety of areas. In cases where the neuropsychological evaluation is the first step in the dementia assessment, your recommendations may direct the patient and referral source to the next step in the diagnostic process, which could include further diagnostics (e.g., neuroimaging, neurological evaluation, or specialty recommendation such as a movement disorder's specialist) or indicate a watch and wait approach (e.g., in the case of MCI), whereby reevaluation at a later time is the most reasonable next step. However, keep your referral source in mind when making recommendations to ensure you are working together for the patient and that you are not overstepping boundaries that could interfere with your relationship with your referral sources. For example, instead of recommending a specific medication to treat dementia, you might recommend that the patient discuss medication treatment options with their physician for their dementia. When questions about legal capacity, work, driving, and independent living arise, neuropsychologists are often in the best position to make recommendations in each of these areas. Given the potential implications of these recommendations, they should not be made lightly, but also should not be shied away from even though they might not be well received by the patient.

Examples

Additional Testing or Evaluation

LESS DESIRABLE: DOCTOR A

Ms. X should probably undergo a brain scan.

MORE DESIRABLE: DOCTOR B

Neuroimaging, such as MRI, is recommended to rule out other potential contributing causes for her dementia.

COMMENT

Dr. B explains why an MRI is being recommended and is more definitive in his statement, which may garner more support for the recommendation.

Referrals

LESS DESIRABLE: DOCTOR A

Mrs. X is referred to neurology to further evaluate and clarify her diagnosis.

MORE DESIRABLE: DOCTOR B

Given her slow gait and frequent falls, it is recommended that Mrs. X see a movement disorder's specialist to further clarify her diagnosis and determine treatment options.

COMMENT

Given the particular concern for an underlying movement disorder, Dr. B specifies the type of neurologist that is being recommended and what symptoms support the need for the referral.

Treatment Considerations

LESS DESIRABLE: DOCTOR A

Treatment of Mr. X's depression is recommended.

MORE DESIRABLE: DOCTOR B

Mr. X may benefit from a trial of an antidepressant medication to address his depressive symptoms.

COMMENT

There are different ways to treat depression, and Dr. B's recommendation is more specific than Dr. A's.

Functional Considerations

LESS DESIRABLE: DOCTOR A

Caution when driving is recommended, and some oversight should be provided.

MORE DESIRABLE: DOCTOR B

Given reduced visual memory and processing speed, Mrs. X is advised to limit her driving to familiar, low-traffic neighborhoods, review routes in advance, and use external aids such as a GPS navigation system.

Or

Given the extent of Mrs. X's cognitive deficits and recent instances of getting lost, it is recommended that she cease driving for safety and liability reasons.

COMMENT

Dr. A's recommendations of caution and oversight of driving may not be restrictive enough, and the wording is vague and open for interpretation. In contrast, Dr. B. gives more specific restrictions for the patient's driving and provides some basis for the recommendation.

Cognitive Compensation

LESS DESIRABLE: DOCTOR A

Mr. X should use memory aids.

MORE DESIRABLE: DOCTOR B

Mr. X may benefit from the use of memory aids such as a memory notebook he carries on his person, in which to record daily "to do" lists, appointments, details from conversations, and other information.

COMMENT

Both Dr. A and Dr. B recommend memory aids, but this is too vague for patients. The clearer you can be about how the aids should be used, the more likely the individual is to adopt the practice.

REEVALUATIONS

Serial evaluations are an integral aspect of neuropsychological assessment of MCI and dementia when clarification of the diagnosis is needed, as well as assessment of cognitive change over time related to a disease process or response to treatment/intervention. Effective reevaluation requires an appropriate determination of what constitutes clinically meaningful test–retest change and may involve the use of statistical procedures such as reliable change methods (Chelune, 2002). Report history can be abbreviated in such instances to avoid redundant or unnecessary information. Usually, an interim history will suffice, only repeating aspects of the history that are relevant to the referral question. There should be a clear comparison of current results to past findings to illustrate what changes have occurred, with accompanying statements as to the likely reason for the changes (e.g., decline, response to treatment, questionable effort). Presenting data in a table or graph form can be helpful in some situations to facilitate ease in interpreting changes. Figure 4.1 represents baseline and follow-up results,

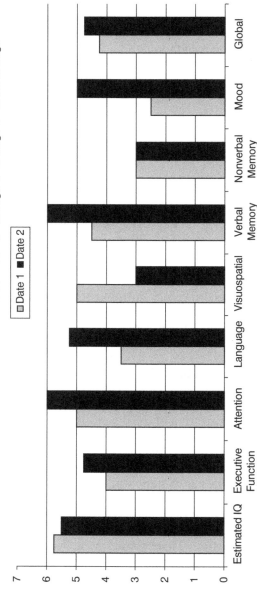

FIGURE 4.1. Example of using a graph to depict reevaluation results. The graph represents clinical ratings for each cognitive domain assessed, including an index of depression, and takes into account qualitative aspects of the patient's performance as well as standard scores in comparison with prior levels. The overall pattern of results reflects primary deficits in problem solving, processing speed, visuospatial abilities, and visual memory. Most aspects of language, attention, and verbal memory were relatively preserved. In comparison with 2012 levels, these results reflect improvement in problem solving, language functioning, attention, and verbal memory, whereas visuospatial abilities are slightly reduced and visual memory remains impaired. In addition, the patient has had a reduction in depressive symptoms and is taking much better care of himself, including better treatment compliance with his medications. The overall pattern results suggest primary dysfunction of frontosubcortical systems, consistent with what can be seen in some individuals with Parkinson's disease, but with improvement from his prior evaluation. These improvements in addition to lifestyle changes (e.g., better diet and medication treatment compliance, alcohol cessation) are all positive indicators for his ability to participate in the deep brain stimulation (DBS) process if he continues on to surgery.

with a brief description of the results in a patient with Parkinson's disease who is being considered for deep brain stimulation for treatment of his motor symptoms as an example of how graphs can be used in your reports to convey results.

COMMON REPORT-WRITING MISTAKES

- Telling the referral sources what they already know.
- Giving a lengthy history that includes irrelevant information for referral question (e.g., detailed description of academic history with question of dementia).
- Writing reports that give lengthy descriptions of tests (and associated brain functioning) prior to or rather than describing the individual's test performance.
- Providing a lengthy summary that just reiterates results.
- Introducing new information in the summary (e.g., emotional problems, sleep disturbance) that was not addressed earlier in the report.
- Not giving a diagnostic opinion when possible (e.g., saying the person has cognitive impairment, but not whether it satisfies the criteria for dementia and what is the suspected etiology).
- Not taking into consideration other possible risk factors that could contribute to cognitive impairment (e.g., medications, psychiatric factors, pain).
- Presenting canned recommendations that are not tailored to the individual.
- Recommending retesting without a good rationale.

The keys to writing an effective report in the assessment of dementia is to know your referral sources and what they want from you, figure out what "story" needs to be told to answer the referral question(s), be as clear about your opinions as the data will allow, and provide cogent and specific recommendations to make the results of your evaluation meaningful.

REFERENCES

Chelune, G. J. (2002a). Assessing reliable neuropsychological change. In R. Franklin (Ed.), *Prediction in forensic and neuropsychology: New approaches to psychometrically sound assessment* (pp. 123–148). Mahwah, NJ: Erlbaum.

Cordell, C. B., Borson, S., Boustani, M., Chodosh, J., Reuben, D., Verghese, J., et al. (2013). Alzheimer's Association recommendations for operationalizing the detection of cognitive impairment during the Medicare Annual Wellness Visit in a primary care setting. *Alzheimers and Dementia, 9*(2), 141–150.

Cullum, C. M., Saine, K., Chan, L. D., Martin-Cook, K., Gray, K. F., & Weiner,

M. F. (2001). Performance-based instrument to assess functional capacity in dementia: The Texas Functional Living Scale. *Neuropsychiatry, Neuropsychology, and Behavioral Neurology, 14*(2), 103–108.

Farias, S. T., Mungas, D., & Jagust, W. (2005). Degree of discrepancy between self and other-reported everyday functioning by cognitive status: Dementia, mild cognitive impairment, and healthy elders. *International Journal of Geriatric Psychiatry, 20*(9), 827–834.

Grisso, T. (2003). *Evaluating competencies: Forensic assessments and instruments* (2nd ed., Vol. 16). New York: Kluwer Academic/Plenum Publishers.

Heaton, R. K., Ryan, L., Grant, I., & Matthews, C. G. (1996). Demographic influences on neuropsychological test performance. In I. Grant & K. M. Adams (Eds.), *Neuropsychological assessment of neuropsychiatric disorders* (2nd ed., pp. 141–163). New York: Oxford University Press.

Hebert, L. E., Beckett, L. A., Scherr, P. A., & Evans, D. A. (2001). Annual incidence of Alzheimer disease in the United States projected to the years 2000 through 2050. *Alzheimer Disease and Associated Disorders, 15*(4), 169–173.

Koepsell, T. D., & Monsell, S. E. (2012). Reversion from mild cognitive impairment to normal or near-normal cognition: Risk factors and prognosis. *Neurology, 79*(15), 1591–1598.

Lucas, J. A., Ivnik, R. J., Willis, F. B., Ferman, T. J., Smith, G. E., Parfitt, F. C., et al. (2005). Mayo's Older African Americans Normative Studies: Normative data for commonly used clinical neuropsychological measures. *Clinical Neuropsychologist, 19*(2), 162–183.

Marson, D. C., Schmitt, F. A., Ingram, K. K., & Lindy, H. (1994). Determining the competency of Alzheimer patients to consent to treatment and research. *Alzheimer Disease and Associated Disorders, 8*(Suppl. 4), 5–18.

Moye, J., Marson, D. C., & Edelstein, B. (2013). Assessment of capacity in an aging society. *American Psychologist, 68*(3), 158–171.

Schulz, R., Cook, T. B., Beach, S. R., Lingler, J. H., Martire, L. M., Monin, J. K., et al. (2013). Magnitude and causes of bias among family caregivers rating Alzheimer disease patients. *American Journal of Geriatric Psychiatry, 21*(1), 14–25.

Temple, R. O., Carvalho, J., & Tremont, G. (2006). A national survey of physicians' use of and satisfaction with neuropsychological services. *Archives of Clinical Neuropsychology, 21*(5), 371–382.

Tremont, G., Westervelt, H. J., Javorsky, D. J., Podolanczuk, A., & Stern, R. A. (2002). Referring physicians' perceptions of the neuropsychological evaluation: How are we doing? *The Clinical Neuropsychologist, 16*(4), 551–554.

Wechsler, D. (2009). *WMS-IV: Wechsler Memory Scale—Administration and scoring manual.* San Antonio, TX: The Psychological Corporation.

Sample Neuropsychological Report for Ms. Smith

Patient name: Ms. Smith   *Date of evaluation:*   XXX

Date of birth: XXX   *Handedness:*   Right

Referral: XXX   *Education:*   16 years

Neurobehavioral Status Examination

Ms. Smith is a 50-year-old Caucasian female with a 1-year history of short-term memory loss that has progressively worsened
over time. She loses her train of thought, has word-finding
difficulty, and gets lost when driving. She is indecisive, and
her husband has taken over the finances because she was allowing bills to pile up. Additional information obtained through
a phone interview with her husband indicates that she forgets conversations, is slower to complete tasks, and has trouble using her GPS, with greater functional difficulties when
"stressed out." There may be some cognitive fluctuations, but
this was hard to ascertain. Ms. Smith was referred for this
evaluation to assess her current cognitive functioning and
assist with differential diagnosis of her symptoms.

Medical history appears noncontributory, and she takes no
medication. Head CT on XXXX was read as normal. She consumes
one to three glasses of wine per week and denied past history
of substance-related problems. Family history includes dementia in a maternal grandfather. Emotionally, she reported some
difficulty with mood. She stated that she has always been a
sensitive person, but that now she becomes upset more readily, especially when others point out her memory loss. She also
described frequent worrying and anxiety. She believes that her
family is frustrated with her. She was previously very involved
with her husband's business, and she feels guilty that she is
no longer helping. She states that she wakes up in the middle
of the night and has trouble returning to sleep, often worrying about things she needs to do. There is no indication of REM
behavioral symptoms. There was no report of hallucinations,
delusions, or suicidal thoughts.

Psychosocial history indicates that she completed high
school and college, making mostly A's and B's, with no history of learning problems. She has primarily worked in sales
and marketing positions and last worked in her husband's business, but quit to be a full-time homemaker. She is active at
her children's school in a variety of leadership positions that
take up to 2 to 3 hours of her time per week. She currently
lives with her husband of 19 years and two children, ages 14
and 11.

Behavioral Observations

Ms. Smith presented as a neatly dressed female with normal speech and gait. No gross motor difficulties were observed, though slight left/right confusion was evidenced on one test. She had mild difficulty understanding test instructions, necessitating repetition and simplification of directions on some tasks. She moved slowly through the testing, but appeared to put forth good effort. Therefore, these results are considered to be a valid representation of her current functioning.

Tests Administered

Wechsler Adult Intelligence Scale–IV (WAIS-IV; selected subtests), Test of Premorbid Functioning (TOPF), Dementia Rating Scale-2 (DRS-2), Wisconsin Card Sorting Test (WCST), Trail Making Test (TMT), Boston Naming Test (BNT), Verbal Fluency, Cookie Theft Description, Clock Drawings, Wechsler Memory Scale–IV (WMS-IV; Logical Memory and Visual Reproduction), California Verbal Learning Test–II (CVLT-II), Rey-Osterrieth Complex Figure, Finger Tapping, Word Choice, Computerized Assessment of Response Bias (CARB), Personality Assessment Inventory (PAI)

Results

Ms. Smith performed below expectation on one forced-choice measure of test engagement (Word Choice = 36/50), but scored adequately on other tests of motivation and effort (CARB = 98.6%; CVLT-II Forced Choice = 16/16; Reliable Digit Span = 8). As such, overall effort was deemed adequate, and these results are considered to be valid.

Ms. Smith was oriented to the day, month, city, and place, but had difficulty expressing the date and year, eventually stating it was the 10th of October 2014. She performed in the moderately impaired range on a test of global cognitive abilities (DRS-2 = 120/144), with greatest difficulty on construction and memory items. Intellectual abilities were estimated to fall in the borderline to low average range, with better verbal than nonverbal skills, the latter of which is moderately below estimated longstanding levels in at least the average range.

Problem solving and concept formation were mildly to moderately impaired, as she completed only 1/6 categories on a card-sorting test, with severe perseveration and confusion on the task. She had trouble following instructions on a processing speed task involving digit-symbol substitution, only completing two items in the time allotted. Processing speed on a visual scanning and numerical sequencing test was severely impaired (< 1st percentile), and she was unable to complete a similar task that additionally involves mental set shifting, being provided with heavy coaching before the task was discontinued due to time constraints. Attention to simple auditory information was moderately impaired (5 digits forward, 3 digits in reverse, 2 digits in sequence).

Expressive vocabulary skills were average, and verbal abstract reasoning in the form of identifying similarities between objects was average. Confrontation naming was mildly to moderately impaired (BNT = 48/60; *T*-score = 31), with minimal benefit from phonemic cuing. Verbal fluency was low average for letters and moderately to severely impaired for categories (11animals in 1 minute). Her written description of a pictorial scene was adequate, aside from 2 misspelling errors.

Visuospatial abilities were markedly impaired. She had mild difficulty copying simple figures on the DRS-2, and slight number asymmetry was noted on her spontaneous drawing of a clock face. In addition, she required extended time to set the hands to a designated time (~5 minutes for entire task), but was able to do so correctly. Her copy of a more complex geometric figure was severely impaired, and she was unable to complete her drawing even with extended time. Performance on a block construction test was moderately to severely impaired (< 1st percentile), with a broken configuration and stacking of blocks. Motor speed was average using her dominant right hand and low average on the left.

Immediate and delayed recall of short stories was mildly to moderately impaired (5th percentile), with retention of 64% of the minimal amount of story details initially learned after a delay. Recognition of story details was also impaired (17/30). Overall learning on a 16-item list-learning task was mildly to moderately impaired, as she learned from 5 to 9 words across trials (with some variability across trials), and recalled 3 items after a delay (4 with cues), which is moderately to severely impaired. In addition, she made 31 intrusion errors across recall attempts. Performance on recognition testing was mildly to moderately impaired, with more false-positive errors (17) than correct recognitions (15/16). Immediate recall of simple figures was severely impaired (< 1st percentile), and she only recalled two design details after a delay, with perseveration from an earlier task. Recall of a more complex geometric figure was severely impaired, with recall of only isolated design details after a delay, likely due in part to initial difficulties copying and organizing the design.

Emotional Functioning

Ms. Smith completed the PAI to provide an assessment of her current emotional functioning. She responded in an open and forthright manner, indicating only modestly elevated levels of stress and anxiety. She seems to have a positive self-image and is likely viewed by others as warm and friendly. There do not appear to be any contributing emotional factors that would account for her current cognitive difficulties.

Summary and Recommendations

Ms. Smith was mildly disoriented and demonstrated low average intellectual abilities, with significantly better verbal than nonverbal skills. She demonstrated global cognitive deficits, with greatest difficulty in problem solving, processing speed, visuospatial abilities, and memory (visual worse than verbal). Overlearned verbal skills and single-word reading were relatively preserved, though she had some difficulty with naming and verbal fluency. Fine motor speed was largely intact, but slightly lower than expected using her nondominant left hand compared to the right. There do not appear to be any contributing emotional factors that would account for these deficits. The overall pattern of results suggests global cognitive dysfunction, with somewhat greater involvement of right-hemisphere systems. These results are consistent with a mild to moderate dementia, with the pattern most consistent with early-onset Alzheimer's disease. Given more pronounced visuospatial difficulty, Lewy body disease could also be considered, and she does report some cognitive fluctuations, though she does not have other prototypical symptoms of Lewy body disease (e.g., parkinsonism, visual hallucinations, REM behavioral symptoms), and it is not unusual for early-onset cases of AD to have some atypical features.

Given her young age and level of deficits, a complete neurological evaluation is recommended, if not already conducted, to rule out other potential contributing causes for her deficits. After this evaluation, treatment options can be reviewed with her physician. Current visuospatial, visual memory, and processing speed deficits raise concerns about driving safety. She acknowledged occasionally getting turned around, but denied any other problems. Nonetheless, given these results, it is recommended that she stop driving. She will likely do best with routine and structure and is encouraged to minimize additional responsibilities (e.g., leadership roles in her community). Making use of a notebook in which she can write down important information and setting reminders on her phone or in other places will be important to help with memory, particularly for time-sensitive items. She and her family may benefit from support services from the Alzheimer's Association. In addition, individual and family counseling may be beneficial to help with adjustment issues given her young age and young children still at home. I would be happy to see Ms. Smith and her family back to review other compensatory strategies once her diagnosis has been confirmed and she has had time to assimilate the information.

Thank you for referring this interesting individual for evaluation. If I can be of further assistance to you or the patient, please do not hesitate to contact me.

CHAPTER 5

Psychopathology and Psychiatric Comorbidity

Robert M. Roth
Laura A. Flashman

Neuropsychology plays a unique role within the discipline of the clinical neurosciences because it integrates neuroscience, clinical psychology, and cognitive psychology. When considering psychopathology, we are able to conceptualize disorders not simply by their clinical features, but also by their cognitive and neurobehavioral features. In the past, typical referral questions for neuropsychologists within psychiatric settings focused on whether cognitive deficits were "functional" or "organic" (the correct answer is "yes"). With advances in the field of neuroscience, it has become clear that this conceptualization of cognitive impairment in individuals with psychopathology is not particularly helpful or relevant. This chapter illustrates more useful approaches to assessment of such individuals and the associated report preparation. Contemporary assessment approaches focus on identifying neuropsychological strengths and weaknesses. Referral questions, particularly in the inpatient setting, typically involve issues related to an individual's current cognitive status and its impact on daily functioning, with an emphasis on identifying what types of services might be appropriate while in the hospital and in the community (as a crucial part of discharge planning). This may include questions pertaining to a person's safety (i.e., "Can this person be left alone in his or her home?"), functional independence (e.g., "Can this person manage his or her own money?"), and employability (i.e., "Can this person work, and, if so, in what type of job would he or she be most likely to succeed?"). Results of the neuropsychological evaluation form part of the repertoire of data used to address these issues, and provide insights into what supports might be needed in order to provide the least restrictive environment and/or what accommodations can be made in the workplace to maximize success.

Referrals may also be made to help address issues related to recovery from a psychiatric episode, support or clarify a diagnosis, or aid in differential diagnosis (especially when there are unusual symptoms or concerns regarding comorbidities such as dementia in an aging patient). In addition, neuropsychological evaluations may be conducted in the context of concern about deterioration in functioning over time, to assess for cognitive changes as a result of medication or other interventions (e.g., electroconvulsive therapy [ECT]), and to help guide rehabilitation, educational, vocational, or other services. Neuropsychological data can also serve important forensic and other legal purposes, such as contributing to the determination of decision-making capacity, and results may be used to help determine disability.

Results of neuropsychological evaluation may indicate the need for referral to other specialists, such as rehabilitation professionals, neurologists, vocational counselors, or educational services, to further inform differential diagnosis and make sure any potentially treatable problems are addressed. Finally, recommendations regarding appropriate compensatory strategies as well as environmental and other modifications are made. Feedback can be provided to the patient, the patient's family, the inpatient team, and community support services, including outpatient providers.

LIFESPAN ISSUES

Although we focus primarily on evaluation of adults with psychopathology, lifespan issues need to be taken into account when conceptualizing a case and when discussing report writing. Some psychiatric disorders begin in childhood (e.g., attention-deficit/hyperactivity disorder [ADHD]), others have a common onset in late adolescence or early adulthood (e.g., schizophrenia), and some typically have a later age of onset (e.g., bipolar disorder). Age of onset of psychiatric illness may have a negative impact on a person's educational and occupational achievement, and this factor should be taken into account when estimating premorbid/baseline level of functioning. For example, demographically based estimates of premorbid functioning may not be appropriate for an individual who experienced the onset of symptoms of schizophrenia in adolescence with resulting significant impact on his or her educational attainment. In such cases, performance-based measures (e.g., vocabulary or word reading) may be preferable, although even these may be affected by the disorder. There is as yet no consensus as to which measure provides the best estimate of baseline functioning in this cohort.

Individuals with psychiatric disorders may also have psychiatric and nonpsychiatric comorbidities that can vary across the lifespan and impact cognition. Age affects the probability of cerebral disorder, and the impact of factors such as substance use, learning disabilities, and head injury can vary based on the age of an individual. For example, there can be overlap between the cognitive impairments associated with psychiatric illnesses and traumatic brain injury (TBI); thus details regarding the injury (e.g., age when it occurred, severity, onset, and course of any cognitive changes) are crucial in determining whether or not the TBI is contributing to an individual's current cognitive profile. Comorbidities that were successfully managed prior to the onset of the psychiatric illness may contribute less to the current cognitive profile than those that developed in parallel with or as a result of the psychiatric disorder. Because potentially confounding premorbid or comorbid factors can account for impairments or exacerbate them, failure to address them can result in misinterpretation or misattribution of impairments to the primary psychiatric illness. Finally, it is important to be mindful of medications that can disrupt cognition through their subtle and sometimes not so subtle effects on cognition.

Profiles of specific symptoms can change across the lifespan as well. For example, there is evidence to suggest a decrease in the severity and frequency of positive symptoms in schizophrenia as individuals with this disorder get older (Arndt, Andreasen, Flaum, Miller, & Nopoulos, 1995). Similarly, symptoms in ADHD tend to change over time, with decreases in hyperactivity and increases in attention span and impulse control (Kessler et al., 2010). Furthermore, symptoms can worsen when individuals leave high school or college, with the loss of built-in supports and accommodations.

Finally, lifespan considerations also affect statements that can be made in the report about prognosis. For example, older individuals with psychiatric illness can develop dementia, which will result in further cognitive deficits and decreased functional independence. The literature is mixed, however, as to whether certain psychiatric illnesses have a neurodegenerative component (Harvey, 2014). This complicates the determination of whether cognitive decline, especially in older individuals, is related to a separate process such as Alzheimer's disease.

NEUROPSYCHOLOGICAL FUNCTIONING IN SELECTED PSYCHIATRIC DISORDERS

A large and often complex literature exists on the neuropsychological characteristics of many psychiatric disorders. Here, we provide a brief overview of cognitive functioning in a selection of disorders for which referral for neuropsychological evaluation is relatively common.

Schizophrenia

Neuropsychological deficits are very common in patients with schizophrenia and are associated with a variety of poor outcomes, even after severity of psychiatric symptoms such as delusions and hallucinations are taken into account. Cognitive deficits are considered by many to be a core feature of the disorder, and in DSM-5, assessment of cognitive functioning is seen as vital for informing differential diagnosis. One of the most consistent findings, however, is the presence of considerable neuropsychological heterogeneity in samples of patients with schizophrenia (Ammari, Heinrichs, & Miles, 2010). Many patients show deficits across cognitive domains assessed, though this finding does not necessarily imply that they have a true *generalized deficit*, as they may have areas of preserved functioning that may not always be observed using standard neuropsychological measures. Furthermore, prominent deficits have been reported in domains such as verbal learning and memory, executive functions (including working memory), and sustained attention and processing speed, even in the context of generalized difficulties (e.g., Saykin et al., 1994). Patients with schizophrenia have also been reported to show considerable intraindividual variability across cognitive tasks (similar in concept to subtest scatter) (Cole, Weinberger, & Dickinson, 2011). Thus, employing multiple measures involving similar or related abilities is desired in order to confidently identify areas of impairment in this population.

Up to 30% of patients with schizophrenia demonstrate little or no impairment when classified based on normative data (Wilk et al., 2005). These "neuropsychologically normal" patients, however, typically show deficits relative to their estimated premorbid intellectual ability or in comparison to healthy controls when matched closely for Full Scale IQ. Some have higher estimated premorbid ability than healthy comparison participants (e.g., Kremen, Seidman, Faraone, Toomey, & Tsuang, 2000). Such findings further highlight the importance of taking premorbid ability into account and have led to the suggestion that these individuals may be more appropriately referred to as having "high-functioning" schizophrenia.

The effect of potential mediator and moderator variables (e.g., gender) on neuropsychological functioning in schizophrenia tends to be small to modest. Atypical antipsychotic medications may have cognitive-enhancing effects, though this remains controversial and there is no differential benefit of one medication over the others (Keefe et al., 2007). The severity of positive symptoms does not account for cognitive impairment in schizophrenia, but symptoms such as poorer awareness of illness and apathy have been associated with worse cognition (e.g., Chan et al., 2012). Patients with a *deficit syndrome*, characterized by persisting negative symptoms despite periods of clinical stability, tend to be more globally cognitively impaired than those without this syndrome (Cohen et al., 2007). Furthermore, chronicity of illness cannot account for impairments given the similarities of functioning in first-episode and chronic patients (Mesholam-Gately, Giuliano, Goff, Faraone, & Seidman, 2009). Interestingly, a history of substance use disorder in patients with schizophrenia is not associated with worse cognition relative to patients without such a history, and in some studies cognition was better in the nonuser cohort (Potvin, Joyal, Pelletier, & Stip, 2008). The reasons for this are unclear, though better premorbid social and/or cognitive functioning in users than nonusers with schizophrenia may play a role.

In most adults with schizophrenia, cognitive deficits are generally stable over time, though there appears to be two periods when cognitive deterioration is more likely to be observed (Harvey, 2014). The first is sometime before the first psychotic episode, and the second is after approximately 65 years of age, with progressive decline in older patients being associated with an extensive history of illness and protracted institutionalization, even if tested when not institutionalized. A wealth of data indicates that neuropsychological difficulties may be present well before illness onset in patients with schizophrenia. Thus, when interpreting neuropsychological findings in a patient with the disorder, one needs to be mindful that (some) difficulties may be longstanding and possibly a core feature of the illness.

Major Depressive Disorder

Individuals with major depressive disorder (MDD) commonly report cognitive problems. There is substantial inconsistency in the neuropsychological literature, however, owing to methodological differences between studies, including variability in patient characteristics. Attentional impairments in MDD are more often seen on more demanding tests, such as those involving sustained attention or working memory (e.g., Ilamkar, 2014). Executive dysfunction has been observed on measures involving cognitive flexibility, inhibition, working memory, and verbal fluency (Snyder, 2013). Memory impairment may appear as a prominent difficulty with encoding (Basso & Bornstein, 1999), although difficulties with retrieval and recognition memory have also been reported; other studies have failed to find impaired memory. Furthermore, the hypothesis that impaired memory in depression is more likely to be observed on tasks that require effortful encoding has generally not been supported. Nonetheless, there is evidence that inadequate use of organizational strategies during encoding may contribute to poor recall (Behnken et al., 2010), and poorer performance has been noted on information-processing tasks when greater effort is required (e.g., Hammar, Lund, & Hugdahl, 2003). In addition, patients with MDD often have slowed processing speed across a variety of cognitive tasks, although this may be more readily observed in older than younger patients and tends to improve with amelioration of mood (e.g., Lee, Hermens, Porter, & Redoblado-Hodge, 2012).

A recent literature review indicated that poorer test performance is associated with greater depression severity at the time of testing as well as longer and recurrent depressive episodes (McClintock, Husain, Greer, & Cullum, 2010). There is considerable heterogeneity in the literature, however, and impairment has been reported in euthymic patients (Schmid & Hammar, 2013); thus, severity of depression cannot fully account for impairments. Having a history of psychotic depression and more psychotic episodes is also associated with poorer cognitive functioning (Hasselbalch, Knorr, Hasselbalch, Gade, & Kessing, 2013).

Psychiatric comorbidities may impact cognitive functioning in MDD. Decreased working memory, long-term memory, executive function, and slowed psychomotor speed have been reported in patients with comorbid MDD and "anxiety disorder" versus MDD only (e.g., Lyche, Jonassen, Stiles, Ulleberg, & Landro, 2011). Similarly, poorer verbal memory was observed in patients with comorbid MDD and posttraumatic stress disorder (PTSD) than in those with MDD only (Scheiner et al., 2014). In contrast, equivalent effect sizes for executive functions were noted for studies that did and did not exclude patients with a comorbid Axis I disorder (Snyder, 2013).

Treatment with antidepressants may be associated with improvement in cognition, but there is no consistent pattern in terms of domains affected, and very few studies show a benefit relative to placebo (Keefe et al., 2014). Augmentation strategies, such as the use of a stimulant in addition to antidepressant medication, have been reported to yield some benefit for cognition (e.g., Keefe et al., 2014).

Finally, the presence of depression in a variety of clinical populations, even when severe, has generally not been associated with poor scores on performance validity tests (e.g., Iverson, Le Page, Koehler, Shojania, & Badii, 2007). Thus, although there is increasing evidence that MDD involves abnormality in motivation-related brain circuitry, this does not appear to translate into invalid cognitive test performance. It should be noted that lack of motivation occurs in both depression and apathy, which are dissociable, but apathy may be more closely related to effort. Specifically, apathy involves a loss of motivation characterized by a quantitative reduction of self-generated goal-directed behavior that can manifest as reduced effort, but that is not accounted for by emotional distress, cognitive impairment, or diminished level of consciousness. Unfortunately, the impact of apathy per se on performance validity tests (PVTs) is unknown at this time.

Bipolar Disorder

Patients with bipolar disorder (BPD) in either a depressive or hypomanic/manic phase show a variety of cognitive deficits relative to euthymic patients, with difficulties in verbal memory and executive functions being especially prominent (e.g., Ha et al., 2014). Nevertheless, cognitive deficits have been found to be largely independent of mood state in BPD (Lee et al., 2014). This finding is supported by research showing poor performance in euthymic patients across cognitive domains, with the largest effects for verbal memory and executive functions (Bourne et al., 2013). A similar pattern of findings has been reported for first-episode BPD (Lee et al., 2014).

The relationship between age and cognition in BPD is unclear. Cognitive impairments have been reported to be less pronounced with increasing age in some work (Mann-Wrobel, Carreno, & Dickinson, 2011), but longitudinal studies suggest stability of cognition over time (Samame, Martino, & Strejilevich, 2014). This may be due in part to an interaction with age of onset. Early onset of illness is associated with more severe impairment of verbal memory and psychomotor speed, but in older patients, later onset is related to more severe and extensive deficits (Martino, Strejilevich, & Manes, 2013). The association between duration of illness and cognitive functioning has been inconsistent (Mann-Wrobel et al., 2011).

A number of other factors appear to be related to cognitive functioning in BPD. Patients with BPD-I and BPD-II tend to show a similar pattern of deficits, though some have noted worse verbal fluency, executive function, and/or memory in BPD-I (e.g., Xu et al., 2012). The relationship between having a history of psychosis and worse cognitive functioning has been inconsistent (Basso et al., 2009). Those with a history of alcohol/substance use disorder tend to show worse memory and executive functions than patients without such a history (e.g., van Gorp, Altshuler, Theberge, Wilkins, & Dixon, 1998). Treatment with antidepressants and anticonvulsants do not appear to have a significant impact on cognitive functioning in patients with BPD (Bourne et al., 2013). Lithium, in contrast, appears to have a subtle negative effect on psychomotor speed and verbal memory (Dias et al., 2012). Some antipsychotics have also been associated with poorer test performance in such patients (Torrent et al., 2011).

Attention-Deficit/Hyperactivity Disorder

Cognitive problems are a core feature of attention-deficit/hyperactivity disorder (ADHD). Although there is no pathognomic neuropsychological test profile, studies across age groups have commonly reported executive dysfunction, most commonly on the measure of response inhibition (Boonstra, Oosterlaan, Sergeant, & Buitelaar, 2005), but also on other measures emphasizing cognitive flexibility, verbal fluency, working memory load, and organization strategy use (e.g., Lin, Chen, & Gau, 2013). The Stroop Task, however, has shown limited sensitivity to ADHD (Schwartz & Verhaeghen, 2008). Executive dysfunction may persist into adulthood even when other symptoms of the disorder have remitted (Miller, Ho, & Hinshaw, 2012). Continuous performance tests (CPTs) often reveal prominent difficulties with vigilance, impulse control, and consistency of reaction time, but diagnosing ADHD based on CPT scores alone is a *faux pas* given that such measures lack evidence for specificity (Riccio & Reynolds, 2001). In addition, because individuals diagnosed with ADHD may not show deficits on performance-based tests of executive function, the use of rating scales of executive functioning (as manifested in everyday life) can be informative and allow for the assessment and identification of different aspects of functioning than provided by cognitive tests alone (Isquith, Roth, & Gioia, 2013).

Impairments in memory, more for verbal than for visual material, have also been reported (e.g., Andersen, Egeland, & Oie, 2013), while visuospatial skills and receptive and expressive language skills are generally intact. When the full scale intelligent quotient [FSIQ] is lower in ADHD than in healthy comparison groups, the scaled score discrepancy is typically on the order of only a few points, is not considered clinically meaningful, and may be accounted for by comorbidities (Bridgett & Walker, 2006). Furthermore, both children and adults with ADHD tend to show lower scores on working memory and processing speed indices. In such cases, the General Ability Index (GAI) may better reflect core intellectual ability than FSIQ.

Children with the combined inattention and impulsive/hyperactive type (ADHD-C) often perform worse than those with the predominantly inattentive type (ADHD-I) on measures requiring inhibitory control, working memory, and processing speed (Nikolas & Nigg, 2013). Parent-reported executive functioning has also been found to differentiate children with ADHD-C and ADHD-I (McCandless & O' Laughlin, 2007). More recently, the "sluggish cognitive tempo" subtype of ADHD (characterized by symptoms such as low energy, hypoactivity, daydreaming, and mental confusion) has been reported to be related to cognitive functioning independent of other symptoms of ADHD (Willcutt et al., 2014).

Studies comparing those with ADHD and a comorbid learning disorder or specific language impairment versus those with ADHD-only have generally reported worse cognitive functioning in the dual diagnosis groups (e.g., Katz, Brown, Roth, & Beers, 2011). The presence of significant depression or anxiety may be associated with poorer test performance in ADHD on measures of processing speed, executive functions, and memory (e.g., Larochette, Harrison, Rosenblum, & Bowie, 2011). In contrast, those with comorbid ADHD and disruptive behavior disorders (conduct disorder, oppositional defiant disorder) generally perform similarly to those with ADHD alone (e.g., Munkvold, Manger, & Lundervold, 2014).

Stimulant medications can improve cognitive functioning in ADHD, but effects are dependent in part on the dose and nature of the tasks employed (e.g., Swanson, Baler, & Volkow, 2011), with some studies suggesting greater amelioration on tasks without an executive component (e.g., spatial recognition memory) (Coghill, Rhodes, & Matthews, 2007). Importantly, the literature indicates that medications do not completely eliminate the cognitive deficits associated with ADHD. Thus, although persons tested when receiving a stimulant medication may perform somewhat better than if they were unmedicated, significant residual difficulties may remain.

Posttraumatic Stress Disorder

There is considerable evidence for reduced learning and memory in posttraumatic stress disorder (PTSD) (Scott et al., 2015). Performance tends to be worse for verbal than visual memory, more prominent for encoding than delayed recall, and is found in both civilian and military trauma samples (Samuelson, Krueger, Burnett, & Wilson, 2010). Although variability is seen, a recent meta-analysis indicated that impaired processing speed has one of the largest effect sizes when comparing PTSD and control groups (Scott et al., 2015). Deficits in sustained and divided attention have also been observed (e.g., Koso & Hansen, 2006). Impaired auditory attention has been reported and may contribute to deficits in other cognitive domains (Gilbertson, Gurvits, Lasko, Orr, & Pitman, 2001). Evidence for executive dysfunction in PTSD has been mixed. Performance on tests of working memory or tasks requiring cognitive flexibility has generally shown mild or no impairment, although a recent meta-analysis indicated a relatively large effect for a composite "attention/working memory" (Scott et al., 2015). In contrast, there is evidence of problems with response inhibition, especially during sustained attention tasks (Koso & Hansen, 2006). In addition, poor use of organizational strategies may contribute to memory deficits in PTSD, though findings have been inconsistent (Johnsen & Asbjornsen, 2009). Significant impairment in other domains of cognitive functioning in PTSD, including visuospatial and constructional ability, and motor skills without executive demands, has generally not been reported. The relationship between PTSD and intellectual ability is unclear, with some studies reporting weaknesses in verbal relative to perceptual skills (Vasterling, Brailey, Constans, & Sutker, 1997).

Cognitive deficits also have been reported in studies of persons with trauma exposure who do not subsequently develop PTSD (e.g., Samuelson et al., 2010). Furthermore, some cognitive weaknesses may be a premorbid factor in PTSD, potentially increasing the risk for developing the disorder (Betts, Williams, Najman, Bor, & Alati, 2012). Such findings raise questions about the extent to which chronic PTSD has a "neurotoxic" effect on cognitive functioning. Nonetheless, severity of current PTSD symptoms is associated with poorer cognitive functioning, particularly verbal memory (Scott et al., 2015). Thus, both premorbid characteristics and symptom severity need to be taken into consideration. Furthermore, mood can have a significant impact on cognition in PTSD, though impairments in verbal memory, attention, and processing speed are seen even when major depression is accounted for (Scott et al., 2015). Recently, comorbid ADHD was found to be associated with poorer cognitive functioning in those with PTSD (Antshel, Biederman, Spencer, & Faraone, in press). There has also been a surge of research examining the effects of PTSD and comorbid mild TBI. Large-scale reviews have found generally comparable performance in patients with PTSD only and those with PTSD and mild TBI (Scott et al., 2015). Nonetheless, the presence of a history of mild TBI can have a significant impact on the development, course, and treatment of PTSD and thus should be taken into account in case conceptualizations.

COLLABORATING WITH AND WRITING FOR PSYCHIATRISTS

Psychiatry and neuropsychology have a long history of clinical and scientific collaboration. Collaborative care of a given patient starts with the neuropsychologist ensuring that there is a clear understanding between the clinicians with respect to the referral issues at hand, including the context and the specific information sought (e.g., recommendations for discharge planning). Referral questions could involve a variety of issues, as noted above. The neuropsychological evaluation of patients referred by psychiatry typically involves obtaining some degree of overlapping information about cognition, mood, behavior, and background history. Nonetheless, the perspective from which the neuropsychologist approaches a clinical interview is also quite different from the approach of a psychiatrist, providing a more detailed and nuanced investigation into the temporal relationships between reported cognitive changes and other factors (e.g., symptoms, stressors, medical history, and development history). In addition to quantitative and qualitative test data tapping neuropsychological domains, the evaluation may provide the psychiatrist with complementary information about psychiatric symptoms or psychological traits (e.g., using personality measures such as the Personality Assessment Inventory [PAI] or the MMPI-2-RF), enhancing clinical conceptualization as well as providing objective assessment of symptom validity in a manner often used inconsistently or not at all in psychiatric settings.

In writing a neuropsychological report for psychiatrists, detailed information regarding the individual's psychiatric history is typically unnecessary, as the referring psychiatrist is already quite familiar with it. It is also important to be mindful that psychiatrists, as well as other physicians, strive for excellent clinical care but are often hard pressed for time. Thus, a report that is well organized, clear, and concise is highly valued. This is especially important for one's summary and recommendations, as this is truly the bottom line of what the referring psychiatrist is seeking. This report should include clear statements with respect to any neuropsychological impairments present and other relevant findings (e.g., IQ, mood, effort), followed by clinical conceptualization including diagnostic considerations and any clearly or potentially contributing factors (e.g., comorbid medical conditions), using standard diagnostic labels familiar to psychiatrists (e.g., DSM-5) when clinically relevant. Recommendations should follow clearly from the background history, behavioral observations, test results, and clinical conceptualization.

CASE EXAMPLE

To illustrate some of the less and more desirable ways of presenting information in a neuropsychological report concerning a patient with a psychiatric disorder, let us consider the case of Mr. D, a 52-year-old, right-handed, Caucasian man with chronic schizophrenia. His psychiatrist referred him for assessment because Mr. D had been getting reviews at work indicating that he was making more errors and forgetting to complete tasks, and thus Mr. D was concerned about losing his job. The psychiatrist was also wondering whether depression might be contributing to the reported difficulties in functioning. Mr. D has had no prior cognitive testing. The psychometric data are presented in Table 5.1. We first compare different ways of presenting parts of the history, observations, test results, and recommendations. Finally, we demonstrate how the more desirable descriptions can be integrated into a complete report.

Example 1: Reason for Referral

LESS DESIRABLE: DOCTOR A

Mr. D, a 52-year-old, right-handed Caucasian schizophrenic male, was referred for neuropsychological evaluation because of possible cognitive problems.

MORE DESIRABLE: DOCTOR B

Mr. D is a 52-year-old, right-handed man with a history of chronic schizophrenia. He was referred by his psychiatrist for evaluation in the context of reports that cognitive problems have been impacting his functioning at work, and to determine whether depression may be contributing.

TABLE 5.1. Neuropsychological Test Scores for Mr. D

Test variable	Test result
WAIS-IV[a]	
Full Scale IQ	74
GAI	83
Verbal Comprehension Index	91
Perceptual Reasoning Index	81
Working Memory Index	71
Processing Speed Index	62
Test of Premorbid Functioning[a]	
Obtained Score	98
WMS-IV[b]	
Logical Memory I	3
Logical Memory II	3
CVLT-II	
Total[c]	22
Trial B[d]	−1
Short delay free recall[d]	−2
Short delay cued recall[d]	−1
Long delay free recall[d]	−2
Long delay cued recall[d]	−1
Recognition hits[d]	−1.5
Forced-choice, raw score	16/16
BVMT-R[e]	
Total recall	16
Delayed recall	12
Recognition hits	3–5
Recognition false alarms	6–10
WAIS-IV	
Digit Span[b]	3
Coding[b]	3
Trail Making Test	
Part A[d]	−2.06
Part B[d]	−2.81
Letter Fluency[d]	−1.30
Category Fluency[d]	−0.80
Wisconsin Card Sorting Test (128 trials)[c]	
Categories Completed, raw score	0 (<.1%ile)
Perseverative Errors	53
Nonperseverative errors	26

(continued)

TABLE 5.1. *(continued)*

Test variable	Test result
CPT-II[f]	
Omissions	72.86
Commissions	58.60
Hit RT	68.52
Hit RT Standard Error	60.48
BDAE Sentence Comprehension[d]	0.2
Boston Naming Test, total correct[d]	−0.9
Grooved Pegboard[d]	
Right hand	−.89
Left hand	−1.13
Beck Depression Inventory–II, raw score	14
Beck Anxiety Inventory, raw score	3

Note: BDAE, Boston Diagnostic Aphasia Examination; BVMT-R, Brief Visuospatial Memory Test–revised; CVLT-II, California Verbal Learning Test–Second Edition; CPT-II, Conner's Continuous Performance Test—Second Edition; D-KEFS, Delis–Kaplan Executive Function System; WAIS-IV, Wechsler Adult Intelligence Scale—Fourth Edition; Wechsler Memory Scale—Fourth Edition.
[a]Standard score, without demographic correction ($M = 100$, $SD = 15$; higher scores reflect better performance).
[b]Scaled score ($M = 10$, $SD = 3$; lower scores reflect worse performance).
[c]T-score ($M = 50$, $SD = 10$; lower scores reflect worse performance).
[d]z-score ($M = 0$, $SD = 1$; lower scores reflect worse performance).
[e]Percentile (lower score reflects worse performance).
[f]Higher T-score reflects worse performance.

Comment on Reason for Referral

Throughout the report, beginning with the reason for referral, one should be mindful of using person-focused language. For example, one should not refer to patients as their illness (e.g., schizophrenic) but rather as an individual who has a given condition (e.g., "person with schizophrenia").

Dr. A states that the reason for referral is "cognitive complaints." Although that is one of the reasons, it fails to provide the necessary and adequate context for the assessment. Dr. B indicates clearly and concisely that the patient is being referred because he is reporting cognitive problems that he believes have been worsening and impacting his ability to perform his role at work. In addition, it is important to keep in mind that there may be more than one reason for a referral and that the doctor and the patient may have different primary concerns. For example, in this case the referring doctor is specifically asking whether depression is contributing to the reported cognitive changes.

Example 2: Interview/Background (excerpt)

LESS DESIRABLE: DOCTOR A

Mr. D has a history of schizophrenia, including hospitalizations in 2003 due to command hallucinations, in 2005 due to delusions and hallucinations, and in 2012 due to disruptive and aggressive behaviors in his apartment complex. He also has longstanding negative symptoms, including flat affect, apathy, and anhedonia. He reported feeling "a bit down" over the past month. He stated that his supervisor at work has commented that he is making more errors during tasks and at times forgets to complete tasks. Mr. D denied having cognitive problems other than being occasionally distracted at work, though he noted that this problem has worsened over the past month or so.

MORE DESIRABLE: DOCTOR B

According to records, Mr. D has a history of chronic schizophrenia resulting in multiple hospitalizations, the last in 2012. He has longstanding negative symptoms that have been minimally responsive to medications and are present irrespective of mood. He reported feeling "a bit down" over the past month, but during that time has not been less motivated or experienced worse anhedonia than usual. Mr. D's mother reported that he has longstanding difficulties with memory and attention that have worsened over the past few weeks. She stated that he seemed a bit more irritable during that period but not depressed. Mr. D stated that his supervisor at work has commented that he is making more errors during tasks and at times forgets to complete tasks. On interview, his supervisor confirmed these problems and indicated that they have been seen in the context of a recent increase in Mr. D's workload due to staff attrition. Mr. D denied having cognitive problems, other than being occasionally distracted at work, though he noted that this has worsened over the past month or so. He indicated that his functioning outside of work is unchanged.

Comment on Interview/Background

Dr. A provides more details about Mr. D's psychiatric history than is necessary given that the patient is well known to the referring psychiatrist. Furthermore, although mood and negative symptoms are mentioned, Dr. A provides no information that would help differentiate whether the current presentation is more consistent with chronic negative symptoms, depression, or some combination. In contrast, Dr. B provides a succinct summary of Mr. D's psychiatric diagnosis and clarifies that some of his negative symptoms, which can also be features of depression (e.g., poor motivation and anhedonia), have been no worse during the period in which an additional diagnosis of depression is being considered. Drs. A and B appropriately report the patient's cognitive concerns, but Dr. B further notes that Mr. D does not believe he has any cognitive problems outside of work, which contrasts with his mother's report. This reflects the importance of determining whether cognitive problems are context specific or more general, and has implications for diagnosis and recommendations.

Dr. B goes an important step further than Dr. A by interviewing knowledgeable informants: his supervisor (the source of the patient's concern about his job, and who mentions a possibly important environmental factor for increased cognitive problems at work) and his mother (who provides valuable information about his cognitive functioning). Patients with schizophrenia may be poor historians due to cognitive problems and/or limited insight. Thus, information gained could inform the understanding of the patient's cognitive and other problems.

Although not detailed in the sample above, reports pertaining to patients with psychiatric illness should also clearly indicate current and previous medical and psychiatric diagnoses (including alcohol and substance use history) and any associated treatments that could impact cognitive functioning. Listing all current prescribed and nonprescription medications is also vital, as some patients may be taking medications that could have beneficial or deleterious effects on cognition. Also not detailed here in this abbreviated example is the patient's educational and occupational history. This background is of considerable importance to help the clinician gauge the patient's estimated premorbid level of functioning, provide insight into possibly longstanding cognitive or behavioral problems, as well as to inform recommendations (e.g., with respect to academic/vocational counseling).

Example 3: Behavioral Observations

LESS DESIRABLE: DOCTOR A

Mr. D was tested as an outpatient at the Neuropsychological Laboratory. He arrived on time and was unaccompanied. He was poorly dressed and his hair was messy. He was alert and oriented to person, place, and situation but not time. Motor skills appeared intact. He did not speak much during the interview or testing, and prosody of speech was flat. Thought processes were mostly linear and goal-directed. Thought content was free of delusions and hallucinations.

He reported his mood as being "occasionally sad" and affect was blunted. Mr. D was cooperative with the evaluation and appeared motivated to perform well during testing. Thus, the results are considered to be a valid representation of his current level of functioning.

MORE DESIRABLE: DOCTOR B

Mr. D was tested as an outpatient at the Neuropsychological Laboratory. He arrived on time and was unaccompanied. His appearance was disheveled. He was alert and oriented to person, place, and situation but not time, stating that it was the 3rd rather than the 5th. Gross motor skills were intact on informal observation. There was a paucity of spontaneous speech, but he was fluent when speaking, though prosody was flat. Thought processes were notable for occasional tangentiality. Thought content appeared normal, with no evidence of delusional thinking or hallucinations. He reported his mood as being "occasionally sad" and affect was blunted. He was cooperative with the evaluation, appeared motivated to perform well during testing, and scored within expectation on performance validity tests. Thus, the results are considered to be a valid representation of his current level of functioning.

Comment on Observations

This is a very important section when working with psychiatrically ill patients, as their symptoms can result in low frustration tolerance or difficulty attending to the tasks at hand (e.g., due to depression, active hallucinations) that can significantly impact their ability to complete testing. Such detrimental effects of psychiatric symptoms are not a given, however, and thus close clinical attention to their presentation (behaviors, emotions and thoughts) is essential. This will also help determine whether one has accurately captured the person's best level of functioning, the person's current level of functioning but not his or her best level, or if the results likely underestimate the person's true abilities.

Dr. A's behavioral observations are lacking in relevant detail. The patient is reported to be disoriented to time, but the extent to which he is disoriented is not stated. Dr. B clarified that the person was off by two days. This may or may not be clinically meaningful. In this case, it could have implications for being at work on appropriate days (especially if the person's schedule is inconsistent or part-time). In outpatients who have few activities or in long-term inpatients, the specific date may simply be something that they do not track closely. Dr. A indicated that the patient's thought processes were "mostly linear and goal-directed." Although that may be technically correct, the term "mostly" leaves the reader questioning what his thought processes were like otherwise. Dr. B succinctly indicates that tangentiality was occasionally noted. Dr. A mentions that no delusions or hallucinations were observed, but those are not the only types of disturbances in thought content possible (e.g., obsessions). Therefore, it would be more helpful to state that thought content appeared normal and then to specify that delusions and hallucinations were not observed (such specification being especially helpful in cases where the patient has a history of such symptoms). Finally, unlike Dr. B, Dr. A fails to indicate whether performance validity testing was conducted and if, so what, the results were.

Example 4: Test Results (excerpt)

LESS DESIRABLE: DOCTOR A

Mr. D demonstrated estimated intellectual functioning in the borderline range (WAIS-IV). Vocabulary, Information, Similarities, and Block Design were in the low average range, while Matrix Reasoning and Visual Puzzles were in the borderline range. Processing speed and working memory were in the extremely low range with no variability. Baseline intellect was estimated to be in the low average to average range based on a word reading test (TOPF) and demographics.

MORE DESIRABLE: DOCTOR B

Mr. D demonstrated estimated overall intellectual functioning in the borderline range (WAIS-IV), with comparable verbal comprehension and perceptual reasoning skills. Processing speed (PRI) and working memory (WMI) were relative weaknesses (extremely low range); thus the GAI (which excludes the PSI and WMI) may be a better reflection of his core intellectual abilities and was estimated to be in the low average range. Premorbid intellect was estimated to be in the average range based on a word reading test (TOPF) and parental demographics, which is significantly higher than his estimated current overall intellectual functioning (as reflected by the GAI).

Comment on Results

The excerpt from Dr. A shows both technical problems and stylistic issues. In terms of the technical problems, it is important to consider the impact of variability in performance on measures that involve multiple subtests such as the WAIS-IV. In this case, Dr. A alludes to the PSI and WM indices being lower than VCI and PRI, but does not then discuss the impact of that discrepancy on interpretation. In addition, Dr. A provides excessive detail that does not significantly contribute to one's understanding of performance on the measure. Finally, in some psychiatric patient groups such as schizophrenia, estimation of premorbid intellectual functioning can be complicated because onset of the disorder may disrupt educational performance and achievement. Thus, use of parental rather than the patient's own demographic information may be more accurate, and combining with an established measure of premorbid functioning (e.g., WRAT, ANART, TOPF) may increase confidence in one's estimate.

Example 5: Summary

LESS DESIRABLE: DOCTOR A

On the present evaluation, Mr. D demonstrated moderately impaired encoding and retrieval of a word list but mildly impaired encoding and retrieval for stories. In addition, he showed mildly slowed processing speed on Trail Making and Coding tasks, as well as poor accuracy and speed on a CPT. Executive functions were impaired for working memory (WMI), ability to think flexibly, and problem solving (WCST). He performed within normal limits on measures of memory designs, verbal fluency, three-dimensional block construction, receptive language, object naming, finger tapping, and grooved pegboard. These findings were observed in the context of borderline-range intellectual abilities, good effort on testing, and mild depression per self-report. The present pattern of performance is generally consistent with Mr. D's history of schizophrenia.

MORE DESIRABLE: DOCTOR B

On the present evaluation, Mr. D demonstrated impairments in memory for verbal information, processing speed, sustain attention, as well as for aspects of his executive functioning (working memory, ability to think flexibly, and solve novel problems). He performed within normal limits on measures of memory for visual information, visuospatial skills, receptive and expressive language, and motor dexterity. These findings were observed in the context of estimated low average range core intellectual abilities, good effort on testing, and mild depression per self-report.

> The present pattern of test performance is generally
> consistent with Mr. D's history of schizophrenia. Although
> he endorsed a mild level of depression, this cannot
> account for his test profile. Rather, his history suggests
> the presence of a "deficit syndrome" that can be associ-
> ated with cognitive impairments and has clinical features
> that are similar to depression.

Comment about Summary

Dr. A provides excessive detail and often focuses on specific tests. For example, Dr. A speaks of levels of impairment (mild, moderate, severe) on different memory measures, whereas Dr. B states that they are impaired without referring to level. As performance on measures within a given domain may show variability, providing a concise description of the overall picture is more helpful to the referring physician, unless the variability is truly clinically meaningful. Overall, Dr. B's summary provides an integration of the findings that focuses on neuropsychological domains rather than on a "laundry list" of individualized test findings. Furthermore, Dr. A's report of the patient's intellectual functioning is suboptimal. That the GAI is likely to provide a better estimate (as noted above) is ignored, and there is failure to specify the fact that the IQ is an estimate.

A vital part of the summary of findings is the integration of the test results, behavioral observations, and background. Here, both Drs. A and B identify the pattern of findings as generally consistent with Mr. D's history of schizophrenia, but Dr. A fails to address the referring psychiatrist's specific question about the potential impact of depression on the patient's cognitive functioning. Dr. B also provides the referring psychiatrist with a statement integrating the clinical history and presentation (i.e., chronic negative symptoms that were also observed during the evaluation) with the test findings to indicate that the patient's cognitive problems and mood symptoms appear more consistent with a deficit syndrome rather than with a mood disorder.

Example 6: Recommendations Sample

LESS DESIRABLE: DOCTOR A

- Mr. D was noted to be making more errors and being forgetful at work. His deficits in attention and memory are likely exacerbated by increased demands at work. Thus, accommodations must be made.
- Mr. D denies having cognitive problems, and therefore psychotherapy is recommended to address this issue.

MORE DESIRABLE: DOCTOR B

- Mr. D was noted to be making more errors and being forgetful at work. His deficits in attention and memory are likely exacerbated by increased demands at work. He would likely be able to maintain employment and perform more successfully if his employer would be willing to make some accommodations. These could include more frequent breaks, written instructions, and routinizing work as much as possible.
- There is a discrepancy between Mr. D's report of his cognitive problems on the one hand, and his mother's report and test results on the other. This indicates limited awareness, which is common in schizophrenia. In a supportive manner, those working with him could help him to recognize when he makes errors or is forgetful, and help him identify appropriate strategies to enhance his ability to compensate for deficits.

Comments about Recommendations

Dr. A recognized that Mr. D's cognitive problems and the increase in workload likely contributed to his recent difficulties, but his recommendation for accommodations is vague. Furthermore, the statement that accommodations "must" be made is rather demanding and may not be realistic given the employer's situation. Dr. B's recommendations are concrete, provide specific suggestions, and use phrasing that will hopefully increase the likelihood that efforts will be made to adopt them (i.e., make constructive suggestions rather than demands).

Dr. A points out that Mr. D denied having cognitive deficits and recommended psychotherapy to address this denial. Unawareness of symptoms is common in schizophrenia and likely related to its underlying neurobiology. Direct confrontation is typically unproductive. Dr. B. points this out and provides suggestions to help Mr. D and others identify cognitive lapses and develop compensatory strategies.

More generally, when making recommendations for patients with psychiatric disorders, it is best to provide as specific recommendations as possible, as the referrer is often looking for assistance in order to develop additional community supports as needed. Furthermore, the extent of basic cognitive deficits, even with reading or listening comprehension, may not always be evident to those who interact with these individuals (e.g., caregivers, family), especially since many patients learn to present in a manner that is at least superficially socially appropriate and/or are unaware of their limitations. The neuropsychologist is in a prime position to help others understand the appropriate level at which information should be presented and what are reasonable expectations of the person given their profile of strengths and weaknesses. The latter can be especially important because a mismatch between demands and abilities can result in considerable stress, symptom exacerbation, challenging behaviors (e.g., aggression) that may result in hospitalization, or professionals' misconstrual of an individual's lack of compliance with requests or task demands as oppositional behavior.

In summary, a well-written, user-friendly neuropsychological report for psychiatrists incorporates the same essential characteristics as reports prepared for other professionals (i.e., clearly addresses the referral question, is written in a clear and concise manner, etc.). In addition, the report should include careful consideration of the characteristics of the patient's psychiatric disorder(s) that can impact on clinical presentation and interpretation of neuropsychological test results (e.g., clinical state, duration of illness), as well as the temporal relationship between psychiatric symptoms and cognitive and functional difficulties; cognitive and functional difficulties are especially important when attempting to make a differential diagnosis of cognitive problems due to psychiatric versus neurological illness (e.g., depression versus TBI). Finally, the writer should be especially careful to provide practical recommendations that take into account the patient's level of functioning, with a focus on identifying resources, services, and interventions that will help maximize the patient's independent functioning in the community.

REFERENCES

Ammari, N., Heinrichs, R. W., & Miles, A. A. (2010). An investigation of 3 neurocognitive subtypes in schizophrenia. *Schizophrenia Research, 121*(1–3), 32–38.

Andersen, P. N., Egeland, J., & Oie, M. (2013). Learning and memory impairments in children and adolescents with attention-deficit/hyperactivity disorder. *Journal of Learning Disabilities, 46*(5), 453–460.

Antshel, K. M., Biederman, J., Spencer, T. J., & Faraone, S. V. (in press). The neuropsychological profile of comorbid post-traumatic stress disorder in adult ADHD. *Journal of Attention Disorders.*

Arndt, S., Andreasen, N. C., Flaum, M., Miller, D., & Nopoulos, P. (1995). A longitudinal study of symptom dimensions in schizophrenia: Prediction and patterns of change. *Archives of General Psychiatry, 52*(5), 352–360.

Basso, M. R., & Bornstein, R. A. (1999). Relative memory deficits in recurrent versus first-episode major depression on a word-list learning task. *Neuropsychology, 13*(4), 557–563.

Basso, M. R., Lowery, N., Ghormley, C., Ward, T., Purdie, R., Neel, J., et al. (2009). Neuropsychological impairment and psychosis in mania. *Journal of Clinical and Experimental Neuropsychology, 31*(5), 523–532.

Behnken, A., Schoning, S., Gerss, J., Konrad, C., de Jong-Meyer, R., Zwanzger, P., et al. (2010). Persistent non-verbal memory impairment in remitted major depression: Caused by encoding deficits? *Journal of Affective Disorders, 122*(1–2), 144–148.

Betts, K. S., Williams, G. M., Najman, J. M., Bor, W., & Alati, R. (2012). Pre-trauma verbal ability at five years of age and the risk of post-traumatic stress disorder in adult males and females. *Journal of Psychiatric Research, 46*(7), 933–939.

Boonstra, A. M., Oosterlaan, J., Sergeant, J. A., & Buitelaar, J. K. (2005). Executive functioning in adult ADHD: A meta-analytic review. *Psychological Medicine, 35*(8), 1097–1108.

Bourne, C., Aydemir, O., Balanza-Martinez, V., Bora, E., Brissos, S., Cavanagh, J. T., et al. (2013). Neuropsychological testing of cognitive impairment in euthymic bipolar disorder: An individual patient data meta-analysis. *Acta Psychiatrica Scandinavica, 128*(3), 149–162.

Bridgett, D. J., & Walker, M. E. (2006). Intellectual functioning in adults with ADHD: A meta-analytic examination of full scale IQ differences between adults with and without ADHD. *Psychological Assessment, 18*(1), 1–14.

Chan, S. K., Chan, K. K., Lam, M. M., Chiu, C. P., Hui, C. L., Wong, G. H., et al. (2012). Clinical and cognitive correlates of insight in first-episode schizophrenia. *Schizophrenia Research, 135*(1–3), 40–45.

Coghill, D. R., Rhodes, S. M., & Matthews, K. (2007). The neuropsychological effects of chronic methylphenidate on drug-naive boys with attention-deficit/hyperactivity disorder. *Biological Psychiatry, 62*(9), 954–962.

Cohen, A. S., Saperstein, A. M., Gold, J. M., Kirkpatrick, B., Carpenter, W. T., Jr., & Buchanan, R. W. (2007). Neuropsychology of the deficit syndrome: New data and meta-analysis of findings to date. *Schizophrenia Bulletin, 33*(5), 1201–1212.

Cole, V. T., Weinberger, D. R., & Dickinson, D. (2011). Intra-individual variability across neuropsychological tasks in schizophrenia: A comparison of patients, their siblings, and healthy controls. *Schizophrenia Research, 129*(1), 91–93.

Dias, V. V., Balanza-Martinez, V., Soeiro-de-Souza, M. G., Moreno, R. A., Figueira, M. L., Machado-Vieira, R., et al. (2012). Pharmacological approaches in bipolar disorders and the impact on cognition: A critical overview. *Acta Psychiatrica Scandinavica, 126*(5), 315–331.

Gilbertson, M. W., Gurvits, T. V., Lasko, N. B., Orr, S. P., & Pitman, R. K. (2001). Multivariate assessment of explicit memory function in combat veterans with posttraumatic stress disorder. *Journal of Traumatic Stress, 14*(2), 413–432.

Ha, T. H., Chang, J. S., Oh, S. H., Kim, J. S., Cho, H. S., & Ha, K. (2014). Differential patterns of neuropsychological performance in the euthymic and depressive phases of bipolar disorders. *Psychiatry and Clinical Neurosciences, 68*(7), 515–523.

Hammar, A., Lund, A., & Hugdahl, K. (2003). Long-lasting cognitive impairment in unipolar major depression: A 6-month follow-up study. *Psychiatry Research, 118*(2), 189–196.

Harvey, P. D. (2014). What is the evidence for changes in cognition and functioning over the lifespan in patients with schizophrenia? *Journal of Clinical Psychiatry, 75*(Suppl. 2), 34–38.

Hasselbalch, B. J., Knorr, U., Hasselbalch, S. G., Gade, A., & Kessing, L. V. (2013). The cumulative load of depressive illness is associated with cognitive function in the remitted state of unipolar depressive disorder. *European Psychiatry, 28*(6), 349–355.

Ilamkar, K. R. (2014). Psychomotor retardation, attention deficit and executive dysfunction in young non-hospitalised un-medicated non-psychotic unipolar depression patients. *Journal of Clinical Diagnosis and Research, 8*(2), 124–126.

Isquith, P. K., Roth, R. M., & Gioia, G. (2013). Contribution of rating scales to the assessment of executive functions. *Applied Neuropsychology: Child, 2*(2), 125–132.

Iverson, G. L., Le Page, J., Koehler, B. E., Shojania, K., & Badii, M. (2007). Test of Memory Malingering (TOMM) scores are not affected by chronic pain or depression in patients with fibromyalgia. *The Clinical Neuropsychologist, 21*(3), 532–546.

Johnsen, G. E., & Asbjornsen, A. E. (2009). Verbal learning and memory impairments in posttraumatic stress disorder: The role of encoding strategies. *Psychiatry Research, 165*(1–2), 68–77.

Katz, L. J., Brown, F. C., Roth, R. M., & Beers, S. R. (2011). Processing speed and working memory performance in those with both ADHD and a reading disorder compared with those with ADHD alone. *Archives of Clinical Neuropsychology, 26*(5), 425–433.

Keefe, R. S., Bilder, R. M., Davis, S. M., Harvey, P. D., Palmer, B. W., Gold, J. M., et al. (2007). Neurocognitive effects of antipsychotic medications in patients with chronic schizophrenia in the CATIE Trial. *Archives of General Psychiatry, 64*(6), 633–647.

Keefe, R. S., McClintock, S. M., Roth, R. M., Doraiswamy, P. M., Tiger, S., & Madhoo, M. (2014). Cognitive effects of pharmacotherapy for major depressive disorder: A systematic review. *Journal of Clinical Psychiatry, 75*(8), 864–876.

Kessler, R. C., Green, J. G., Adler, L. A., Barkley, R. A., Chatterji, S., Faraone, S. V., et al. (2010). The structure and diagnosis of adult ADHD: An analysis of expanded symptom criteria from the adult ADHD Clinical Diagnostic Scale (ACDS). *Archives of General Psychiatry, 67*(11), 1168–1178.

Koso, M., & Hansen, S. (2006). Executive function and memory in posttraumatic stress disorder: A study of Bosnian war veterans. *European Psychiatry, 21*(3), 167–173.

Kremen, W. S., Seidman, L. J., Faraone, S. V., Toomey, R., & Tsuang, M. T. (2000). The paradox of normal neuropsychological function in schizophrenia. *Journal of Abnormal Psychology, 109*(4), 743–752.

Larochette, A. C., Harrison, A. G., Rosenblum, Y., & Bowie, C. R. (2011). Additive neurocognitive deficits in adults with attention-deficit/hyperactivity disorder and depressive symptoms. *Archives of Clinical Neuropsychology, 26*(5), 385–395.

Lee, R. S., Hermens, D. F., Porter, M. A., & Redoblado-Hodge, M. A. (2012). A meta-analysis of cognitive deficits in first-episode major depressive disorder. *Journal of Affective Disorders, 140*(2), 113–124.

Lee, R. S., Hermens, D. F., Scott, J., Redoblado-Hodge, M. A., Naismith, S. L.,

Lagopoulos, J., et al. (2014). A meta-analysis of neuropsychological functioning in first-episode bipolar disorders. *Journal of Psychiatric Research, 57,* 1–11.

Lin, Y. J., Chen, W. J., & Gau, S. S. (2013). Neuropsychological functions among adolescents with persistent, subsyndromal and remitted attention deficit hyperactivity disorder. *Psychological Medicine,* 1–13.

Lyche, P., Jonassen, R., Stiles, T. C., Ulleberg, P., & Landro, N. I. (2011). Verbal memory functions in unipolar major depression with and without co-morbid anxiety. *The Clinical Neuropsychologist, 25*(3), 359–375.

Mann-Wrobel, M. C., Carreno, J. T., & Dickinson, D. (2011). Meta-analysis of neuropsychological functioning in euthymic bipolar disorder: An update and investigation of moderator variables. *Bipolar Disorders, 13*(4), 334–342.

Martino, D. J., Strejilevich, S. A., & Manes, F. (2013). Neurocognitive functioning in early-onset and late-onset older patients with euthymic bipolar disorder. *International Journal of Geriatric Psychiatry, 28*(2), 142–148.

McCandless, S., & O' Laughlin, L. (2007). The clinical utility of the Behavior Rating Inventory of Executive Function (BRIEF) in the diagnosis of ADHD. *Journal of Attention Disorders, 10*(4), 381–389.

McClintock, S. M., Husain, M. M., Greer, T. L., & Cullum, C. M. (2010). Association between depression severity and neurocognitive function in major depressive disorder: A review and synthesis. *Neuropsychology, 24*(1), 9–34.

Mesholam-Gately, R. I., Giuliano, A. J., Goff, K. P., Faraone, S. V., & Seidman, L. J. (2009). Neurocognition in first-episode schizophrenia: A meta-analytic review. *Neuropsychology, 23*(3), 315–336.

Miller, M., Ho, J., & Hinshaw, S. P. (2012). Executive functions in girls with ADHD followed prospectively into young adulthood. *Neuropsychology, 26*(3), 278–287.

Munkvold, L. H., Manger, T., & Lundervold, A. J. (2014). Conners' continuous performance test (CCPT-II) in children with ADHD, ODD, or a combined ADHD/ODD diagnosis. *Child Neuropsychology, 20*(1), 106–126.

Nikolas, M. A., & Nigg, J. T. (2013). Neuropsychological performance and attention-deficit hyperactivity disorder subtypes and symptom dimensions. *Neuropsychology, 27*(1), 107–120.

Potvin, S., Joyal, C. C., Pelletier, J., & Stip, E. (2008). Contradictory cognitive capacities among substance-abusing patients with schizophrenia: A meta-analysis. *Schizophrenia Research, 100*(1–3), 242–251.

Riccio, C. A., & Reynolds, C. R. (2001). Continuous performance tests are sensitive to ADHD in adults but lack specificity: A review and critique for differential diagnosis. *Annals of the New York Academy of Sciences, 931,* 113–139.

Samame, C., Martino, D. J., & Strejilevich, S. A. (2014). Longitudinal course of cognitive deficits in bipolar disorder: A meta-analytic study. *Journal of Affective Disorders, 164,* 130–138.

Samuelson, K. W., Krueger, C. E., Burnett, C., & Wilson, C. K. (2010). Neuropsychological functioning in children with posttraumatic stress disorder. *Child Neuropsychology, 16*(2), 119–133.

Saykin, A. J., Shtasel, D. L., Gur, R. E., Kester, D. B., Mozley, L. H., Stafiniak, P.,

& Gur, R. C. (1994). Neuropsychological deficits in neuroleptic naive patients with first-episode schizophrenia. *Archives of General Psychiatry, 51*(2), 124–131.

Scheiner, D. L., Keilp, J., Mindt, M. R., Burke, A. K., Oquendo, M. A., & Mann, J. J. (2014). Verbal learning deficits in posttraumatic stress disorder and depression. *Journal of Traumatic Stress, 27*(3), 291–298.

Schmid, M., & Hammar, A. (2013). Cognitive function in first episode major depressive disorder: Poor inhibition and semantic fluency performance. *Cognitive Neuropsychiatry, 18*(6), 515–530.

Schwartz, K., & Verhaeghen, P. (2008). ADHD and Stroop interference from age 9 to age 41 years: A meta-analysis of developmental effects. *Psychological Medicine, 38*(11), 1607–1616.

Scott, J. C., Matt, G. E., Wrocklage, K. M., Crnich, C., Jordan, J., Southwick, S. M., et al. (2015). A quantitative meta-analysis of neurocognitive functioning in posttraumatic stress disorder. *Psychological Bulletin, 141*(1), 105–140.

Snyder, H. R. (2013). Major depressive disorder is associated with broad impairments on neuropsychological measures of executive function: A meta-analysis and review. *Psychological Bulletin, 139*(1), 81–132.

Swanson, J., Baler, R. D., & Volkow, N. D. (2011). Understanding the effects of stimulant medications on cognition in individuals with attention-deficit hyperactivity disorder: A decade of progress. *Neuropsychopharmacology, 36*(1), 207–226.

Torrent, C., Martinez-Aran, A., Daban, C., Amann, B., Balanza-Martinez, V., del Mar Bonnin, C., et al. (2011). Effects of atypical antipsychotics on neurocognition in euthymic bipolar patients. *Comprehensive Psychiatry, 52*(6), 613–622.

van Gorp, W. G., Altshuler, L., Theberge, D. C., Wilkins, J., & Dixon, W. (1998). Cognitive impairment in euthymic bipolar patients with and without prior alcohol dependence. A preliminary study. *Archives of General Psychiatry, 55*(1), 41–46.

Vasterling, J. J., Brailey, K., Constans, J. I. A. B., & Sutker, P. B. (1997). Assessment of intellectual resources in Gulf War veterans: Relationship to PTSD. *Assessment, 4*, 51–59.

Wilk, C. M., Gold, J. M., McMahon, R. P., Humber, K., Iannone, V. N., & Buchanan, R. W. (2005). No, it is not possible to be schizophrenic yet neuropsychologically normal. *Neuropsychology, 19*(6), 778–786.

Willcutt, E. G., Chhabildas, N., Kinnear, M., DeFries, J. C., Olson, R. K., Leopold, D. R., et al. (2014). The internal and external validity of sluggish cognitive tempo and its relation with DSM-IV ADHD. *Journal of Abnormal Child Psychology, 42*(1), 21–35.

Xu, G., Lin, K., Rao, D., Dang, Y., Ouyang, H., Guo, Y., et al. (2012). Neuropsychological performance in bipolar I, bipolar II and unipolar depression patients: A longitudinal, naturalistic study. *Journal of Affective Disorders, 136*(3), 328–339.

CHAPTER 6

Personal Injury Forensic
Neuropsychological Evaluation

Glenn J. Larrabee

This chapter provides an overview of the issues unique to forensic neuropsychological evaluation and report writing in a personal injury context. I contrast the difference in roles between the clinical and forensic evaluation, the differing referral questions that are asked, and the importance of an evidence-based scientific approach to forensic neuropsychological practice. Evidence-based practice underlies preparation of an effectively worded report, which serves to communicate one's analysis of the neuropsychological evidence specific to the forensic questions posed in the original referral. Effective forensic practice provides additional evidence for the case that is in dispute.

THE NATURE OF FORENSIC NEUROPSYCHOLOGICAL PRACTICE

Forensic neuropsychology refers to the application of neuropsychology to answer legal questions. In the civil court, these questions pertain to damages in personal injury litigation—for example, presence or degree of acquired brain damage following traumatic brain injury (TBI; Larrabee, 2012a; Roebuck-Spencer & Sherer, 2012), or neurotoxic injury (Bolla, 2012), as well as issues regarding various capacities in activities of daily living, including the ability to make medical decisions, enter into contracts, and issue a last will and testament (Marson, Hebert, & Solomon, 2012). In the criminal courts these questions pertain to issues of various competencies within the legal system, as well as issues of criminal responsibility

(Denney, 2012a, b; Denney & Sullivan, 2008). Sweet, Ecklund-Johnson, and Malina (2008) provide additional discussion of issues specific to the practice of forensic neuropsychology.

The neuropsychologist in a forensic setting plays a significantly different role from the neuropsychologist in a clinical setting. Denney (2012a, p. 440, citing Heilbrun, 2001) lists several differences between the therapeutic and forensic use of neuropsychological evaluation. In the clinical setting, the purpose of the examination is diagnosis and treatment of illness, whereas in the forensic setting the purpose is assisting the decision maker or attorney. The clinician plays a helping role, whereas the forensic examiner maintains an objective or quasi-objective role. Clinically, it is the patient who is being served, whereas in the forensic setting, the entity can be the court, the attorney, and/or the patient–examinee. Typically, the client is not the patient, and the forensic neuropsychologist's alliance is with the truth rather than the patient or referral source (Denney, 2012b). Other differences that impact the forensic report include the need to clarify the reasoning involved in reaching conclusions in the forensic setting, whereas factors justifying conclusions are optional in the clinical setting. Of particular relevance to the present chapter on report writing is that in the clinical setting, the written report is often brief, with emphasis on conclusory statements, whereas forensic reports are typically lengthy and detailed, documenting findings, reasoning, and conclusions. As an example, the summary and conclusions section of some of my more complicated forensic reports may be longer than an entire clinical report on a patient diagnosed with stroke, brain tumor, or dementia.

In the forensic setting, issues of attorney–expert interaction are critical, as delineated by Greiffenstein and Kaufmann (2012). I can still recall my first testamentary capacity case in the late 1980s in which I was contacted by counsel and asked to evaluate his client for capacity to execute a valid will. I completed the initial interview and testing, contacted counsel, and informed him that his client was demented. His response was "But does he have the capability to execute a valid will?" In this scenario, I had made what Denney and Wynkoop (2000) refer to as the "forensic leap of faith"—that is, assuming that demonstration of neuropsychological impairment sufficiently addresses the legal issue. Further conversation with counsel clarified the contours of testamentary capacity, which I addressed in a follow-up examination of his client.

The above vignette shows why it is paramount that at the moment of being contacted by counsel you gain a clear understanding as to why you are being retained; specifically, what issues does counsel wish for you to address? In personal injury cases, the reason for evaluation is most commonly establishment of damages; that is, does the litigant have neuropsychological impairment as a result of the litigated accident, alleged malpractice, toxic exposure, or assault? It is insufficient to merely document the presence of neuropsychological impairment, if indeed such impairment is present. Impairment, if present, must be causally linked to the event causing the alleged injury. In addition, the forensic neuropsychologist must also characterize the functional consequences of the impairments manifested by the litigant.

Greiffenstein and Kaufmann (2012) list five basic principles of effective neuropsychologist–attorney interactions:

1. Understand legal bases (i.e., have a working knowledge of key law and legal practices).
2. Practice competent neuropsychology.
3. Support board certification.
4. Adhere to ethical principles.
5. Be courtroom familiar.

Practicing competent neuropsychology is particularly relevant to the neuropsychological report. As defined by Greiffenstein and Kaufmann, this principle simply means that the forensic neuropsychologist functions as a scientist–practitioner by combining the body of scientific knowledge with sound clinical judgment while performing medicolegal evaluations involving predictions about persons. The scientific aspect of the forensic neuropsychologist's work requires placing the legal question and evaluation methods in the context of the peer-reviewed scientific literature. An example offered by Greiffenstein and Kaufmann is considering the neuropsychological test results obtained from an individual in the context of the well-established dose–response relationship between duration of coma and neuropsychological outcome (Dikmen, Machamer, Winn, & Temkin, 1995; Rohling, Meyers & Millis, 2003). The examinee with a history of 2 weeks of coma following a TBI should perform similarly to the published group data for persons with similar injury characteristics, thereby establishing a causal link of current test performance with a history of TBI. By contrast, an examinee with no loss of consciousness should not be producing scores at the level seen in association with a month or more of coma following TBI.

I have also written about the scientific aspects of forensic neuropsychological practice (Larrabee, 2012b). I reviewed Hill's (1965) nine factors for establishing that there is a causal link between a particular environmental condition and causation of a particular disease. Although Hill's factors were posited for evaluation of the relationship between toxins and disease, the basic principles also apply to other conditions seen by forensic neuropsychologists including TBI (e.g., Hill's causal factor 5 is the biological gradient or dose–response curve).

Boone (2013) provides a comprehensive discussion of a scientific, evidence-based approach to forensic neuropsychological practice. Her book is focused entirely on civil forensic practice, and covers this area in detail, including a chapter devoted to mild TBI, the most commonly litigated case seen by forensic neuropsychologists. One chapter provides discussion of seven common flaws in forensic neuropsychological reports:

1. Failure to assess appropriately for response bias.
2. Use of inappropriate tests or norms.
3. Failure to draw conclusions consistent with published research.
4. Failure to consider all possible etiologies.
5. Overinterpretation of lowered scores.
6. Claims that low cognitive scores document brain injury.
7. Misinterpretation of the MMPI-2/MMPI-2-RF validity scales.

Boone provides an example of an entire neuropsychological report for a noncredible examinee from her forensic practice that includes a reanalysis of the data obtained on a prior neuropsychological evaluation.

THE FORENSIC NEUROPSYCHOLOGICAL REPORT

Melton, Petrila, Poythress, and Slobogin (2007) note that virtually all cases referred from a court and most cases referred from attorneys will result in the preparation of a written report. This report serves the important function of documenting that an evaluation has taken place, and it includes the nature of the evaluation, data considered, findings, and limitations in the clinical data. The audience for the forensic report usually consists of officers of the court or laypersons rather than medical practitioners involved in patient care; therefore, use of professional jargon is not advisable. Moreover, since the substance of the report is more likely to become public knowledge, special care must be taken to minimize any infringement on the privacy rights of persons mentioned in the report. Melton et al. (2007) also note that the medicolegal report will undergo careful scrutiny in an adversarial setting; consequently, attention to detail and accuracy of information conveyed are crucial. As a result, well-written reports may obviate the need for courtroom testimony, whereas a poorly written report, when placed in the hands of a skilled lawyer, can become an instrument to discredit or embarrass the expert neuropsychologist.

The forensic report is not just based on interview and psychological and neuropsychological testing; rather, it also incorporates extensive record review, commonly including reanalysis of prior test data obtained by another neuropsychologist. With experience I have found that it works best to review the records of a case before conducting the examination, which makes the interview flow better; that is, having preexisting knowledge of the case provides an underlying temporal structure to the interview. My own order of examination starts with a written informed consent. This is followed by a verbal description of the examination process describing the nature of the interview, the background interview, the structured interview, and test procedures, in general.

My typical forensic report in a personal injury case has eight sections. The first is the referral and current complaints, in which the incident leading to the alleged injury is described, including the date, a brief statement as to what other health care providers have found, and the litigant's current primary symptoms, "leading to referral for the current neuropsychological evaluation." The second section is essentially a verbatim review of the clinical interview, followed by the third section covering personal, educational, social, and occupational background (preaccident factors). The fourth section is the structured interview, which differs from the clinical interview by asking pointed, structured questions as opposed to the open-ended format of the clinical interview which is meant to elicit spontaneous production of information. This is followed by sections on procedures, observations, neuropsychological test results, and the final section on summary and conclusions. I will now comment on information included in sections two through eight.

The clinical interview starts with the accident/incident that is the basis of the litigation, for example, car accident, toxic exposure, or alleged medical malpractice. The examinee is drawn into a lengthy description of the incident in what, unbeknownst to them, provides information about the presence/absence of posttraumatic amnesia (PTA; in the case of an alleged TBI), or the presence/absence of evidence for acute encephalopathy (in the case of alleged carbon monoxide exposure or anesthesia incident causing alleged hypoxic brain insult). During this detailed discussion, the examiner can also monitor for evidence of arousal or distress, as might occur if a PTSD is present. This portion of the interview is critical, for it usually enhances rapport with the examinee, in addition to serving the purpose of gathering information relevant to determining whether there was evidence of cerebral insult.

The above discussion of the event leading to the claim of injury can take up to 30 minutes. In the case of an alleged TBI, I will even inquire as to the time of day the event occurred, and how long the litigant was in the hospital (information that is later cross-checked and verified with accident report records and hospital records). As demonstrated by High, Levin, and Gary (1990), orientation to time is the last component of orientation to recover during clearing of PTA in about two-thirds of TBI cases. Hence, demonstration of accurate recollection of the time of the accident, verified against accident records and hospital records, can provide a marker of the presence and duration of PTA. Similarly, if there is a significant gap in recall following a severe TBI for which the accident is not recalled, and the first few days during hospitalization are also not recalled, return of ongoing memory, as reported in the interview, can be linked to nurses' notes describing the patient as alert and oriented times three.

LESS DESIRABLE

When asked if he experienced loss of consciousness in the accident, Mr. X reported this experience, and also endorsed being stunned and dazed, when queried about these features suggestive of posttraumatic amnesia.

MORE DESIRABLE

Mr. X was asked to describe the events leading up to, during and following the accident and could state these in great detail, including the time of day, weather, hearing the sound and feeling the force of the crash, and identifying who he spoke to at the scene, as well as the order of arrival of the EMS and police. Following this detailed description, he specifically denied loss of consciousness as well as any gaps in recall.

What is obvious here is that the less desirable report shows information gathered by leading questions. The more desirable report shows information obtained by open-ended questioning. Only after it has been established that there is no apparent loss of consciousness or PTA are the questions then asked regarding these alterations in functional status.

Following discussion of the accident and its immediate aftermath, the examinee is questioned about their medical follow-up, in chronological order, including health care providers seen, diagnostic procedures performed, what the health care provider has conveyed about their diagnosis (to check for potential for iatrogenesis), as well as the treatments that have been provided. This portion of the interview also provides an opportunity for clinical evaluation of memory function, verified of course with the medical records. Following this review, the examinee is then asked about current providers and current continuing problems from their alleged injury. This is done in an open-ended fashion, rather than inquiring as to specific symptoms.

The interview about the preaccident background includes questioning about the examinee's nuclear family, whether or not the examinee ever experienced significant physical or emotional trauma as a child, and early school history, including questioning about learning disability and attention and behavior problems. Ultimate level of education is determined, as well as work history, social history, and health history. Again, this information is checked against available records.

Following the clinical interview, I then conduct a structured interview, asking specific questions about specific problems the examinee may or may not be experiencing. I deliberately conduct the structured interview after the open-ended main clinical interview, to avoid "leading" the examinee. It is not uncommon to see more symptoms elicited during structured interview, particularly in suggestible examinees.

The above interview process is captured in my report as verbatim as possible. Although this is more detail than many offer in their own clinical reports, it serves the record formation purpose of the report; that is, I am creating a record of the examination, so that all who take the time to read the report know well what actually transpired in the examination.

The same amount of detail is taken in the record review, so that the reader can make comparisons between the interview information and the actual records (comparisons that I will make in this section as well as in the summary and conclusion section of the report). Significant apparent inconsistencies in medical history can also be pointed out, such as the examinee specifically denying loss of consciousness, confusion, or disorientation according to ER records, only later to report all three to a physician seen one year posttrauma.

The record review section is followed by a detailed list of the examination procedures (clinical interview, structured interview, record review, and the actual psychological and neuropsychological tests administered). In Florida, we are required to list any persons utilized in conducting the examination (i.e., nondoctoral technicians, referred to as "assistants to a licensed psychologist" in Florida). In my own evaluations, I conduct the interview, structured interview, and record review, and I also administer about 1½ hours' worth of testing myself, including assessment of performance validity (i.e., is the examinee providing an accurate measure of actual level of ability?), phonemic and semantic fluency, processing speed, and verbal learning and memory, in order to obtain a sample of the examinee's test behavior. My assistant administers the remaining test procedures and scores the entire test battery. I perform the data analysis and prepare the written report.

In a separate observations section, I describe basic mental status and behavioral observations (e.g., was there any arousal or distress when discussing the accident; is there evidence for pain behavior such as grimacing, wincing, or repositioning in the chair). The second half of the observations section includes a description of the performance validity test (PVT; is the examinee providing an accurate measure of actual ability; Larrabee, 2012c) and symptom validity test (SVT; is the examinee providing an accurate description of actual symptom experience; Larrabee 2012c) results. This is followed by a comment as to whether the test results are to be considered valid or invalid.

LESS DESIRABLE

1. The examinee appeared engaged and invested in doing her best, and the current test results are considered to represent an accurate measure of her neuropsychological strengths and weaknesses. In addition, the examinee passed the Rey 15 Item test, and did not produce any elevations on the Personality Assessment Inventory validity scales. Therefore, the current examination results provide an accurate picture of her current strengths and weaknesses.

MORE DESIRABLE

1. The examinee failed three free-standing and four embedded/derived measures of performance validity, and also showed significant elevations on the Response Bias scale of the MMPI-2-RF and on the Modified Somatic Perception Questionnaire. These multiple indicators of invalid performance and symptom report, in the context of the current litigation, are consistent with probable malingering to a high degree of confidence (or alternatively, consistent with invalid assessment results, to a high degree of confidence). This means that current poor test results are more likely the result of intentional underperformance, whereas normal range performances may well be an underestimate of actual level of ability.

2. The examinee passed all but two PVTs, one free standing and one embedded/derived, as well as all SVTs administered. His two PVT failures were just beyond cutoff and in the range where false positives can occur. His clinical history of a month of coma, need for supervised living, and inability to drive a motor vehicle, all demonstrate characteristics of false-positive cases on PVTs. Hence, his current test results are considered to be an accurate measure of his actual level of ability.

The less desirable example relies heavily on clinical judgment, which is notoriously poor regarding determination of motivated performance (see Heaton, Smith, Lehman, & Vogt, 1978). It also relies on a procedure, the Rey 15-Item Test, that is less sensitive to invalid performance than forced choice PVTs (Vickery, Berry, Inman, Harris, & Orey, 2001), and relies on the Personality Assessment Inventory (PAI; Morey, 1991), which does not include validity scales that parallel those more sensitive to symptom exaggeration in personal injury settings, including the FBS-r and RBS of the MMPI-2-RF. This same examinee (1) produced invalid PVT and SVT results on my own subsequent examination. Moreover, my own evaluation of the raw test data from these other examinations reflected evidence of invalid test performance on embedded derived PVTs for motor function, working memory, verbal supraspan learning, and problem solving. The second of the two desirable cases (2–different examinee) demonstrates how to address one's interpretation of failed PVTs as representing false-positive identification.

The next section of the report contains the results of the actual direct testing portion of the forensic evaluation. I break this down by functional domain, including:

- Language and verbal symbolic functions.
- Perceptual spatial judgment and problem solving.
- Gross and fine motor skills.
- Memory and related functions (broken down into subcategories including orientation to time, attention/concentration/working memory and processing speed, verbal learning and memory, visual learning and memory, and recent/remote memory function).
- Intellectual and problem-solving skills (broken down into subcategories, including estimation of premorbid level of function, and whether WAIS-IV Index scores are consistent or inconsistent with estimated premorbid level of function, verbal intellectual skills, visual–nonverbal intellectual skills, problem solving and set shifting, and academic skills).

The final section of the report describes personality testing, as well as pain scale findings (if appropriate to the case).

Each of the above-mentioned domains of ability/symptoms is essentially a "mini-report" on the function, for example, verbal learning and memory, describing the basic nature of the task (without risking test security) and the percentile of performance on each task, with a conclusory statement about the level of function in the domain.

LESS DESIRABLE

> 1. The examinee showed impaired performance on phonemic fluency, normal semantic fluency, poor discrimination of faces but normal performance on Block Design. Memory was very poor for text recall and paired associate learning, but normal for learning a list of 15 unrelated words. These findings are consistent with traumatic brain injury.

Headings are used, but each heading only delineates test scores as preserved or impaired, with no reference to the history or severity of injury or attempt to integrate performance with other factors.

MORE DESIRABLE

> 1. The examinee showed evidence of poor text recall and verbal paired associate learning, but performed normally on the more sensitive supraspan list learning test for learning and retention of 15 unrelated words. This inconsistency in performance is seen in the context of failed free-standing PVTs, as well as failure of the Delayed Recognition scores for text recall and paired associate learning, in a pattern indicative of invalid test performance.

The integration of all of the test results takes place in the summary, but each section of the results describes the function in that section, as well as an explanation as to why.

A similar section on a person with severe TBI might read as follows:

> 2. The examinee showed evidence of poor text recall, paired associate learning, and supraspan list learning and recall of 15 unrelated words. This performance is consistent with his history of 2 weeks of coma, with acute CT scan showing left temporal hemorrhagic contusion, with persisting structural change evident on MRI done 6 months posttrauma.

The final section of the report is entitled "Summary and Conclusions" and is the real meat of the evaluation. If the preceding sections have been appropriately described and reviewed, the reader is able to follow the summary well, and the conclusions, as stated, are as the reader would expect. In other words, the reader's reaction should be "of course." I typically start out this section by referring to the acute medical records. For example:

> EMS records show the examinee's denial of loss of consciousness and record a Glasgow Coma Scale of 15, consistent with ER records showing denial of loss of consciousness, and description of the examinee as alert and oriented to person, place, time and circumstances. These medical records are consistent with the examinee's current interview in which they provided a detailed rendition of the events of the accident, with no gaps in recall, and ability to actually report within 30 minutes the time of day the accident occurred.

Alternatively, the EMS records may show someone described as unconscious and posturing, with Glasgow Coma Scale of 7 on admission to the ER, with progress notes showing one week of coma and one week of PTA.

Although the examinee may report loss of consciousness of two weeks in the interview, it is fairly common for patients to confuse PTA with coma, since they have no recollection of ongoing events while they are in PTA.

The patient's postaccident follow-up is then documented, followed by a summary of the interview, which is integrated with the medical record summary. For example, a severely injured patient shows no recall during the interview for his or her subacute hospitalization, with recall returning when in a separate inpatient rehabilitation facility, yet this is consistent with the medical records which show posttraumatic amnesia continuing until their second week of treatment in rehabilitation, whereas they were either in coma or PTA all the time they were in subacute hospitalization.

In addition to the freely reported symptoms during the main interview, the symptoms elicited during structured interview are repeated. Any preexisting relevant history is noted (e.g., childhood abuse, learning disability, or ADHD). This is followed by a summary of the examination findings. For example:

> The examinee failed three PVTs and two independent SVTs, which, in the context of external incentive, is consistent with the presence of probable malingering, to a high degree of confidence. In view of the data showing no acute evidence for loss of consciousness or PTA, this indicates that current poor performances are more likely the result of intentional underperformance, whereas normal range scores themselves may be underestimates of actual level of ability. Current test results are variable, likely due to invalid performance; however there are select test procedures that contradict acquired impairment, including Controlled Oral Word Association, Trail Making B, and both the learning and delayed recall trials of the Auditory Verbal Learning Test, with entirely normal learning and delayed recognition on the CVMT.

The summary section is then followed by the statement "Overall, I have the following conclusions: . . ." First, in the case of a patient with an alleged mild TBI who also produced evidence of invalid test performance:

> 1. EMS records showing no loss of consciousness, with Glasgow Coma Scale of 15, and ability to recall and relate the events of the accident, with ER records showing the same evidence, do not support that a significant brain injury occurred. Although the examinee two months later reported to Dr. G that they were initially "stunned," this is a nonspecific complaint that can occur in conditions other than traumatic brain injury. Thus, either no brain

injury occurred, or at worst, the examinee sustained an uncomplicated mild TBI. It should be noted that the typical outcome of uncomplicated mild traumatic brain injury (mTBI) is full and complete recovery, in some cases as early as 1 week posttrauma, but in almost all cases, by 90 days posttrauma.

2. In the current case, normal brain function and/or complete recovery is shown in particular by normal Controlled Oral Word Association, Trail Making B at the 84th percentile, superior range, normal Auditory Verbal Learning Test performance, and above-average CVMT delayed recognition, at the 75th percentile. On Dr. X's earlier neuropsychological evaluation, normal brain function is supported by normal learning and delayed recall on the CVLT-II, normal TPT total time, and above-average TPT Location, with normal Trail Making B and Category Test performance.

3. In spite of the above, the examinee still complains of continuing cognitive impairment and shows variably impaired performance on current testing. The same is seen in Dr. X's earlier examination. The current and prior test score fluctuations in performance both occur in the context of evidence for invalid test performance, with abnormally low Finger Tapping Performance, poor Reliable Digit Span and Failure of the TOMM and MMPI-2-RF Response Bias Scale on the current test results, and Elevated MMPI-2-RF Response Bias Scale, failure of the Word Memory Test, poor Reliable Digit Span, and Excessive Failure to Maintain Set and "other" responses during the earlier evaluation conducted by Dr. X.

4. The results in paragraph 3, in the context of the current litigation, are consistent with the presence of probable malingering, to a high degree of confidence. This suggests significant caution in depending upon this person's symptomatic complaints in determining presence/degree of acquired impairments, such as claimed pain. Rather, such determinations are best made on the basis of objective examination procedures.

In paragraph 4, note that use of the term "probable malingering" refers to the occurrence of multiple invalid performances, in the context of external incentive, with no viable alternative clinical reason for the invalid test performance (Slick, Sherman, & Iverson, 1999). In a case of alleged mild TBI, there is no reason to expect gross neuropsychological impairment, nor did this examinee manifest a history of severe psychiatric disturbance, such as schizophrenia, or have a history of mental retardation. In other words, there was no viable clinical explanation for the multiple PVT failure.

In an alternative case of severe TBI, the conclusion section might read as follows:

> 1. EMS records describe complicated extrication, with a GCS of 3 at the scene. On admission to ER, GCS remained 3. Acute CT scan showed left subdural hematoma, with slight midline shift. After admission to inpatient care, the examinee did not follow commands for 3 weeks. At time of discharge to inpatient rehabilitation, he was still only oriented times two, with full orientation not returning for an additional 2 weeks. This information, showing 3 weeks of coma and 2 weeks of PTA is consistent with the occurrence of a severe traumatic brain injury.
>
> 2. Consistent with paragraph 1, the examinee remains in a supervised living arrangement, two years posttrauma. He has continuing disturbance in gait, borderline memory ability, and impaired judgment. He has a court-appointed guardian. Although he passes all but two measures of performance validity, his scores on these two measures are in the range associated with false positives in examinees with need for 24-hour supervision. Consequently, these two failures should be considered false-positive results. His test results show widespread impairment, across all domains, consistent with his history of prolonged coma and posttraumatic amnesia. Similar results were obtained by Dr. X, on testing done 1 year posttrauma. The persisting impairments and lack of change on current testing, conducted 2 years posttrauma, bodes poorly for any additional significant recovery.
>
> 3. Based on conclusions 1 and 2 above, the examinee will need a closely supervised setting for the foreseeable future. He is not likely ever to return to any competitive employment.

COMMON ERRORS IN FORENSIC NEUROPSYCHOLOGICAL REPORTS

I actually developed my four-part consistency analysis (Larrabee, 1990, 2012b) based on my experience examining litigants, including my careful review of the evaluation reports prepared by other psychologists. This analysis includes:

1. Are the data consistent within and between neuropsychological domains?
2. Is the neuropsychological profile consistent with the suspected etiological condition?
3. Are the neuropsychological data consistent with the documented severity of injury?
4. Are the neuropsychological data consistent with the subject's behavioral presentation?

The primary problem in forensic neuropsychological reports is the lack of integration of data from all sources, including direct examination (interview and testing), observations of the behavior of the examinee, and medical records. In a poorly conducted evaluation, history as provided by the examinee may be accepted as accurate, with no checking of other records. For example, an examinee may report blow to the head, and being "stunned and dazed," information that is contradicted by the medical records showing no blow to the head, no loss of consciousness, and no confusion and disorientation, with a description of the litigant as alert and oriented to person, place, time and situation. Yet, this "new history" of being "stunned and dazed" now becomes part of the medical record.

It is not uncommon to see inadequate assessment of performance and symptom validity. On multiple occasions, I have seen cases where only two or fewer PVTs were administered and passed, whereas multiple embedded and derived PVT measures were failed, as well as elevations on MMPI-2-RF validity scales such as FBS and RBS. I have seen use of the Validity Indicator Profile (VIP) (developed in criminal forensic settings wherein feigned intellectual impairment and psychosis are more likely to occur) in civil cases, with no administration of memory paradigm PVTs such as the TOMM or Word Memory Test. Or the Personality Assessment Inventory (PAI) substituted for the MMPI-2-RF, when the PAI only contains validity assessment relevant to feigned psychosis and does not include scales sensitive to feigned injury or illness, such as the MMPI-2-RF Fs, FBS-r, or RBS.

Another error is the failure to consider how commonly statistically "abnormal" scores occur in normative populations comprising lengthy neuropsychological test batteries. For example, in a group of 40 separate neuropsychological test scores and using a cutoff of –1 SD, 27% of normal persons will have more than eight scores below this cutoff (Binder, Iverson, & Brooks, 2009, Table 5). Some neuropsychologists may interpret these normal variability performances as evidence of acquired impairment secondary to injury to the brain.

It is common to see evidence for confirmation bias, only seeking evidence for impairment, and ignoring evidence contradicting impairment, such as evidence for normal verbal supraspan learning on the Auditory

Verbal Learning Test (AVLT) or California Verbal Learning Test–II (CVLT-II) and normal performance on the Rey Complex Figure Test as well as on Trail Making B. This type of bias fails to take into account the principle of consistency within domains and between domains. Within domains, impaired text recall on WMS-IV Logical Memory is not consistent with entirely normal AVLT performance and evidence of normal memory during the clinical interview. Between domains, examples of inconsistencies include normal memory occurring in the context of impaired attention; and normal processing speed and memory in the context of gross reductions in the WAIS-IV Verbal Comprehension Index and Perceptual Reasoning Index. In Larrabee (2012b), I further discuss sources of bias in test score interpretation.

It is also common to see a lack of integration of test scores with actual behavior—for example, the litigant who produces a combined Finger Tapping score of 20 (right and left hands added together), but who is able to drive a stick shift car; or the examinee who lives independently, manages his finances, and drives a car without additional accidents or tickets, yet produces a WAIS-IV Processing Speed Index of 65, with a Trail Making B score at the 1st percentile.

Expected levels and patterns of performance with the alleged cause of brain damage are often ignored—for example, a litigant alleging sequelae of carbon monoxide exposure, who produces normal verbal and visual learning and memory scores, and demonstrates normal fine motor skills. Note that carbon monoxide preferentially damages the hippocampi, basal ganglia, and cerebellum.

When I encounter these errors of interpretation, I deal with them in two sections of the report: the record review, and the summary and conclusions. In the record review, after I have summarized the interpretive report of the opposing neuropsychologist, I then reinterpret the test data, relating it to the original severity of trauma, as per EMS and ER records, and discuss any apparent inconsistencies, before offering my own interpretive conclusions regarding their data. In the summary and conclusions, when I am making conclusions about my own data, I include aspects of their data that support these conclusions. This may include normal performances matching my own results, as well as invalid performances, matching my own performance and symptom validity findings.

Appendix 6.1 (pp. 163–165) presents the summary, impressions, and conclusions sections from one of my civil forensic evaluations, with identifying information removed. This was a medical malpractice case. Test data are displayed in Table 6.1 and follow an interpretive schema of < 5th percentile = impaired, 6th–16th percentiles = borderline, 17th–39th percentiles = low average, 40th–59th percentiles = average, 60th–85th percentiles = high average, and 86th + percentiles superior.

TABLE 6.1. Data for Medical Malpractice Case Example

Test domain	Score	Percentile/interpretation
Performance validity		
Rey 15-Item with Recognition	21	Pass
Dot Counting Test	20	Pass (stroke ≤ 21)
b Test	107	Pass (stroke ≤ 169)
TOMM	50/50/50	Pass
Word Memory Test	100/95/95	Pass
Language		
Benton Visual Naming	Adjusted score = 40	2nd percentile/impaired
Benton Controlled Oral Word Association	Adjusted score = 39	56th percentile/average
Semantic Category Fluency (animals, fruits, vegetables)	Raw total = 27	9th percentile/borderline
Benton Sentence Repetition	Adjusted score = 5	< 1st percentile/impaired
Benton Aural Comprehension of words and phrases	18/18	71th+ percentile/preserved
Benton Reading Comprehension of words and phrases	18/18	59th+ percentile/preserved
Benton Token Test	39/44	15th percentile/borderline
Visuoperceptual/visuospatial		
Benton Visual Form Discrimination	22/32	< 1st percentile/impaired
Benton Facial Recognition	45	59th percentile/average
Benton Judgment of Line Orientation	13 adjusted score	1.5th percentile/impaired
Manual motor function		
Finger Tapping, right hand	38 taps	21st percentile/low average
Finger Tapping, left hand	33.4 taps	18th percentile/low average
Grip Strength, right hand	22 kg	5th percentile/impaired
Grip Strength, left hand	18.5 kg	5th percentile/impaired
Purdue Pegboard, right hand	9	< 1st percentile/impaired
Purdue Pegboard, left hand	12	8th percentile/borderline
Purdue Pegboard, both hands	8	< 1st percentile/impaired
Grooved Pegboard, right hand	127 seconds	4th percentile/impaired
Grooved Pegboard, left hand	110 seconds	24th percentile/low average
Manual tactile function		
Benton Finger Localization, right hand	24/30	< 4th percentile/impaired
Benton Finger Localization, left hand	29/30	57th percentile/average
Benton Tactile Form Perception, right hand	5/10	< 1st percentile/impaired
Benton Tactile Form Perception, left hand	3/10	< 1st percentile/impaired
Benton Temporal Orientation	Zero errors	34th percentile/preserved

(continued)

TABLE 6.1. *(continued)*

Test domain	Score	Percentile/interpretation
Working memory		
WAIS-III Working Memory Index	80	9th percentile/borderline
Digit Span	Scaled score = 10	50th percentile/average
Arithmetic	Scaled score = 6	9th percentile/borderline
Letter Number Sequencing	Scaled score = 4	2nd percentile/impaired
Processing speed		
WAIS-III Processing Speed Index	79	8th percentile/borderline
Digit Symbol–Coding	6	9th percentile/borderline
Symbol Search	6	9th percentile/borderline
Trail Making A	67 seconds, zero errors	4th percentile/impaired
Trail Making B	198 seconds, (discontinued)	Impaired
Stroop (Trenerry version)	70/112	15.5th percentile/borderline
Verbal learning and memory		
Serial Digit Learning	4	8th percentile/borderline
Expanded Paired Associate Test		
Immediate	16	15.5th percentile/borderline
Delayed	8	31.3rd percentile/low average
WMS-III Logical Memory		
Immediate	7	16th percentile/borderline
Delayed	12	75th percentile/high average
California Verbal Learning Test–II		
Trial 1–5	$T = 45$	31st percentile/low average
Interference	$z = -.5$	31st percentile/low averge
Short Delay Free Recall	$z = -1.5$	7th percentile/borderline
Long Delay Free Recall	$z = -1.5$	7th percentile/borderline
Verbal Selective Reminding Test (six-trial version)		
Long-Term Storage	38	18th percentile/low average
Consistent Long-Term Retrieval	27	16th percentile/borderline
Delayed Recall	9	10th percentile/borderline
Visual learning and memory		
Visual Reproduction (WMS figures with Trahan normative data)		
Immediate Reproduction	4	5.9th percentile/borderline
Delayed Reproduction	2	2nd percentile/impaired
WMS-III Faces I	10	50th percentile/average
WMS-III Faces II	11	63rd percentile/high average
Hannay–Levin Continuous Recognition Memory Test, total correct	65	<1st percentile/impaired
Continuous Visual Memory Test		
Total Correct	59	<5th percentile/impaired
Delayed Recognition	4/7	58th percentile/average

(continued)

TABLE 6.1. *(continued)*

Test domain	Score	Percentile/interpretation
Recent/remote memory		
Presidents Test		
Verbal Naming	2	< 1st percentile/impaired
Verbal Sequencing	Rho = 1.0	64th+ percentile/preserved
Picture Naming	6	51th+ percentile/preserved
Picture Sequencing	Rho = .94	16th percentile/borderline
Verbal intellectual and problem-solving skills		
WAIS-III Verbal Comprehension Index	89	23rd percentile/low average
Vocabulary	7	16th percentile/borderline
Similarities	10	50th percentile/average
Information	10	50th percentile/average
Visual intellectual and problem-solving skills		
WAIS-III Perceptual Organization Index	74	4th percentile/impaired
Picture Completion	6	9th percentile/borderline
Block Design	4	2nd percentile/impaired
Matrix Reasoning	7	16th percentile/borderline
Problem solving and set shifting		
Wisconsin Card Sorting Test		
Number of Categories	3	6th percentile/borderline
Perseverative Responses	37	8th percentile/borderline
Perseverative Errors	35	6th percentile/borderline
Academic skills		
WRAT-3		
Reading	Standard score = 107	68th percentile/high average
Spelling	Standard score = 100	50th percentile/average
Arithmetic	Standard score = 90	25th percentile/low average
Pain scales and depression		
Beck Depression Inventory–II	13	Minimal
McGill Pain Questionnaire	21	Below average re pain sample
Pain Disability Index	41	Closer to low than high disability
Modified Somatic Perception Questionnaire	6	Average for female back pain patients
MMPI-2		
Valid	F, Fb, Fp all < 60; FBS raw = 20; K = 72	MMPI-2 scores and the Beck Depression Inventory–II suggest the presence of a mild degree of depression
Primary scale elevations	Hs = 67, D = 70; Sc = 66	
RC scale elevations	RC 1 = 66, RC 2 = 70	

CONCLUSIONS

In closing, the practice of forensic neuropsychology is a scientific enterprise, and the report itself reflects this emphasis. The interview and record review sections of the report are analogous to the literature review of a scientific publication. The listing of test procedures as well as observations (including PVT and SVT evaluations) are analogous to the methodology section, and test results are parallel to the results section of a scientific paper, with the summary and conclusions section equivalent to the summary of a proper scientific publication.

The forensic neuropsychological evaluation report integrates all that is known about the examinee and the examinee's alleged condition that is the focus of litigation. Comprehensive neuropsychological test results are integrated with clinical interview and medical record review in a scientifically defensible manner to answer the forensic question. In my opinion, forensic practice represents the highest level of practice of our profession.

REFERENCES

Bolla, K. I. (2012). Neurotoxic injury. In G. J. Larrabee (Ed.). *Forensic neuropsychology: A scientific approach* (pp. 281–301). New York: Oxford University Press.

Boone, K. B. (2013). *Clinical practice of forensic neuropsychology. An evidence-based approach*. New York: Guilford Press.

Denney, R. L. (2012a). Criminal forensic neuropsychology and assessment of competency. In G. J. Larrabee (Ed.). *Forensic neuropsychology: A scientific approach* (pp. 438–472). New York: Oxford University Press.

Denney, R. L. (2012b). Criminal responsibility and other criminal forensic issues. In G. J. Larrabee (Ed.). *Forensic neuropsychology: A scientific approach* (pp. 473–500). New York: Oxford University Press.

Denney, R. L., & Sullivan, J. P. (Eds). (2008). *Clinical neuropsychology in the criminal forensic setting*. New York: Guilford Press.

Denney, R. L., & Wynkoop, T. F. (2000). Clinical neuropsychology in the criminal forensic setting. *Journal of Head Trauma Rehabilitation, 15*, 804–828.

Dikmen, S. S., Machamer, J. E., Winn, H. R., & Temkin, N. R. (1995). Neuropsychological outcome at 1-year post head injury. *Neuropsychology, 9*, 80–90.

Greiffenstein, M. F., & Kaufmann, P. M. (2012). Neuropsychology and the law: Principles of productive attorney-neuropsychologist relations. In G. J. Larrabee (Ed.), *Forensic neuropsychology: A scientific approach* (pp. 23–69). New York: Oxford University Press.

Heaton, R. K., Smith, H. H., Lehman, R. A. W., & Vogt, A. T. (1978). Prospects for faking believable deficits on neuropsychological testing. *Journal of Consulting and Clinical Psychology, 46*, 892–900.

Heilbrun, K. (2001). *Principles of forensic mental health assessment*. New York: Kluwer Academic/Plenum Publishers.

High, W. M., Levin, H. S., & Gary, H. E. (1990). Recovery of orientation following closed-head injury. *Journal of Clinical and Experimental Neuropsychology, 12,* 703–714.

Hill, A. B. (1965). The environment and disease: Association and causation. *Proceedings of the Royal Society of Medicine, 58,* 295–300.

Larrabee, G. J. (1990). Cautions in the use of neuropsychological evaluation in legal settings. *Neuropsychology, 4,* 239–247.

Larrabee, G. J. (2012a). Mild traumatic brain injury. In G. J. Larrabee (Ed.). *Forensic neuropsychology: A scientific approach* (pp. 231–259). New York: Oxford University Press.

Larrabee, G. J. (2012b). A scientific approach to forensic neuropsychology. In G. J. Larrabee (Ed.). *Forensic neuropsychology: A scientific approach* (pp. 3–22). New York: Oxford University Press.

Larrabee, G. J. (2012c). Performance validity and symptom validity in neuropsychological assessment. *Journal of the International Neuropsychological Society, 18,* 625–630.

Marson, D. C., Hebert, K., & Solomon, A. C. (2012). Assessing civil competencies in older adults with dementia. Consent capacity, financial capacity, and testamentary capacity. In G. J. Larrabee (Ed.). *Forensic neuropsychology: A scientific approach* (pp. 401–437). New York: Oxford University Press.

Melton, G. B., Petrila, J., Poythress, N. G., & Slobogin, C., with Lyons, P. M., & Otto, R. K. (2007). *Psychological evaluations for the courts* (3rd ed.). New York: Guilford Press.

Morey, L. C. (1991). *The personality assessment inventory.* Odessa, FL: Psychological Assessment Resources.

Roebuck-Spencer, T., & Sherer, M. (2012). Moderate and severe traumatic brain injury. In G. J. Larrabee (Ed.). *Forensic neuropsychology: A scientific approach* (pp. 260–280). New York: Oxford University Press.

Rohling, M. L., Meyers, J. E., & Millis, S. R. (2003). Neuropsychological impairment following traumatic brain injury: A dose–response analysis. *The Clinical Neuropsychologist, 17,* 289–302.

Slick, D. J., Sherman, E. M. S., & Iverson, G. L. (1999). Diagnostic criteria for malingered neurocognitive dysfunction: Proposed standards for clinical practice and research. *The Clinical Neuropsychologist, 13,* 545–561.

Sweet, J. J., Ecklund-Johnson, E., & Malina, A. (2008). Forensic neuropsychology: An overview of issues and directions. In J. E. Morgan & J. H. Ricker (Eds.). *Textbook of clinical neuropsychology* (pp. 869–890). New York: Taylor and Francis.

Vickery, C. D., Berry, D. T. R., Inman, T. H., Harris, M. J., & Orey, S. A. (2001). Detection of inadequate effort on neuropsychological testing: A meta-analytic review of selected procedures. *Archives of Clinical Neuropsychology, 16,* 45–73.

Sample Summary, Impressions, and Conclusion Sections from a Civil Forensic Evaluation Report

In summary, this 55-year-old widowed right-handed African American former health care worker with 14 years of education was referred by Attorney D for neuropsychological evaluation of the consequences of a stroke occurring on 05/17/08. Review of medical records shows an earlier visit to X Memorial Hospital on 05/15/08 with chief complaints of weakness and impaired speech. Initially, there was a right-sided sensory motor impairment that appeared to resolve during the time she was in the hospital. Following neurological consultation, it was felt that she had probable somatization disorder as the events had occurred during a period of high stress related to her brother's funeral. She was provided discharge instructions for TIA and anxiety reaction. CT scan on this visit was interpreted by Dr. V as showing no measurable acute cerebrovascular accident.

On 05/17/08, she was readmitted to X Memorial Hospital and noted to have right-sided facial weakness and slurred speech. CT scan of the brain was interpreted by Dr. W as showing recent infarct in the left basal ganglia, probably within the caudate nucleus. She was assessed with left MCA/CVA with ischemic basal ganglia and external capsular lesions. She was hospitalized from 05/17/08 to 05/21/08. She underwent speech and language evaluation and received occupational and physical therapy services. On 05/18/08, MRI of the brain with and without contrast was interpreted as showing high signal intensity along the left internal capsule, basal ganglia region, consistent with acute infarction. Following her inpatient stay, she was transferred to outpatient treatment with therapies ultimately discontinued due to lack of attendance.

On current direct interview, the patient was able to report her medical history in broad strokes and with a reasonable degree of accuracy. There was some difficulty in time-tagging of events, for example, stating that she had back surgery five years ago when it had occurred 3 years ago. Current medications were Verapamil, Aprinox, Regulon, and Celexa, and Lortab for injury to her left wrist. Primary current complaints were pain in the left wrist and right arm, worsening of preexisting migraines, and persistent, periodic speech difficulty. On direct questioning, she acknowledged word-finding problems and occasional comprehension difficulties. Word-finding problems were more pronounced than her comprehension problems. She reported occasional trouble reading, some difficulty writing, but denied trouble spelling. She also reported calculation difficulties since her stroke. She acknowledged increased weakness and clumsiness in the right compared to the left side of her body, but did not report any numbness or tingling on the right. She denied left body side changes. She reported concentration was a little bit off, with some difficulty remembering what she was told or what she read, but denied problems remembering where she puts things or where the car is parked. Problems were described in both recent and remote memory, but remote was superior to recent memory functioning. Also, she noticed her thinking and decision-making skills had changed, and that it requires more mental effort to make decisions at present. She reported her spirits were down. Appetite has been up and down, and she is more emotional than she used to be. She reported difficulty sleeping, in part due to thinking repeatedly about how the stroke had occurred. Also, she had increased anxiety and worry, with occasional temper difficulty.

On current direct assessment, she passed a wide range of free-standing performance validity tests (PVTs), and showed no evidence for symptom exaggeration on the Symptom Validity Scales (SVTs) of the MMPI-2, or on pain scale assessment. Consequently, the current test findings are thought to be an accurate measure of her actual level of ability.

Detailed language assessment showed persistent confrontation naming difficulties and semantic category fluency difficulties, along with impaired sentence repetition. Auditory and reading comprehension were generally preserved, though auditory comprehension declined somewhat on a measure of complex comprehension, the Token Test. Perceptual skills were preserved for facial discrimination but impaired for form discrimination and particularly impaired for judgment of spatial orientation. Gross motor skills were variably performed, with normal range tapping but impaired grip strength. There were no focal deficits on gross motor testing, but focal deficits were apparent on fine motor skills with better performance of the left compared to right upper extremity on both the Purdue Pegboard and Grooved Pegboard. She showed errors for double simultaneous stimulation for finger localization on the right hand that were not apparent on the left, consistent with the original left-hemisphere location of her stroke. On Tactile Form Perception, she showed bilateral impairment suggestive of bilateral stereognostic difficulties, which are typically seen with right posterior hemisphere disease.

She was oriented to time. She performed poorly on attentional tasks, but this was confounded by her language impairment. By contrast, her verbal and learning and memory skills were in the low end of the normal range, whereas visual memory performance was typically poor. Recent and remote memory performance was generally preserved.

Intellectual and problem-solving skills showed decline relative to premorbid level of function for perceptual/

organizational skills. Working memory and processing speed, as well as problem solving and set-shifting were poor. Basic academic skills for oral reading, spelling, and written computations were consistent with premorbid estimate.

Pain scale assessment did not show any evidence for pain symptom exaggeration. Personality testing showed evidence for mild degree of depression.

Overall, I have the following conclusions:

1. She is presenting with evidence of persistent language impairment characterized by impaired visual confrontation naming, semantic category fluency, and sentence repetition. This pattern of deficits is characteristic of conduction aphasia, which is consistent with the left subcortical location of her stroke. She is also showing reduced right compared to left upper extremity fine motor performance, and poor right-hand finger localization skills, which are also consistent with residual effects of her left-hemisphere stroke. In addition to these findings, she is also showing impairment in visual/ intellectual and problem-solving skills that is strongly suggestive of additional right posterior hemisphere dysfunction. In particular, her spatial judgment is poor, she has bilateral stereognostic impairment, poor visual memory and reduced performance on the Perceptual Organization Index of the Wechsler Adult Intelligence Scale III, all features that are consistent with the presence of nondominant (i.e., right-) hemisphere disease.

2. Her current language impairment and right-hand sensorimotor problems correlate with medical information regarding the stroke occurring on 05/17/08. The pattern of performance suspicious for right posterior hemisphere dysfunction suggests additional disease in the right hemisphere of the brain. Given her history of vascular disease, this is a likely etiological factor. I am unable to determine whether or not this occurred at the time of her left-hemisphere stroke. Further neurologic consultation may be helpful in this regard.

3. Language and right upper extremity fine motor impairment are going to be handicapping factors regarding her participation in the competitive workforce. This is compounded by additional neuropsychological evidence of nondominant righthemisphere dysfunction, manifesting as impaired spatial judgment, poor visual memory, and reduced visual intellectual skills. Although she reports no difficulties driving a car (i.e., no tickets or accidents), it would be prudent to have her undergo a driving safety evaluation in light of her current perceptual and spatial deficits. Such an examination can be performed at Y Rehabilitation Institute.

CHAPTER 7

Criminal Forensic
Neuropsychological Evaluation

Joel E. Morgan
Bernice A. Marcopulos

Neuropsychological consultation to the legal profession has grown exponentially over the past decade in both civil litigation and criminal venues (Kaufmann, 2013). These forensic assessment contexts bring numerous challenges to the neuropsychologist that go well beyond those in clinical settings. While to the competent, experienced neuropsychologist every examination of every examinee is a serious endeavor that strives for truth and accuracy, the "stakes" of some criminal forensic evaluations are at the very highest level. Most would agree that there are no higher stakes than in death penalty cases.

In this chapter we first review the important distinctions between criminal and civil assessment venues. We next discuss the major assessment questions typically sought in these two legal settings—that is, what exactly are attorneys and the court requesting of the neuropsychologist? We then cover important aspects of writing for the legal system and, finally, offer examples of report components illustrating some ways in which these issues are expressed in writing for the courts.

First, some legal terminology: The language used by the legal profession and that of clinical neuropsychology may not always be identical. Attorneys and courts are interested in a defendant's *capacity*. Neuropsychologists provide information about the functional abilities and psychological status of examinees. This is true whether we provide clinical or forensic services. Neuropsychologists understand the term "functional abilities." In the legal sense, this refers to a person's capacity. In the legal system, the term "capacity" refers to the ability, capability, or fitness to be able to do something; a capacity to perform some act, an ability to comprehend both the nature and consequences of one's acts. It relates therefore to soundness of mind (Clark, 2013). For a neuropsychologist, this refers to cognition, especially reasoning ability, judgment, decision making, and the like. One's capacity in the legal sense obviously relates to the concept of *competency*. We will elaborate this discussion of capacity and competency in later sections of this chapter.

CIVIL AND CRIMINAL FORENSIC EXAMS

Forensic neuropsychology refers to the provision of neuropsychological consultation services to the legal profession. These services may involve medicolegal issues such as disability exams, civil matters (e.g., personal injury, medical malpractice), or criminal matters that include a host of misdemeanors and felonies from the banal (e.g., criminal trespassing, disorderly conduct) to the most heinous (e.g., kidnapping, sexual assault, murder). All forensic exams involve potential *secondary gain* for the examinee. Secondary gain differs from primary gain in that, with primary gain, examinees typically experience some type of distress. They desire to understand what is causing their difficulties for the purpose of getting better. In standard clinical neuropsychological exams, examinees seek to answer the question of what is wrong with them, what is their diagnosis, if any, and what can be done about it. The primary gain is to improve their health. Secondary gain refers to the fact that the outcome of the neuropsychological exam may benefit the examinee in ways beyond determining a diagnosis and providing treatment recommendations (Heilbronner, Sweet, Morgan, Larrabee, & Millis, 2009). In civil litigation, the outcome of the exam my result in a large monetary payout for alleged damages. Examinations for disability may result in a lifetime monthly annuity. In criminal settings, the outcome of the exam may release the examinee from proceeding to trial, if deemed incompetent to stand trial, or may relieve him or her from criminal responsibility if he or she is deemed not guilty by reason of insanity. The exam may also mitigate penalties in cases of diminished mental capacity or in death penalty cases (so-called Atkins cases; *Atkins v. Virginia*, 2002; Chafetz & Biondolillo, 2012).

There are significant differences between civil and criminal settings. In civil cases involving personal injury and malpractice, a plaintiff makes allegations about some putative wrongdoing by the defendant. Defendant is *liable*. Plaintiff seeks *judgment* by the court in his or her favor and *damages* for the alleged wrongdoing. For civil matters of this kind involving neuropsychological consultation, the examinee is alleged to have some type of cognitive or psychological impairment, presumably caused by the defendant and about which the neuropsychologist is expected to shed light. The putative cause of the alleged impairment is the nature of the civil suit—that is, defendant did something wrong. For example, suppose a plaintiff alleges that his doctor failed to correctly diagnose a stroke, delaying treatment, and plaintiff went on to develop significant cognitive impairment. It is easy to see how neuropsychological consultation for either side fits into this type of scenario. In civil cases, it is often the plaintiff who first consults with a neuropsychologist. Plaintiff expert renders a neuropsychological report, which is served to the defendant by plaintiff counsel. The defense then has an opportunity to retain its own expert, who may prepare a report, rebutting plaintiff expert's opinion.

In the following section, we define and review some specific concepts that are relevant in the context of criminal forensic neuropsychological examinations. These concepts entail the mental status of the defendant. As such, they represent the core differences between criminal and civil assessment contexts.

Civil versus Criminal Settings

The reader should be aware that there are significant differences between civil and criminal venues and that these differences often have implications for the work of the forensic neuropsychologist. Criminal cases have greater consequences, including incarceration, even the possibility of a death sentence. There are other differences:

- In civil cases, the alleged wronged party files the case; in criminal cases, the prosecutor files the case as a representative of the government (society).
- Civil cases typically result in monetary awards, while criminal cases may involve both incarceration and monetary damages.
- The standard of proof is more stringent in criminal cases ("beyond a reasonable doubt"), while in civil cases it is the "preponderance of evidence" (essentially understood to mean more likely than not that something occurred in a certain way).
- Criminal cases almost always have trial by juries, while civil cases may be tried by either a judge or jury.
- Defendants in criminal cases are entitled to an attorney, provided by the government should they be unable to afford one on their own. In civil cases, the individual must pay for his or her attorney.
- Greater protections are afforded criminal defendants that are not afforded to defendants in a civil case, that is, stricter standards of proof and due process, among others (Garner, 2014). As an example, in cases where prosecutors ask for the death penalty (capital punishment), the defendant is entitled to "extended" due process under the

Fourteenth Amendment's Due Process Clause. This includes mental health expert testimony, as well as any other expert testimony that may mitigate the sentence of death (Dipps, Boyce, & Perkins, 2013).

Slightly more than half of forensic cases referred to neuropsychologists are criminal in nature (Kaufmann, 2008). The involvement of neuropsychologists in these matters relates to the fact that the demands placed on defendants are largely cognitive; defendants require a specific level of functional mental ability—that is, the capacity to participate in the proceedings (Denney, Fazio, & Greiffenstein, in press). In criminal settings, charges are brought against a defendant; he or she is facing prosecution for allegations of violating the law. Neuropsychologists consult both with prosecutors and defense attorneys. In criminal settings, it is often the case that the defense attorney first raises issues of psychological/neuropsychological relevance; that is, is the defendant mentally impaired in some meaningful way? If so, does that impairment diminish his ability to participate in the legal proceedings or somehow excuse or explain wrongful behavior? Defense attorneys raise these issues for a variety of reasons, the most common of which are that their defendant has a mental health or neurological history; that the defendant acts strangely—there appears to be something wrong with the defendant mentally such that the attorney has difficulty communicating with or understanding him or her, or vice versa; and that the defendant doesn't seem to understand the nature of his or her situation and/or the charges. In each of these scenarios, defense attorneys may seek counsel from a neuropsychologist to examine their client and render an expert opinion.

This chapter does not explicitly deal with malingered cognitive or psychological presentations. Nevertheless, the reader should be aware that experience shows that upwards of 50% or more of criminal defendants may malinger cognitive and/or psychiatric illness in an effort to avoid trial, mitigate penalties, or escape punishment entirely (Ardolf, Denney, & Houston, 2007; Morgan & Sweet, 2009). Similarly, it is not uncommon for defense attorneys to contact a neuropsychologist in cases where there is no actual, *credible* defense relative to the facts and evidence of the case, in the hopes of finding some extant cognitive or psychological abnormality to pursue, if only to help mitigate a harsh penalty. In one recent case. for example, there were numerous eyewitnesses to the defendant's assault of a store clerk. There was no real defense. However, the defendant had a long history of substance abuse, as well as a developmental disability and several traumatic brain injuries with a well-documented medical record. Defense counsel attempted to use the neuropsychological evaluation that showed cognitive impairment to mitigate the harsh penalty of 10 years in prison sought by the prosecution. Ultimately, this defense was successful in that the prosecutor offered a plea bargain of seven years' probation with the completion of drug treatment.

TYPICAL CRIMINAL REFERRAL QUESTIONS

Competency

This is the most common referral to a neuropsychologist in criminal proceedings (Melton, Petrila, Poythress, & Slobogin, 2007). Competency essentially entails the defendant's capacity to understand the nature of the legal proceedings and make reasonable decisions in his or her own behalf (Grisso, 2003). The issue of a criminal defendant's competency may arise at any time during the adjudication process. States may differ somewhat in the precise way in which competency is defined. In New Jersey, where one of us (JEM) practices, the competency statute is N.J.S.A. 2C: 4-4(b):

> A person is mentally competent if (1) the defendant has the mental capacity to appreciate his presence in relation to time, place and things; and (2) his elementary mental processes are such that he comprehends (a) he is in a court of law charged with a crime, (b) there is a judge on the bench, (c) there is a prosecutor who will try to convict him, (d) that he has a lawyer who will defend him, (e) that he will be expected to testify as to facts or be silent, (f) the role of the jury and the consequences of a plea bargain, (g) that he has the ability to participate in an adequate presentation of his defense.

There are a number of different types of competency (Denney, 2012). These include competency:

- To confess or waive one's rights to pretrial counsel (i.e., understanding the Miranda warning).
- To plead guilty.
- To waive counsel and represent oneself.
- To stand trial.
- To be sentenced.
- To waive appeal.
- To be executed.

Neuropsychological evaluation of the defendant's cognition is not necessary for a competency evaluation, but it can be salient in making determinations of competency and is particularly helpful in determining whether the defendant is likely to be restored. But test scores on neuropsychological tests of intellect, memory, and so forth may not tell the whole story. The presence of extremely limited abilities is typically accompanied by serious deficits in the ability to comprehend. But many individuals with limited abilities can still be competent. Defendants with acute, serious psychiatric disorders, such as florid psychosis, are most likely to be found incompetent (Nicholson & Kugler, 1991; Pirelli, Gottdiener, & Zapf, 2011). In contrast, chronic, stable psychiatric disorders typically do not result in incompetency. The forensic evaluator must outline a clear link between the mental disorder and impairment of legal competency. The ultimate decision as to whether a defendant is or is not competent is up to the court (the judge). Expert reports addressing the issue of competency are issued by forensic evaluators for both defense and prosecution. Testimony is taken in a hearing in which experts testify as to their findings and the reasoning underlying their opinions.

The following example shows how the issue of competency is expressed in the report. Note that how the test data is presented can make the difference between clarity and obfuscation.

LESS DESIRABLE: DOCTOR A

Mr. Defendant's memory tests scores were two-and-a-half standard deviations below the mean, indicating substantially impaired anterograde memory performance. He earned a Standard Score of 65 on the WMS-IV Delayed Recall—a very low score. In a similar vein, his CVLT-II Long Delayed Recall T-Score of 30, two standard deviations below the mean, reflected impaired anterograde memory. His severe memory impairment renders his ability to assist in his defense quite limited.

MORE DESIRABLE: DOCTOR B

Memory testing of Mr. Defendant resulted in extremely impaired performance. He was unable to learn more than a few words of a brief story of paragraph-length material. Similarly, he showed extreme forgetting over a short delay of the few parts of the story he originally retained. The scores he obtained on memory tests were below the first percentile. This means that 99% of the people who took the test in his age group performed better than he did. The severity of his memory impairment will likely result in extreme difficulty in relating to his attorney, assisting him with details of the alleged crime, his state of mind at the time, and providing him with relevant information necessary to marshal an adequate defense.

The above examples illustrate the lack of clarity in expressing data too literally, as if we were writing for another neuropsychologist. Most nonpsychologists do not have a detailed understanding of psychometrics or statistics, so that it is important to discuss these issues in ways that are more understandable. We suggest that the wording of the findings is best understood when expressed in terms the lay public can understand. With that, it is best to describe not only the meaning of scores, but also how the data translates to the functional limitations of the examinee, obviously with particular relevance to the referral question.

Also note that the assessment of competency is not based simply on an analysis of cognitive tests scores but is a functional assessment of legal capabilities, dependent in part on the nature of the context/situation (Grisso, 2003). One may be competent in one sense, say to waive one's Miranda rights, but not in another, such as to act as one's own attorney. The law understands competency as in a specific context rather than as a general phenomenon across situations. The cognitive underpinnings necessary for each of these competencies vary (Tussey, Marcopulos, & Caillouet, 2013).

Criminal defendants must be considered competent to face criminal proceedings in the United States (Youtsey, 1899). This is a U.S. constitutional requirement, established by the Supreme Court in *Dusky v. United States* (1960). Defendants cannot progress through the adjudication process without understanding the nature of the charges against them and without having the ability to reasonably assist in their own defense. When cognitive impairment impacts competency, neuropsychologists can play an important role in competency evaluations (Marcopulos, Morgan, & Denney, 2008; Denney et al., in press). As is true of the interface between the law and neuropsychology in general, despite the presence of written criteria, the clinician's determination of competency in a given situation is most often a clinical judgment based on a functional assessment linking psychological impairment with the specific demands of the legal situation (e.g., Zapf & Roesch, 2009). It is not simply based on test scores.

When the court rules that a defendant is not competent, the defendant is typically remanded to a mental health facility until that time when he or she is restored to competency. The staff at the facility, often a government forensic hospital, does a competency evaluation, typically followed by private evaluations, and if experts disagree, another hearing ensues. Of course, some individuals can potentially be restored to competency, as in those with acute psychosis. But there are some conditions in which individuals cannot be restored to competency. These would include those with chronic mentally debilitating conditions, often of a neurological or neurodevelopmental origin. An example would be a defendant who has a degenerative dementia. If the defendant is not competent owing to the severe memory impairment associated with the dementia, obviously he or she is unlikely to be restored to competency in the future (Heck & Herrick, 2007). Another example is a case in which a defendant, awaiting adjudication in jail, was severely assaulted by another inmate and sustained serious and debilitating brain damage in the process, rendering him unable to participate in his defense. In one or our cases (JEM), a criminal defendant awaiting trial developed bacterial meningitis and had subsequent serious cognitive impairment, rendering him incompetent to stand trial. His mental status was unlikely to improve. In contrast, there are instances in which defendants might recover from a neurological condition and improve their cognitive functions so that they might become competent—for instance, those defendants suffering a complicated mild or moderate TBI.

Diminished Capacity

This term refers to a plea or defense, not available in all states, in which the defendant asserts that because of his or her mental impairment, defect, or disease, he or she is incapable of reaching the mental state required to commit a particular crime (*mens rea*—guilty mental state, i.e., criminal intent; Garner, 2014). This doctrine recognizes that although, at the time the offense was committed, an accused was not suffering from a mental disease or defect sufficient to completely exonerate him or her from all criminal responsibility—that is, not guilty by reason of insanity—the accused's mental capacity was diminished by intoxication, trauma, or mental disease such that he or she did not possess the specific mental state or *intent* essential to the particular offense charged. For example, in a murder case, a diminished capacity defense asserts that because of the defendant's mental illness, say paranoid schizophrenia, the defendant did not intend to cause death, but because of mental illness, caused death without intent. The precise extent of "diminishment" is not the issue; rather, it is the notion that mental disease or defect is extant, affecting the control and comprehension of behavior. When successful as a plea or defense, as a result the defendant typically is convicted of a lesser offense or the penalty is mitigated at sentencing.

Diminished capacity also arises in cases where the defendant is not classically mentally ill but may be considered so in cases where the neuropsychologist finds significant cognitive impairment. In one case, a teenager with serious neurodevelopmental impairment, seizure disorder, and bipolar disorder physically assaulted the bus driver en route to school. He later said that he didn't want to go to school that day because he was having a test and felt unprepared. In this case, all agreed he was of diminished capacity, and so he was remanded to treatment rather than incarceration. In this case, the expert's report was useful because it explained the mental state of the defendant and showed that his behavior was, to a large extent, beyond his control.

Not Guilty by Reason of Insanity

This is a verdict in criminal cases whereby the defendant is determined to be legally insane. By virtue of mental illness, the defendant argues that he or she should not be held responsible for the crime in question (Williams, 2003). In these cases, the defendant admits to the act but alleges it was caused by the mental disorder at the time. The reader should appreciate that the mere presence of a mental disorder, whether a psychiatric or a cognitive impairment, though necessary, is not sufficient to warrant a determination of insanity and therefore to entertain this defense. In the following example, the neuropsychologist Dr. A implies that this defendant's diagnosis of schizophrenia makes him legally insane.

LESS DESIRABLE: DOCTOR A

Mr. Jones meets the legal definition of insanity because of his diagnosis of schizophrenia. He was not taking his medicine around the time of the crime and was experiencing paranoid delusions and hallucinations. For example, he believed that he had been kidnapped by Al Qaeda. He also has a history of command hallucinations from "Satan." He was out of touch with reality and unable to tell right from wrong.

MORE DESIRABLE: DOCTOR B

Mr. Jones demonstrated escalating psychiatric symptoms just prior to his arrest. For example, Mr. Jones's report that Al Qaeda had kidnapped him. This is best explained as a paranoid delusion, which is consistent with his diagnosis of schizophrenia. Delusions are false beliefs. Therefore, the weight of the evidence suggests that Mr. Jones manifests a serious "mental disease or defect" as a threshold condition necessary to further consider the possibility of legal insanity. According to records, including Mr. Jones's Facebook posts, he has a history of responding to hallucinations that he perceives to be the voice of Satan. Although Mr. Jones understood that robbing the bank was illegal, his primary motivation was to obey a command by "Satan." Thus, his understanding of the nature, character, and consequences of his offense was inextricably related to his delusional beliefs that were part of his psychiatric illness.

Dr. B makes a clearer case as to how Mr. Jones's delusions had a direct impact on his behavior and decision making around the time of the crime.

Insanity is a legal standard, not a psychological or medical diagnosis. Contrary to public opinion, this particular defense is infrequently raised and rarely accepted by the court and juries (Melton et al., 2007). This is because the lay public tends to put great stock in the belief that the vast majority of people are capable of controlling their own behaviors. Similarly, the lay public typically has limited experience with, and even less understanding of, serious psychiatric and neurologic disorders, let alone their impact on judgment and behavior.

Take, for example the recent Florida case of Julie Schenecker, who killed her two teenage children, shooting them to death with a recently purchased handgun. She had the delusional belief that her children were so disrespectful that only God could help them and found it her duty to "send them to God." Despite the fact that this defendant had a nearly lifelong record of severe bipolar disorder, mixed type, with an extensive medical record, numerous inpatient psychiatric hospitalizations, myriad psychotropic medications and opinions from highly regarded psychiatric and neuropsychological forensic experts, the jury found her guilty of murder. The lay public has a hard time understanding how this type of severe mental illness may completely take over one's mind and cloud one's judgment, behavior, and parental love to this extent.

WRITING FOR AND INTERACTING WITH LAWYERS, JUDGES, AND JURIES

There are a number of unique considerations in writing reports in criminal forensic contexts, such as what information to include, how to present the information, and how to present a legal opinion, if this is requested. Many of these considerations are outlined in the recently revised *Specialty Guidelines for Forensic Psychology* (American Psychological Association, 2013) as well as Melton et al.'s (2007) classic source. The most important considerations for writing forensic reports are to specifically address the referral question(s) and to know the particular statutory requirements of the jurisdiction where the report will be submitted. Federal courts follow the Federal Rules of Evidence (see *Daubert v. Merrill Dow Pharmaceuticals,* 509 US 579, 1993). The *Daubert* standard (which superseded the original *Frye* standard in the federal courts) provides for rules of evidence regarding the admissibility of expert witnesses' testimony during federal legal proceedings. The major components of *Daubert* are that (1) the judge has the task of gatekeeping, ensuring that scientific expert testimony proceeds from scientific knowledge; (2) the testimony of the expert is relevant and reliable to the issues at hand: (3) the "scientific knowledge" is a product of sound scientific methodology derived from scientific method; and (4) "scientific methodology" proceeds from empirical testing, that results are subjected to peer review, that there is a known error rate, that there are standards and controls as to the method, and that the degree to which the theory and technique are accepted by the relevant scientific community. Many states have adopted the *Daubert* standard for admissibility of expert scientific testimony.

Although different courts have preferred report formats, a forensic report has several essential components (see Conroy, 2006; Heilbrun, Grisso, & Goldstein, 2009):

- A clear statement of the referral question (e.g., competency to proceed).
- Documentation of notifications (e.g., limit of confidentiality).
- A list of records reviewed and other collateral information.
- A list of tests/procedures.
- Discussion and justification of the conclusions and opinions, as well as consideration of alternate explanations.

Referral Question

The legal questions to be answered should be presented in the beginning of the report and stated as the referral question. This question should include who requested the evaluation (prosecutor, defense, court), dates of contact, date of report, and the subject of the evaluation. These referral questions are listed again at the end of the report, with the answers.

Informed Consent and Mandatory Notifications

This section indicates that the defendant was notified of the nature and purpose of the evaluation and of who will be seeing the report (Bush et al., 2005). This notification can be issued verbally, but Brodsky (2009) strongly recommends that forensic psychologists provide informed consent and notification *in writing* and clearly document that this information was given in their report. Informed consent typically includes defining the role of the neuropsychologist, limits of confidentiality, and the lack of a doctor–patient relationship, which means that the neuropsychologist will not offer treatment recommendations. The defendant is urged to put forth full effort and is informed of the potential consequences of not cooperating with the evaluation.

Prejudicial versus Probative Information

Forensic report writers should include all the data and information they used in forming their opinions, a concept often referred to by attorneys as "reliance"—that is, "Doctor, what information/data did you rely on to arrive at your opinion?" But many forensic evaluators are careful to limit their reports to "probative" information (Grisso, 2010). Probative value of evidence versus prejudicial information is explained in Federal Rule 403. Evidence presented in court should be relevant (i.e., probative) to the legal question and not unfairly prejudicial. Including more information than is necessary to support the opinion relevant to the legal question could be prejudicial and is best avoided. For example, some defense attorneys will object to certain terms describing findings, diagnoses, or references to their client that the neuropsychologist has determined or found in the record such as "antisocial," "sociopathic," or "aggressive." Sometimes neuropsychologists experience an ethical dilemma in dealing with attorneys who request that such prejudicial terms be removed from their reports. The forensic evaluator should present an accurate and well-described portrait of the defendant using language that clearly defines psychological constructs in neutral, unbiased, and nonpejorative terms.

Validity and Reliability of Tests and Procedures Used in Forming Opinions

The forensic neuropsychologist should provide information on the validity and reliability of all the data and information used in the report. For instance, when reporting on symptom and performance validity tests that indicate malingering, or an adaptive behavior level for a death penalty defendant, the evaluator will discuss the psychometric properties of the instrument used, while also taking care not to compromise test security. In the case of interview data, one must also discuss the reliability of the source. The mother or other close relative of the defendant is often interviewed for adaptive behavior scales such as the Vineland Adaptive Behavior Scales (VABS; Sparrow, Cicchetti, & Balla, 2005), but relatives may have a strong bias to find the defendant impaired in an effort to save his or her life. These adaptive behavior interview instruments are also affected by normal memory decay over time. For instance, Tourangeau, Rips, and Rasinski (2000) documented how survey respondents are prone to make systematic errors in recollection of autobiographical information.

LESS DESIRABLE: DOCTOR A

The Vineland Adaptive Behavior Scales was administered to John's mother and his residential counselor at the adult home. The VABS is a valid and reliable structured interview that produces standard scores on Communication, Social, and Activities of Daily Living (ADLs).

MORE DESIRABLE: DOCTOR B

I [JEM] administered the VABS, a structured interview of adaptive behavior, to John's mother and his residential counselor. Ms. Jones admitted that since John was removed from her home as a toddler and spent most of his childhood in foster homes and residential treatment centers,

> she did not have extensive knowledge of his daily func-
> tioning and abilities in independent living. In the past
> few years, she saw him infrequently and briefly. I also
> administered the VABS to John's residential counselor who
> has had daily contact with him during the past 3 months,
> but only in this restricted environment.

In this example, Dr. A reports on the reliability and validity of the VABS based on the psychometric properties reported in the manual. She provides more information regarding the reliability and validity of the informants she relied on for interview data with the VABS.

Preferred Report-Writing Style for Forensic Neuropsychological Reports

Karson and Nadkarni (2013) describe three approaches to forensic report writing: by procedure, issue, and legal argument. Neuropsychological assessment reports are traditionally organized by test (i.e., procedure) and/ or cognitive domain. Karson and Nadkarni caution that this style may not be ideal for focused legal questions such as competency to proceed. Ackerman (2006) also argues that the test-by-test report format is less desirable and less readable; he advocates for an integrated report. A test-by-test clinical neuropsychological report implies that all the neuropsychological data is relevant to the legal question, when in fact, much of it may not be. For instance, in a competency to stand trial evaluation, the defendant's psychomotor speed and visuospatial functioning is unlikely to be specifically germane to their competency. Rather, the examinee's global cognitive functioning as it pertains to issues of competency, such as one's judgment, comprehension, and reasoning, is much more relevant. A report that is primarily organized around the legal question or issue to be addressed, and also uses relevant neuropsychological examination findings to discuss and support the conclusion, is far more appropriate and useful for the courts.

The forensic evaluator's role is to educate the trier of fact (i.e., the judge and jury) in order to help them make their legal decision using important neuropsychological and psychological data. Nonpsychologists read reports for the courts, so professional jargon should be minimized and, if used at all, should be defined. There is some controversy among forensic evaluators as to whether it is appropriate to provide legal opinions (e.g., Heilbrun, 2001). Some jurisdictions prefer that this decision be left to the courts and limit the forensic evaluator to providing supporting information in their reports.

Generally speaking, a forensic report may be lengthier than a typical clinical report because supporting data are often included and justifications are given for each opinion. However, this is not always the case. A competency to proceed report is typically very focused and may consist of a two-page letter to the judge. Unlike a typical clinical report, footnotes and literature citations may be included in forensic reports.

Tests and Procedures

The report should include a list of tests used and a complete list of records reviewed and/or made available to the neuropsychologist writing the report. How much information should be provided about a test, particularly symptom validity and performance validity tests? The forensic neuropsychologist must balance the concerns of test security with the requirements of the legal system and courts that desire transparency and a clear explanation of the procedures and methods underlying an opinion, especially that of malingering. Regarding the determination of malingering, some attorneys believe this is the job of the court and jury and will challenge the expert about this diagnosis. This view relates to the notion that a determination of malingering implies that the expert knows the underlying motivation of the defendant. In such cases, it may be more pragmatic to discuss issues of validity and credibility. Often, appending a reference list of peer-reviewed publications to the report illustrating the scientific merit and acceptance of such opinions, tests, and procedures is sufficient, particularly if the literature citied includes published legal decisions.

Should test data be included in the report? If so, are data listed in the body of the report or in an appendix? Given that the "raw" data will invariably be requested, some argue that it should be provided in the report. However, others argue that this endangers test security. We recommend that test data be incorporated into the report—but in an *explanatory or interpretive fashion* rather than as a mere listing of scores on tests. The same logic applies to explanations of what a test actually assesses. Provide examples to make your point, but be careful not to endanger test security by revealing specific test items. Here is an example.

LESS DESIRABLE: DOCTOR A

The defendant's scores on neuropsychological tests suggested his cognition was grossly impaired. But comparison of his current scores to the same tests a year ago would suggest a serious decline. He earned Scaled Scores of 8 and 11 on Similarities and Matrix Reasoning last year, but now scored 6 and 9 on those same tests. But there is no justification in his medical history for this decline, and the scores must therefore be invalid.

MORE DESIRABLE: DOCTOR B

> The defendant scored significantly lower in the cur-
> rent exam than he did last year on the same tests, tests
> assessing verbal and spatial reasoning. Declining test
> scores in the absence of progressive neurological or psy-
> chiatric illness makes little sense, particularly in a
> secondary gain setting where defendant may have much to
> gain by appearing more impaired than he actually is.

Forensic Conclusions and Opinions

Forensic neuropsychologists should identify the source of all their information (e.g., records, collaterals interviews). The report should be very
clear about what information presented is factual and what is conjecture or
inference. Be clear about when you are relying on actuarial data versus your
clinical judgment. Present your findings in a neutral, unbiased way. The
forensic evaluator must be mindful of confirmation bias and "cherry picking" data. It is important to present confirming as well as disconfirming
data and to explain why you are coming to your conclusion. The findings
should be reported in terms of level of neuropsychological certainty and
discussed in terms of base rates in the population of interest.

REPORT EXAMPLES

The following examples may not contain all the elements that can be
included in a criminal forensic neuropsychological report, or be written in
the preferred style of the reader's jurisdiction. The reader should consult
with the courts and more experienced forensic colleagues to ensure that the
report they write meets local statutory and regulatory requirements as well
as conforming to the preferred report styles for the particular setting and
particular legal question (Karson & Nadkarni, 2013).

Notification/Informed Consent

> Mr. Defendant was informed that my psychological and
> neuropsychological evaluation had been ordered by the
> court and that I was being retained by the prosecuting
> attorney's office. He was informed that nothing we dis-
> cussed would remain confidential, and that information
> he provided during our clinical interview and the test
> results from my examination of him would become a part
> of my report, to be used in upcoming proceedings. He was

informed that a copy of any report I produced would be sent to his attorneys, the prosecuting attorneys, and the court. Mr. Defendant indicated that he understood the purpose of the evaluation, and the limitations of confidentiality of our interview and the testing I conducted.

Competency to Proceed to Trial—Considered Competent

This is a man with an extensive history of psychiatric hospitalizations for acute manic episodes of bipolar disorder. Historically, he presents as acutely psychotic and out of contact with reality with grandiose, paranoid delusions, expansive mood, pressured speech, flight of ideas (rapid flow of the mind from one thought to another) and irritability, hostility, and combativeness. These are all classic symptoms of the manic state of bipolar disorder. In previous competency evaluations that I reviewed, some of these symptoms remained, particularly delusional, disorganized thinking and impaired judgment, necessitating the doctors to conclude that he was not competent to proceed to trial.

At the present time, Mr. Doe's clinical condition shows considerable improvement. He was rational, logical, cooperative, in good spirits, and recognized his previous delusional and grandiose symptoms. It could not be reliably determined if his statements regarding his educational attainment and book authorship are truthful or not. If not, he may still manifest some degree of grandiose delusional thinking or he could simply be lying. But, as will be discussed below, nonetheless I believe him to be competent to proceed to trial. My current diagnosis is bipolar disorder, type I, in remission.

Mr. Doe is aware of his current surroundings, the hospital building, city, state, and his doctors. He was aware of the date and time. He knows the president and vice president. He remembered me from a previous examination of several months ago.

Mr. Doe correctly stated the charges against him. He correctly stated the judge, the roles of the judge, prosecutor defense attorney, and jury. He understands the term "plea bargain" and the consequences. He understands he has the right to testify or not.

These understandings were also apparent in the most recent previous examination for competency conducted in

April of 20XX. But at that time he was felt to be too disorganized, delusional and unrealistic to adequately participate in his own defense.

At this time, however, Mr. Doe is far less disturbed, shows considerably less delusional thinking, and is rational, coherent and logical. Mr. Doe demonstrates sufficient factual and rational understanding of courtroom procedures and of his legal case for competency to proceed to trial. He can assist his attorney to a reasonable degree in his own defense, and his mental disorder will not impede him from doing so.

Competency to Proceed to Trial—Considered Not Competent

On direct questioning about the aspects of legal proceedings, Mr. Defendant provided the following information: He understood that the judge is in charge of the courtroom. He did not know that the judge rules on questions of the law; this concept entirely escaped him.

He did not fully comprehend the role of the prosecuting attorney. He insisted that the prosecutor did not want to convict him or prosecute him and did not know that the prosecutor charged him and tried to convict him.

He understood that his attorney, Ms. Jayne Doe, was there to help him. He indicated that he thought a jury was composed of 10 to 12 people, and he said, "If you do something serious like steal they convict you." His understanding of a plea bargain was also quite limited. "If they want me to have a one-trial intervention or anything."

Although Mr. Defendant seems to understand aspects of legal proceedings, especially with regard to the professionals involved in a trial, he is clearly incapable of assisting his attorney on his own behalf. He was diagnosed with "schizophrenia schizoaffective type" [sic] and until recently has not been identified by mental health professionals. He presents as a grossly disturbed and disorganized individual with rapid, irrelevant speech, flight of ideas, and illogical and irrational mental status. He shows extremely limited ability to focus and maintain his attention on anything. He repeats himself numerous times. He is highly anxious and is unaware of normal social discourse. He is clearly mentally ill despite the fact that he has not received a formal mental health diagnosis or treatment until recently, that is, in conjunction with the

charges pending against him. He nonetheless presents a
history that is consistent with that of untreated persistent mental illness.

Therefore, within a reasonable degree of scientific
psychological certainty, I find Mr. Criminal Defendant
does not demonstrate the factual and rational understanding required to proceed to trial. He has only the most
elementary, rudimentary understanding of the principles
of the legal system and because of his marked schizophrenic disorder, his inability to focus, his irrelevant
speech, and tangential thinking, he is unable to assist
his attorney on his own behalf. Further, he does not fully
comprehend the charges against him or the seriousness of
the behaviors, which are alleged against him.

He would strongly benefit from a comprehensive psychiatric examination, inpatient hospitalization for restoration, followed by a day treatment program, and regular
medication for schizophrenic/schizoaffective disorder in
the form of antipsychotic medication. This medication will
calm him, help him organize his thoughts, help him stay
focused and on task, and improve his impulse control,
reasoning, and judgment.

Diminished Capacity

As was discussed earlier, diminished capacity refers to a defense plea in
which defendants are considered incapable of forming criminal intent
because of their mental impairment. Although the law does not specify
the *degree* of diminishment of capacity, the law calls for the *presence* of a
mental defect to the extent that it lowers the threshold of one's comprehension of their acts.

Sometimes, expressing complex psychological ideas in forensic reports
requires a good deal of explanation, as most members of the legal profession have limited psychological knowledge, perhaps with the exception of
those with many years of experience. The following report excerpt is from
a rather sad case in which defendant was charged with the wrongful death
of her child by neglect. She became entangled in a religious cult and was
easily exploited because of her limited abilities and strong underlying psychological dynamics:

Results of the neuropsychological evaluation indicate
Ms. X put forth variable effort on cognitive performance
validity tests. Her overall intellectual functioning falls
in the Extremely Low (Mild Mental Retardation) range, however, this may be a slight underestimate of her abilities.

Nonetheless, it is highly unlikely that her abilities fall above the borderline range based on her educational and occupational records. Overall, Ms. X's neurocognitive abilities are generally very limited and in the severely impaired range. She is a woman with general global delays and limited cognitive abilities. The psychological testing results revealed her to be a woman who feels depressed and may be delusional. She tends to think in unusual ways. She is withdrawn, prefers to be alone, and does not desire social relationships. Her profile suggests a tendency toward schizoid personality characteristics.

Opinion: In consideration of Ms. X's neurocognitive and psychological test data coupled with the information obtained via record review and during the clinical interview, the inmate is a woman who is extremely naïve and impressionable. She has limited cognitive abilities. Furthermore, her personality characteristic of social isolation is evident in her interaction with Pastor Y as she willingly cut off the few friendships that she had previously maintained in order to follow him. She is a limited, needy, dependent woman with extremely low self-esteem, who has strong needs for approval, acceptance, and forgiveness.

Ms. X became dependent on this man for guidance, and her strong religious views were distorted by this individual. She became a religious zealot, putting all of her trust in Pastor Y. Because of her limited cognitive abilities, her strong dependency needs, her naïveté, her need for acceptance, and her religious fervor, she was easily exploitable by the "reverend." Several crucial psychological factors are at play here—a woman with limited cognitive abilities, who was vulnerable and naïve, and whose psychological makeup resulted in a strong desire to be taken care of and dependent on someone, to "believe" in someone perceived as having extraordinary powers, who has the answers, who could help her. It is exactly this type of situation that often results in successful brainwashing of members of cults. Ms. X is precisely the type of individual that cult leaders seek out, as they are most vulnerable and easily exploited by the charismatic cult leader. Her judgment was limited due to her lower intellectual functioning, and her psychological needs resulted in someone who was easily convinced, brainwashed, that their life should be drastically changed to follow one man. Given her psychological needs, this created a dynamic, a cult-type worship, where she felt she needed to follow Pastor Y's guidance. Pastor Y was able to prey on these characteristics. He understood Ms. X's vulnerability and her naïve nature, her dependency characteristics, and her desire to be a follower of a religious group. She trusted this man and his judgment. The common theme of isolating oneself from family and friends in order to follow all of the laws of the cult fed into Ms. X's psychological makeup. Unfortunately, she had isolated herself to such a degree that she had no one to rely on to help her find her way out or get help once the situation with her daughter took place. She was taken advantage of by this man who desired to be in power and worshipped. These cult leaders attract the most vulnerable, limited, and needy individuals into their cult. So is the case with her.

It wasn't just her limited cognitive skills that impaired her ability to understand that the situation was dangerous. An individual with a borderline IQ would generally be able to realize this was not the appropriate route to take when a child is ill. However, it is the emotional and personality functioning of Ms. X, the isolation, the brainwashing, and Pastor Y's charismatic power over her, that became an unfortunate dynamic and led to her failed judgment. She did not have a conscious objective to harm her daughter, nor did she believe that her conduct would cause harm to her daughter. But instead she did not possess the capability to speak against this overpowering individual, who exploited her religious zeal and her naïveté. She believed he knew what was best for her and her children, and she followed his guidance. She trusted his judgment above her own and believed that when cooperating with him her daughter would heal and improve. Her cooperation and trust were the key to her daughter getting better, but if she showed she did not believe in the Pastor and sought outside medical treatment, then her daughter was not likely to heal.

It was clear during my interaction with Ms. X that she was slowly beginning to understand the power that Pastor Y held over her. While a part of the cult-like group, living with him and under his watch at all times, she was unable to break away to get help or even leave him. Once physically and emotionally separated from him, it was as if a fog was lifted. Pastor Y's influence was broken. She didn't feel the need to be controlled by him or to seek out his approval for every decision. Time was a factor,

too, because as it passed she gained greater insight into
the lack of power she had over her own life and her children's lives and well-being. Yet she continues to suffer
from delusions, which indicates she is not sound of mind.
She may be gaining insight into the outcome of her failure to leave Pastor Y's overpowering guidance, but the
presence of psychosis also inhibits her ability to fully
remain in contact with reality.

　　Therefore, within a reasonable degree of scientific
psychological certainty, I find the examinee to have had
diminished mental capacity at the time of the alleged
offenses. Thus, the examinee's conduct was neither knowing
nor purposeful under the New Jersey Criminal Code. She
did not have criminal intent.

Not Guilty by Reason of Insanity

In this scenario, defense examiners must convince the court that the defendant was not responsible for the alleged criminal behavior by virtue of
serious mental disease or defect, such that he or she did not know right
from wrong. In the excerpt that follows, defendant was charged with the
brutal murder of his girlfriend. He had a history of psychosis, bipolar disorder, and was a heavy polysubstance abuser. He had also been doing "bath
salts," a synthetic, psychoactive designer drug well known to cause severe
psychosis. In addition, he suffered a small stroke thought to be caused by
the combination of untreated hypertension and cocaine abuse. Clinical
assessment and a careful review of his history and psychiatric treatment
records around the time of the crime strongly suggested that he was almost
totally out of touch with reality at the time of the murder.

Results of the neuropsychological evaluation indicate
that Mr. Defendant put forth adequate effort on cognitive
symptom validity tests. His overall intellectual functioning is high average. There is evidence of some executive
dysfunction, namely, processing speed and inhibition. Psychological testing results are sometimes associated with
severe exaggeration of symptoms, but this man's history
indicates the presence of severe psychosis. Mr. Defendant's responses indicate symptoms consistent with major
depression, paranoid delusional disorder (severe), and a
thought disorder. His reality testing is grossly impaired,
and he is severely psychotic. He also reported chronic
alcohol and drug dependence.

　　In addition to the current neuropsychological results,
Mr. Defendant's records indicate a chronic psychiatric

history dating from 2007 and a reported history of severe substance abuse beginning at age 13. Mr. Defendant's records note ongoing mood instability issues. During several manic episodes, Mr. Defendant was arrested for burglary. It appears that in January 2010 while, under observation at a local hospital, Mr. Defendant was diagnosed with bipolar disorder with psychotic features. He reported that he began to use bath salts in September 2010. The records indicate that he became severely paranoid, and in January 2011 he stated "things just weren't right." A medical work-up revealed that he appeared to have suffered a small stroke thought to be due to cocaine abuse and untreated hypertension. Between January and March 2011, he was hospitalized and placed in rehabilitation and mental health treatment on three separate occasions. In March 2011, specifically March 10, Mr. Defendant met with a social worker seeking assistance with finding a rehabilitation program. The social worker, Mr. X, noted that his patient was paranoid, angry, withdrawn, and experiencing suicidal ideation. His paranoid delusions largely focused on his girlfriend. The social worker documented a diagnosis of delusional episode related to bath salt use. Mr. X informed Mr. Defendant on March 11 that he was accepted into the rehab program beginning March 14, 2011. However, before he could be admitted, he murdered his girlfriend on March 13, 2011.

Opinion: In consideration of Mr. Defendant's documented extensive psychiatric history of severe psychosis and documentation of acute psychotic symptoms around the time of the crime, as well as cognitive impairment from a stroke, it is my professional opinion that, within a reasonable degree of scientific psychological certainty, Mr. Defendant was delusional and out of touch with reality, such that he could not fully appreciate the difference between right and wrong at the time of the alleged crime. He was under the false belief that his girlfriend wanted to kill him and had planned to do so. In an individual with such an extensive psychiatric history, clearly increasing in severity as his drug use (which included amphetamines, i.e., stimulant medications, bath salts, and crack) escalated and became more frequent, as is noted in his psychiatric records, his thinking became more and more unusual, delusional, paranoid, and grossly psychotic. He developed paranoid delusions that his girlfriend was trying to kill him. Thus, he was experiencing a significant mental disorder at the time of the alleged offense. A stimulant psychosis does occur in some individuals and in some cases does not resolve even after use is discontinued. Bath salts are reported in the scientific literature to trigger a severe paranoid psychosis as well. The combined effects of his underlying bipolar disorder and psychosis were exacerbated by drug use, thus resulting in his inability to judge his behavior, actions, and thinking, and his inability to appropriately gauge the nature of reality. It appears that the psychotic episode has not resolved, given Mr. Defendant's presentation during the current evaluation. He clearly has lost touch with reality and remains paranoid despite receiving psychiatric treatment in a structured setting.

THE DEATH PENALTY

Thirty-two states, as well as the U.S. government and the military, sanction capital punishment for serious crimes. However, since the U.S. SupremeCcourt ruled on *Atkins v. Virginia*, that the use of capital punishment violates the Eighth Amendment for "cruel and unusual" punishment for individuals with intellectual disability, assessment of IQ in the criminal forensic case can literally mean the difference between life and death. As such, defendants have extensive due process. Evaluations for "Atkins cases" are tremendously thorough, necessitating that examiners delve into the childhood, education, social, and family background extensively to determine whether intellectual limitations were evident during the developmental period. Critical to this examination process is not only the documentation of IQ below 70, but also a very thorough assessment of the examinee's functional adaptation or "life skills" (Schalock, Borthwick-Duffy, Buntinix, Coulter, & Craig, 2010).

Some forensic neuropsychologists may wish to illustrate their findings in a table of test scores, with appropriate explanatory text, as we previously noted. The use of such a table of test scores would be particularly appropriate in some death penalty cases, where defense and prosecution experts differ on the interpretation and meaning of serial assessments of the IQ of a defendant facing the death penalty. In these cases, some defense experts use the Flynn effect (FE; Flynn, 1984) to opine that the defendant is mentally retarded (MR; now, intellectually disabled [ID]; Schalock et al., 2010). FE refers to an aggregate increase in intelligence test scores over time, since the 1930s, and is a generally accepted phenomenon (Neisser, 1998). The phenomenon illustrates the mean rise in IQ scores of about 0.3 IQ points per year, 3 per decade. Theories about the reasons for the FE are many, but its precise cause is unknown. Although the existence of the FE is well established in the scientific literature, its use in death penalty cases is quite controversial (e.g., Hagan, Drogin, & Guilmette, 2008; Cunningham & Tassé, 2010). A full consideration of the extremely complex issues inherent in neuropsychological evaluation of capital murder defendants is beyond the scope of this chapter (Heilbronner & Waller, 2008).

CONCLUSIONS

The examples in this chapter illustrate typical formats for forensic reports, with language understood by the legal profession. Note that these reports did not focus on the results of test scores and normative data, but rather directly addressed the legal questions. A good criminal forensic neuropsychological report discusses the defendant's symptoms of psychiatric or neurocognitive disorder and how these directly impacted the legal question. The referral questions of the retaining attorney, or court, should be explicitly answered in a language understandable to the legal profession. By doing so, the neuropsychologist serves both the legal system and the public at large.

REFERENCES

Ackerman, M. J. (2006). Forensic report writing. *Journal of Clinical Psychology, 62*(1), 59–72.

American Psychological Association. (2013). Specialty guidelines for forensic psychology. *American Psychologist, 68*(1), 7–19.

Ardolf, B. R., Denney, R. L., &. Houston, C. M. (2007). Base rates of negative response bias and malingered neurocognitive dysfunction among criminal defendants referred for neuropsychological evaluation, *The Clinical Neuropsychologist, 21*(6), 899–916.

Atkins v. Virginia. 536 U.S. 304 (2002) 260 Va. 375, 534 S.E.2d, 312, reversed and remanded.

Brodsky, S. L. (2009). *Principles and practice of trial consultation.* New York: Guilford Press.

Bush, S. S., Barth, J. T., Pliskin, N. H., Arffa, S., Axelrod, B. N., Blackburn, L. A., et al. (2005). Independent and court-ordered forensic neuropsychological examinations: Official statement of the National Academy of Neuropsychology. *Archives of Clinical Neuropsychology, 20*(8), 997–1007.

Chafetz, M. D., & Biondolillo, A. (2012). Validity issues in *Atkins* death cases. *The Clinical Neuropsychologist, 26*, 1358–1376.

Clark, C. R. (2013). Specific intent and diminished capacity. In I. B. Weiner & R. K. Otto (Eds.), *Handbook of forensic psychology* (4th ed., pp. 353–381). Hoboken, NJ: Wiley.

Conroy, M. (2006). Report writing and testimony. *Applied Psychology in Criminal Justice, 2*, 237–260.

Cunningham, M. D., & Tassé, M. J. (2010). Looking to science rather than convention in adjusting IQ scores when death is at issue. *Professional Psychology: Research and Practice, 41*(5), 413–419.

Denney, R. L. (2012). Criminal forensic neuropsychology and assessment of competency. In G. J. Larrabee (Ed.), *Forensic neuropsychology: A scientific approach* (2nd ed., pp 438–472). New York: Oxford University Press.

Denney, R. L., Fazio, R. L., & Greiffenstein, M. F. (in press). Clinical neuropsychology in criminal forensics. In J. E. Morgan & J. H. Ricker (Eds.), *Textbook of clinical neuropsychology* (2nd ed). New York: Psychology Press.

Dipps, D., Boyce, R. & Perkins, R. (2013). *Criminal law and procedures, cases and materials*. St. Paul, MN: Foundation Press.

Dusky v. United States, 362 U.S. 402 (1960).

Flynn, J. R. (1984). The mean IQ of Americans: Massive gains 1932 to 1978. *Psychological Bulletin, 95*(1), 29.

Garner, B. A. (2014). *Black's law dictionary*. Eagan, MN: Thomas West.

Grisso, T. (2003). *Evaluating competencies: Forensic assessments and instruments*. New York: Plenum Publishers.

Grisso, T. (2010). Guidance for improving forensic reports: A review of common errors. *Open Access Journal of Forensic Psychology, 2*, 102–115.

Hagan, L. D., Drogin, E. Y., & Guilmette, T. J. (2008). Adjusting IQ scores for the Flynn Effect: Consistent with the standard of practice? *Professional Psychology: Research and Practice, 39*, 619–625.

Heck, A. L., & Herrick, S. M. (2007). Geriatric considerations in restoration of competence to stand trial: Two cases of impaired cognition. *Journal of Forensic Psychology Practice, 7*, 73–82.

Heilbronner, R. L., Sweet, J. J., Morgan, J. E., Larrabee, G. J., Millis, S., & Conference participants. (2009). American Academy of Clinical Neuropsychology Consensus Conference statement on the neuropsychological assessment of effort, response bias, and malingering. *The Clinical Neuropsychologist, 23*, 1093–1129.

Heilbronner, R. L., & Waller, D. (2008). Neuropsychological consultation in the sentencing phase of capital cases. In R. L. Denney & J. P. Sullivan (Eds.), *Clinical neuropsychology in the criminal forensic setting* (pp. 273–294). New York: Guilford Press.

Heilbrun, K. (2001). *Principles of forensic mental health assessment*. New York: Kluwer Academic/Plenum Publishers.

Heilbrun, K., Grisso, T., & Goldstein, A. M. (2009). *Foundations of forensic mental health assessment*. New York: Oxford University Press.

Karson, M., & Nadkarni, L. (2013). *Forensic report writing*. Washington, DC: American Psychological Association.

Kaufmann, P. M. (2008). Admissibility of neuropsychological evidence in criminal cases. In R. L. Denney & J. P. Sullivan (Eds.), *Clinical neuropsychology in the criminal forensic setting* (pp. 55–90). New York: Guilford Press.

Kaufmann, P. M. (2013). Neuropsychologist experts and neurolaw: Cases, controversies and admissibility challenges. *Behavioral Sciences and the Law, 31*, 739–755.

Marcopulos, B. A., Morgan, J. E., & Denney, R. (2008). Neuropsychological evaluation of competency to proceed. In R. L. Denney & J. T. Sullivan (Eds.), *Clinical neuropsychology in the criminal forensic setting* (pp. 176–208). New York: Guilford Press.

Melton, G. B., Petrila, J., Poythress, N. G., & Slobogin, C. (2007). *Psychological valuations for the courts: A handbook for mental health professionals and lawyers* (3rd ed.). New York: Guilford Press.

Morgan, J. E., & Sweet, J. J. (Eds.). (2009). *Neuropsychology of malingering casebook*. New York: Psychology Press.

Neisser, U. (1998). Introduction: Rising test scores and what they mean. In U. Neisser (Ed.), *The rising curve: Long-term gains in IQ and related measures* (pp. 3–22). Washington, DC: American Psychological Association.

Nestor, P. G., Daggett, D., Haycock, J., & Price, M. (1999). Competence to stand trial: A neuropsychological inquiry. *Law and Human Behavior, 23*, 397–412.

Nicholson, R., & Kugler, K. (1991). Competent and incompetent criminal defendants: A quantitative review of comparative research. *Psychological Bulletin, 109*, 355–370.

Pirelli, G., Gottdiener, W. H., & Zapf, P. A. (2011). A meta-analytic review of competency to stand trial research. *Psychology, Public Policy, and the Law, 17*(1), 1–53.

Schalock, R. L., Borthwick-Duffy, S. A., Buntinix, W. H. E., Coulter, D. L., & Craig, E. M. (2010). *Intellectual disability: Definition, classification, and systems of supports* (11th ed.). Washington, DC: American Association on Developmental Disabilities.

Sparrow, S. S., Cicchetti, D. V., & Balla, D. A. (2005). *Vineland Adaptive Behavior Scale—Second Edition*. Circle Pines, MN: American Guidance Service.

Tourangeau, R., Rips, L. J., & Rasinski, K. (2000). *The psychology of survey response*. Cambridge, UK: Cambridge University Press.

Tussey, C. M., Marcopulos, B. A., & Caillouet, B. A. (2013). Neuropsychological evaluation of competency in criminal forensic contexts. *Psychological Injury and the Law, 6*, 31–40.

Williams, C. (2003). Not guilty by reason of insanity (NGRI). In E. Hickey (Ed), *Encyclopedia of murder and violent crime* (pp. 330–332). Thousand Oaks, CA: Sage.

Youtsey v. United States, 97 F. 937, 941 (6th Cir. 1899).

Zapf, P., & Roesch, R. (2009). *Evaluation of competence to stand trial*. New York: Oxford University Press.

CHAPTER 8

Pre- and Postsurgical Neuropsychological Evaluation
Illustrations in Epilepsy

Chris Morrison
William S. MacAllister

Neuropsychologists are frequently called upon to perform presurgical neuropsychological evaluations in patients scheduled to undergo a variety of procedures (e.g., resective or ablative epilepsy surgery, tumor resection, deep brain stimulator placement, shunt placement, organ transplant, and left ventricular assist device [LVAD] implantation). In the case of epilepsy (Brodie et al., 1997), deep brain stimulation (Bronstein et al., 2011), and select other conditions, a presurgical neuropsychological evaluation is considered part of standard care.

There are multiple potential goals for obtaining standardized objective cognitive and behavioral data in these contexts. The patient's baseline level of general intellectual functioning and pattern of neurocognitive strengths and weakness may be used, in part, to determine surgical candidacy and to guide the specifics of surgical planning. The neuropsychological evaluation often provides information regarding the potential risks/benefits of the procedure, thereby allowing the patient and surgical team to make the most informed decision possible regarding surgical options and also provides an opportunity for the team to integrate treatments and interventions that may reduce the identified potential negative outcomes. Understanding the impact of the procedure on neurocognitive and behavioral functioning, by comparing pre- and postsurgical neuropsychological data, is also critical considering the fact that such information may guide future interventions and/or determine the need for rehabilitative interventions.

UNIQUE ASPECTS OF EVALUATING PATIENTS WITH EPILEPSY

The neuropsychologist's role within the epilepsy surgical team is probably the most established surgical setting for the field of neuropsychology. In this context, neuropsychological test data

- Contributes information about seizure lateralization and localization (Akanuma et al., 2003; Castro et al., 2013; Soble et al., 2014).
- Contributes to an understanding of the potential postoperative cognitive morbidity (Baxendale, Thompson, Harkness, & Duncan, 2006; Chelune et al., 1998; Gargaro et al., 2013; Gleissner et al., 2002; Gleissner, Helmstaedter, Schramm, & Elger, 2004; Gleissner, Sassen, Schramm, Elger, & Helmstaedter, 2005; Sherman et al., 2011).
- Contributes information regarding potential postoperative seizure freedom (Chelune et al., 1998; Hennessy et al., 2001; Sawrie et al., 1998).
- Provides information that may determine if the patient requires and/ or can tolerate other related pre- and perioperative procedures (e.g., Wada, functional magnetic resonance imaging [fMRI], or brain-mapping procedures)
- Provides information that will guide a language mapping procedure if needed (e.g., baseline performance on language tasks to be used should the patient undergo grid placement and mapping of the language-dominant hemisphere).

WRITING FOR AND COLLABORATING WITH NEUROLOGICAL/ NEUROSURGICAL TEAMS

When neuropsychological services are requested as part of a presurgical work-up, they are typically provided within the context of an integrated multidisciplinary team, such as that seen in tertiary care epilepsy centers. In this setting, neuropsychologists commonly enjoy the luxury of direct and frequent verbal communication with team members (e.g., neurologists, neurosurgeons, social workers, nurse practitioners) and shared medical records that include well-documented patient histories.

Neuropsychologists have historically been trained to write comprehensive histories, describe tests and data interpretation in detail, and generate elaborate conclusions with descriptions of differential diagnosis, functional abilities, and appropriate recommendations. Although this format results in comprehensive, lengthy reports, many medical referral sources consider this format onerous, and, as such, reports are rarely read in their entirety. While this format may be appropriate in specific circumstances (e.g., if the neuropsychologist is providing the first description of the patient's clinical history/presentation and the report will be used by numerous subsequent treating providers, outside agencies, and/or school systems), those evaluated in an epilepsy surgical program (or other surgical setting) are generally heavily vetted by the surgical team, which is already quite familiar with the details of the patient's medical background. As such, the history in the neuropsychological consultation report in this setting should focus on brief highlights of the presenting condition, with mention of only the points most salient to their impact on cognitive, behavioral, and affective functioning. The neuropsychologist should focus on the unique biographical/psychosocial history that is often not obtained by other medical providers, as this information can prove helpful when considering risks/benefits and more psychosocially oriented recommendations.

In keeping with the style of our medical colleagues and the soon-to-be uniform use of electronic medical records, a more succinct, bulleted format for reports may be most useful in terms of quickly locating certain types of information (e.g., educational history) and noting relevant findings and conclusions. The example at the end of this chapter and those examples provided on the Neuropsychology ToolKit website (*https://karen-postal. squarespace.com/report*-writing) may be helpful in generating ideas for reconceptualizing long, prose-oriented neuropsychological consultation reports.

Given pressures to write shorter, more concise reports with rapid turnaround, many neuropsychologists have begun to omit detailed descriptions of individual tests from the Test Results section of their reports. This section is the least likely to be read by our referring physician colleagues and is certainly the most likely to be misunderstood by patients and families, as succinct writing here often requires use of professional jargon that is often misconstrued by nonprofessionals.

Although omitting detailed data sections may be appropriate in many settings, individuals undergoing surgery often have a chronic condition that prompts a referral for follow-up neuropsychological evaluations over the course of many years whether or not there was a surgical intervention in the intervening period. For example, it is not uncommon for a patient to undergo a surgical work-up and then not proceed with surgery until several years later. In this situation, the neuropsychological evaluation is repeated to determine if there have been focal or diffuse changes in cognitive functioning. Both such outcomes are valuable to the treatment team and patient in terms of surgical planning. When there are focal changes, the cognitive data suggest that a select region of the brain has been adversely affected by years of additional seizure activity (implicating that brain area as involved in seizure generation). In the case of diffuse cognitive decline, it may become clear that reservations a patient and/or surgical team may have had about postsurgical cognitive morbidity are either nullified or overshadowed by the new cognitive burden that has resulted from not treating the epilepsy surgically.

In these repeat testing scenarios, the neuropsychologist will need the data from earlier evaluation(s) to make optimal use of the current cognitive assessment and be a helpful resource to the surgical team. For example, it is through careful comparison of cognitive and mood data that the neuropsychologist can clarify for the team that memory concerns reported (and identified) prior to surgery have not worsened, but the patient's symptoms of depression and anxiety have. In that scenario, appropriate psychological interventions will be recommended, and the patient can be provided with psychoeducational feedback, while the medical team may choose not to reduce seizure medications that were erroneously presumed to be the cause of new memory/cognitive dysfunction by the patient.

Raw test data (not just prose interpretations such as "intact" or "average" within a report) are necessary in determining whether there truly has been change on objective testing (see the following section, "Measuring Reliable Change"). Regardless of whether the raw and normed neuropsychological test data are provided within the Test Results section or in a table at the end of the report, it is critical that surgical evaluation reports include enough information to allow for appropriate comparisons across assessments. In theory, it is possible to obtain the raw data if it was not provided in the previous report. However, there are often many practical barriers to obtaining this information at all, much less in a timely fashion. Therefore, to ensure optimal care of the patient and the best possible use of the neuropsychological evaluations over time, the test data should be included in some manner when performing surgical evaluations.

In the Summary/Impression section of a presurgical report, the neuropsychologist should address points relevant to the surgical question at hand. In some cases (e.g., deep brain stimulation [DBS] surgery, LVAD placement), the key question may be ruling out dementia and establishing whether the patient has the cognitive ability to manage the devices postoperatively. In contrast, for epilepsy surgery candidates, report impressions generally include statements regarding whether the neuropsychological data suggest lateralized or localized cerebral dysfunction, which, by implication, may suggest location of the seizure focus. Furthermore, the potential for cognitive morbidity may be discussed for patients deemed at risk for cognitive decline following surgical intervention (e.g., potential disruption of verbal memory functioning in a patient with intact verbal memory performance under consideration for left mesial temporal lobe resection). In such cases, the neuropsychologist may recommend further investigations, such as Wada examination, to determine the functional integrity of mesial temporal structures or to elucidate functional reorganization of memory.

It is also important that the neuropsychologist highlight other factors relevant to the peri- and postoperative phase of the procedure when possible. Examples include the need to identify and recommend treatment for prominent mood symptoms, and to clarify psychosocial circumstances, such as the nature of supports the patient will have in the immediate postoperative stage if the patient lives alone and has limited family support, and any other psychosocial concerns identified through the course of the neuropsychological consultation.

As the Summary/Impression section is often the only part of the neuropsychological consultation report read by members of a surgical team, it is important that responses to the key referral questions not get "buried" in a long, prose-oriented paragraph. After concisely summarizing the findings, the specific responses to referral questions should be presented in a concise paragraph or bulleted format.

MEASURING RELIABLE CHANGE

When considering how the patient is performing in a repeat examination (e.g., a postoperative evaluation) relative to their baseline level of ability, special considerations are warranted. Effective evaluation of cognitive change pre- and postsurgically (or over time more generally) can be a challenging task. Although clinicians have historically based decisions regarding change on clinical judgment alone, this approach has proven untrustworthy. In recent years, several methods for assessing change have been advanced (e.g., simple discrepancy scores, standard deviation indices), but most recently, the calculation of "reliable change indices" (RCIs) has gained traction and many advocate for their routine use in clinical decision making (Duff, 2012). RCIs provide an empirically based method by which serially obtained test scores can be evaluated. Accordingly, it can be determined whether apparent change seen across presurgical–postsurgical assessments is reliable, or due to random factors related to the imperfect psychometric properties of tests and/or practice effects. The RCI scores provide the means by which a clinician calculates measurement error around test–retest difference scores. If observed change scores exceed what may be predicted by measurement error alone, it can be said that the change is statistically significant. For a detailed review of the use of reliable change scores, we recommend reviewing the excellent source (Duff, 2012).

Unfortunately, reliable change indices are not without pitfalls, and their use may prove even more challenging in pediatric examinations. RCIs necessitate stability of true scores across time, and as such, differences between pretest–posttest assessment results reflect either improvement or decline across time. In pediatric neuropsychological evaluations, children's scores are expected to change over time throughout development. To some extent, this factor can be controlled for by using normative scores in reliable change calculations rather than raw scores, but the utility of this approach has not been thoroughly investigated. It is also important to note that, as

RCIs are inherently related to the test–retest reliability of a measure, the utility of RCIs may be compromised by test–retest intervals that differ from those reported in the literature and/or technical manuals. In most clinical settings, it is unusual for patients to be evaluated at intervals commonly utilized to determine a task's test–retest reliability as reported in the test technical manuals (often intervals of just a few weeks).

Fortunately, recent work has focused on providing more practical data on commonly utilized neuropsychological instruments in epilepsy evaluations. For example, detailed RCI data have been provided for instruments such as the Wechsler IQ and Memory Scales (Hermann et al., 1996; Martin et al., 2002), the California Verbal Learning Test—Second Edition (Woods, Delis, Scott, Kramer, & Holdnack, 2006), the Rey–Osterrieth Complex Figure (Nakhutina, Pramataris, Morrison, Devinsky, & Barr, 2010), and the Boston Naming Test (Sachs et al., 2012), to name a few. This recent work makes determination of reliable change on specific neurocognitive tasks rapid and easy when working with adults with epilepsy. Unfortunately, similar data for children remain sparse. As such, pediatric-oriented clinicians must exercise caution when making assertions regarding change, decline, or developmental stagnation/plateauing of cognitive skills in follow-up evaluations.

REPORT COMPONENTS AND ANALYSIS WITH SELECTED EXAMPLES

To elaborate on the report-writing strategies discussed above and to highlight some common suboptimal report-writing practices, the following examples for select sections of the typical neuropsychological test report are provided. Various cases are used for these illustrations, and examples for presurgical reports, presurgical evaluations with multiple data sets, and postsurgical evaluations are provided.

History

In addition to the customary information typically included in a neuropsychological report, the neuropsychologist will be including basic disease-specific information that will have an impact on how the cognitive data are interpreted. That said, this history does not need to be extensively detailed for the reasons specified above.

Example 1: Presurgical Report—History

LESS DESIRABLE: DOCTOR A

The patient was born full term after a normal labor and delivery. At the age of 2, he experienced a febrile seizure with a viral infection and fever of 102 degrees.

Thereafter, he was healthy until approximately the age of 20. At that time, he was on vacation with his college friends. After a 6-hour flight home from Cabo San Lucas (with a 3-hour layover), he experienced his first nonfebrile seizure. His college friends/travel companions were able to describe the event as involving staring glassy-eyed, while picking at his shirt with his right hand. They estimated that the entire event lasted about a minute and a half. For the next 20 minutes or so, he appeared dazed and confused, and was unable to speak clearly. They took him to the emergency room of the local hospital. No abnormalities were seen in the blood work, the EEG did not show epileptiform activity, and the MRI was essentially normal. Unfortunately, six months later in the month of August, he experienced a similar event after working long hours as a carpenter; his sleep had been disrupted at that time, with sleep on many nights totaling only 5 hours. This time, however, the event progressed to involve whole-body shaking. He was treated with 250 mg of leviteracetam BID.

MORE DESIRABLE: DOCTOR B

Although he had a febrile seizure at age 2, his first unprovoked seizure occurred at age 20 upon returning home on a long flight. The event was described as unresponsive staring with right-hand automatisms lasting 90 seconds. He was confused with speech disruption for 20 minutes thereafter. A medical work-up was unrevealing. A similar seizure that evolved to include whole-body convulsions occurred 6 months later during a period of high stress and poor sleep. He was treated with leviteracetam. Although seizures were initially rare (1 seizure/6 months), seizure frequency increased despite trials with multiple AEDs. He currently experiences three to four complex partial seizures monthly, with occasional secondary generalization.

COMMENT ON EXAMPLE 1

Although Dr. A's history may be technically correct, much of this information is already known to the surgical team or is irrelevant. In addition, excessive reporting of details, such as medications/dosages, has the high probability of being inaccurate. Patients with conditions that require surgical intervention, particularly epilepsy, may have comorbid memory deficits and frequently report elements of their history incorrectly. Repeating this history with such a high level of specificity (particularly when it is not needed to interpret the neuropsychological data) could be more harmful than beneficial as it may perpetuate flawed information throughout the medical record.

Behavioral Observations

The unique aspect of writing behavioral observations in an epilepsy report relates primarily to the question of whether the patient had a seizure during the evaluation. This is not unusual and may be particularly likely if the evaluation is conducted during an inpatient video/EEG monitoring hospital admission. A common report-writing error made in this setting relates to the examiner noting that the patient experienced a particular type of seizure. Although many seizure types seem "easy" to identify, in the absence of expert epilepsy training and without knowledge of EEG findings during the seizure, an observer can be fooled.

Example 2: Behavioral Observations

LESS DESIRABLE: DOCTOR A

```
Patient had a GTC and then fell asleep.
```

MORE DESIRABLE: DOCTOR B

```
Patient appeared to experience a brief period of cogni-
tive/behavioral disruption (he was no longer as quick to
respond appropriately to questions), which was followed by
head version to the right and subsequent clonic movements
of both upper and lower extremities lasting 45 seconds.
Postictally, he fell asleep and was not arousable.
```

COMMENT ON EXAMPLE 2

Dr. A presumes that "whole-body shaking" is always a generalized tonic–clonic (GTC) seizure. In fact, both the tonic and clonic phases of a seizure can happen in isolation. In addition, Dr. A did not report the potential early complex partial seizure component. As written, Dr. A's description is not only inaccurate but could apply to a patient with primary generalized epilepsy or to a person with focal epilepsy that secondarily generalizes. Furthermore, the event could have been a psychogenic nonepileptic event, which can occur even in individuals with confirmed epilepsy. When reporting seizure semiology, it is better to merely describe the phenomenology that was observed rather than speculate about seizure type. The epileptologists will find the description much more helpful than the neuropsychologist's presumptions about seizure type.

Results

Most methods of presenting results by domain are appropriate. However, pages of detailed comment on test descriptions and every variable of each measure will not serve the treatment team, including the next neuropsychologist who performs the postoperative evaluation and must wade through the prose to find key data points. Although presentation of the data in tabular form is clear and easy to view, in our experience importing Word or Excel tables into electronic medical records often results in distortion of the table, thus defeating the purpose of rendering data points easy to find. Succinct statements about a particular measure or set of measures that ultimately contribute to understanding brain functioning (e.g., localization/lateralization in an epilepsy case or whether patient is demented in another type of presurgical evaluation) are most effective.

Example 3: Presurgical Report—Results

LESS DESIRABLE: DOCTOR A

General cognitive ability is in the average range. There was a statistically significant difference between his stronger visuospatial skills (PRI = 110) and weaker verbal comprehension skills (VCI = 98). The Working Memory Index (WMI = 107) was similar to the PRI but significantly above the VCI. Processing speed (PSI = 95) was significantly worse than working memory abilities.

MORE DESIRABLE: DOCTOR B

General cognitive ability was found to be in the average range and globally consistent with premorbid estimates. The disparity between the verbal/conceptual (VCI = 98) and perceptual reasoning (PRI = 110) domains was not clinically meaningful. Verbal working memory (WMI = 107) and visuomotor processing speed (PSI = 95) are well preserved.

COMMENT ON EXAMPLE 3

Dr. A highlights a series of statistically significant differences; however, none of these differences are clinically meaningful, as they are relatively commonly seen in the normal population (i.e., have a base rate of > 10%). In addition, Dr. A makes comparisons between factor scores that have no particular meaning in terms of functioning or functional neuroanatomy (e.g., the PRI vs. WMI comparison). The failure to review the base rates of these "statistical differences" and the overanalysis of the various combinations of factor score comparisons often leads to spurious conclusions.

Furthermore, Dr. A comments on some comparisons without actually interpreting them (e.g., while the WMI was stronger" than the PSI, is the PSI "normal" or "abnormal"?). Finally, the detail Dr. A includes is irrelevant to our physician colleagues and is not needed by the next neuropsychologist when the premorbid estimate and factor scores are provided. In contrast, Dr. B provides a clear and concise summary of factor scores without over-interpretation of what is essentially normal score variation.

Example 4: Presurgical Report—Results

LESS DESIRABLE: DOCTOR A

The 15-point discrepancy between Mr. Jones's verbal memory and visual memory indices suggests dominant hemisphere dysfunction.

MORE DESIRABLE: DOCTOR B

Mr. Smith shows prominent verbal memory deficits in contrast to preserved visual memory; the 22-point discrepancy between verbal and visual memory indices is large and clinically unusual, occurring in less than 10% of the population.

COMMENT ON EXAMPLE 4

Dr. A is basing decisions on the lateralizing nature of neuropsychological findings on normal score variation. For example, a 15-point discrepancy between verbal and visual memory indices is common in the normal population (e.g., on the WRAML-2, a discrepancy of this magnitude occurs in over 18% of the population) and is therefore of limited clinical relevance. Though obviously a different patient, Dr. B is identifying a large, statistically significant, and, most importantly, an uncommon discrepancy (i.e., base rate of less than 10%) that has more meaningful clinical implications, such as suggesting dominant hemisphere dysfunction.

Example 5: Presurgical Report—Results

LESS DESIRABLE: DOCTOR A

Mr. Smith was able to learn a series of progressively more complex figures presented for passive 10-second viewing trials (ss = 11) and recall the figures after a delay (ss = 10); recognition of the figures was also intact. His memory for a complex figure that he had copied earlier was in the expected average range (RCFT z = 0.1).

In contrast, Mr. Smith demonstrated some difficulty
with initial learning of a noncontextualized word list
presented over serial trials (CVLT-II). His recall after a
single presentation was borderline impaired (4/16); however, he was able to gradually acquire new words over
serial learning trials and ultimately achieved a total
learning score in the average range (T = 43). Review
of his serial and semantic clustering scores suggested
that he used the less efficient serial order method for
learning (high average range) rather than capitalizing
on the inherent semantic clustering method for enhancing recall (low average). There was no obvious suscepti-
bility to proactive or retroactive interference, and he
recalled a normal number of words after a delay (13/16).
Discriminability of the target words when presented in
a recognition trial was also normal. Mr. Smith struggled
with recalling contextually organized verbal information (i.e., story prose) after a single learning trial (ss
= 6). However, when his memory for the story prose was
assessed 30 minutes later, he largely retained what little
had been encoded during the initial learning trial (ss =
8). Although this score is in the "average" range, when
Mr. Smith is compared to a more similar demographic group
(e.g., highly educated individuals), his scores on the
story memory task are clearly below expectations (DemT =
35) and are suggestive of difficulty with learning verbally based information.

MORE DESIRABLE: DOCTOR B

While normal memory was seen in the nonverbal modal-
ity, new learning of verbally based information was very
challenging for the patient, particularly when he was not
afforded multiple learning opportunities.

COMMENT ON EXAMPLE 5

Dr. A carefully reviews and comments on many of the primary and secondary variables provided by the tests being interpreted in this section. Equal
consideration of the various normed scores available for a test can result
in an elevated Type I error rate of sorts. That is, the more scores that are
produced/reviewed, the greater the likelihood that a certain percentage of
scores will be found to be abnormal just by chance alone (Binder, Iverson,
& Brooks, 2009). Reviewing all available scores, and giving primary and
secondary outcome variables "equal value" when interpreting the profile,

can lead to confusing, even complex and spurious overinterpretation of the results.

In addition to these statistical concerns with reviewing all (or most) scores produced by a single test, writing about the full complement of scores will result in pages of dense text that few, if any, referral sources will want to read or have the psychometric background to understand. When data are presented in some sort of tabular format (see the sample report in Appendix 8.1, pp. 217–219), excessive writing is no longer necessary and the neuropsychologist can focus on the key, overarching interpretations, particularly in data profiles that are fairly straightforward. This reduces the length of the reports and makes them easier to read.

Unfortunately, many individuals presenting for epilepsy surgery have significant cognitive impairments or intellectual disability. Accordingly, it is necessary that neuropsychologists writing pre- and postsurgical reports have experience and expertise in the evaluation of very-low-functioning individuals, many of whom may be untestable by traditional means (e.g., have intellectual skills below the "floor" of most IQ measures). Despite the seemingly "untestable" nature of this population, neuropsychologists can provide meaningful information to the team. Evaluations of such patients typically employ behavioral observations and nonstandardized testing, as well as questionnaires/structured interviews to assess adaptive functioning (typically with patient caregivers). Instruments helpful in this population may include the Adaptive Behavior Assessment System–II (Harrison & Oakland, 2003) and the Vineland Adaptive Behavior Scales—Second Edition (Sparrow, Cicchetti, & Balla, 2005).

In these cases, the significance of neuropsychological consultation is not as obvious, but we assert that neuropsychologists, with training and expertise in not only cognitive functioning but also psychological functioning, have much to offer to the patient families, treating epileptologists, and neurosurgeons (Brandling-Bennett, 2014). Most notably here, neuropsychologists are well poised to make meaningful recommendations regarding services needed (e.g., behavioral management in individuals with severe behavioral problems). Further, evaluation of psychological/behavioral functioning provides critical information regarding the likelihood that a low-functioning patient will be able to participate meaningfully in procedures such as Wada procedures, fMRI studies, or brain mapping, or will be able to tolerate lengthy intracranial EEG monitoring without posing a major safety risk. Perhaps most importantly to neurosurgeons operating on such individuals, documenting the profound nature of their cognitive deficits indicates that the patient is at low risk for postsurgical cognitive decline. Moreover, standardized measures of adaptive functioning, behavior, and quality of life provide a meaningful point of reference to which postsurgical improvements can be compared and overall progress measured. In short, assuming that there are no complications during surgery, adverse cognitive outcomes are less likely in these individuals, while improving overall quality of life is possible if seizure frequency and/or severity can be reduced. This should be documented clearly in the neuropsychological report, and the patient caregivers made aware of potential risks from not pursuing the surgery, such as further cognitive or decline with continued uncontrolled seizures (Helmstaedter & Elger, 2009; Hermann, Meador, Gaillard, & Cramer, 2010).

Example 6: Postsurgical Report—Results

LESS DESIRABLE: DOCTOR A

Postsurgically, Mr. Jones has shown a decline in verbal intellectual functioning, as documented by the 4-point decline on the WAIS-III Verbal Comprehension Index.

MORE DESIRABLE: DOCTOR B

Postsurgically, Mr. Smith has shown a decline in verbal intellectual functioning, as documented by the 9-point decline on the WAIS-III Verbal Comprehension Index, which exceeds reliable change indices for statistically significant change.

COMMENT ON EXAMPLE 6

Dr. A's assertion that the patient has experienced a clinically significant decline in functioning is based on normal score variation, as the scores reported are well within the typical variability of what may be seen on reassessment. In contrast, Dr. B has identified a change in functioning that is larger than what can be expected based on random factors alone; according to Martin et al. (2002), a decline of 7 or more points on the WAIS-III Verbal Comprehension Index suggests "reliable change." As such, it can be concluded that the patient experienced a statistically significant and clinically meaningful decline in language-based functions.

Example 7: Postsurgical Report—Results

LESS DESIRABLE: DOCTOR A

Mr. Smith's performance on a timed set shifting task (TMT-B) was slower by 23 seconds in this postoperative exam. In addition, he showed slightly greater interference effect on the Stroop task (declined from the average to low average range). On the WCST-64, although he again completed three categories, he made a somewhat greater

number of perseverative errors relative to his performance last year before the surgery.

In contrast, abstract reasoning and conceptualization
have improved somewhat. His scores on the Similarities
and Matrix Reasoning subtests, previously solidly average
(ss = 10), are now nearer to the high average range (ss =
12 and ss = 13, respectively).

MORE DESIRABLE: DOCTOR B

The degree of change between pre- and postsurgical scores
does not exceed the typical test–retest variance of the
measure or that expected from a clinical population.
Therefore, there does not appear to have been a change in
executive functions relative to presurgical levels.

COMMENT ON EXAMPLE 7

Dr. A is reviewing the raw and normed data and using clinical judgment to
interpret whether a change has occurred. As indicated above, whenever possible, it is preferable to use RCI data to determine if there has been a change
in performance. For example, using the case above, Dr. A comments on the
23-second change from pre- to postsurgical time points, implying that this
reflects a decline in ability. In reviewing data available for this measure in
Hermann et al. (1996), it can be seen that a decline of 67 seconds is needed
to establish that change above and beyond the inherent variability seen in
an epilepsy population has occurred. Thus, that 23-second change is potentially just "noise" in the data. The change in the Wechsler scaled scores
provides another opportunity to highlight how "eye-balling" the data may
result in misinterpretation. In an epilepsy population, Martin et al. (2002,
Table 3) reveal that an improvement of 3 (Similarities) to 5 (Matrix Reasoning) or more scaled score points is needed to show that there has been
actual improvement above and beyond practice effects.

Summary/Impression/Formulation

A brief summation of the referral question and findings should be followed
by an explicit comment that integrates the interpretation of the test results
as they relate to the referral question. Care should be taken to not repli-
cate the entire Background and Test Results (sans scores) sections, if one
has been included. A two-paragraph model for generating an impression is
often a helpful starting place wherein the first paragraph reviews basically
what was found and the second addresses what the findings mean in terms
of the question(s) being asked by the referral source. Elaborations as appropriate can then be made.

In an epilepsy setting, it is essential that the neuropsychologist not try to "fit" the neuropsychological results to specific EEG or MRI findings. The results provided by objective cognitive and behavioral assessment contribute unique information as compared to other diagnostic procedures. As such, inferences from neuropsychological data about the integrity of brain functioning are not "inaccurate" just because there is apparent variance with results from structural or functional procedures. In addition, addressing the epilepsy-specific localization/lateralization question should not be avoided just because none is obvious from the neuropsychological profile. In fact, diffusely normal and diffusely impaired profiles (both are nonlocalizing/lateralizing) do provide the surgical team with very specific and helpful information. When possible, comment should be made regarding the potential for postoperative cognitive morbidity (either high or low risk for change following resective surgery). For example, when nonverbal memory performance is extremely poor (and depending on other factors such as handedness), the neuropsychologist may offer that the patient is at low risk for postoperative cognitive impairment following resection of nondominant mesial temporal structures. Finally, through their lengthy interaction with patients, neuropsychologists often obtain an appreciation for how the patient understands the surgical process, what their expectations are, and what their psychological coping skills may be. Red flags for a poor outcome should be noted and communicated to the team so that appropriate education and intervention can be discussed with the surgical team prior to surgery.

Example 8: Presurgical Report—Summary

LESS DESIRABLE: DOCTOR A

In conclusion, the patient demonstrates preserved general intellectual functioning but impairment in verbal fluency, naming, verbal memory, nonverbal memory, nonverbal fluency, and other aspects of executive functioning. Receptive language and basic visuospatial processes are intact.

Given the patient's known medical condition and the multidomain cognitive impairment, the following diagnoses are appropriate:

ICD-9

   345.91 Medically refractory epilepsy
   294.9 Cognitive impairment secondary to epilepsy

MORE DESIRABLE: DOCTOR B

The globally lower than expected memory performance, in combination with impairments in cognitive flexibility,

problem solving, and generative fluency, suggest frontotemporal dysfunction; however, the profile is not strongly
lateralizing. Although the patient was found to have right
mesial temporal sclerosis, the underlying cerebral dysfunction and/or the secondary effects of frequent GTC seizures seems to be disrupting bilateral frontal and temporal networks.

COMMENT ON EXAMPLE 8

Dr. A summarizes the data and provides a diagnosis in the routinized format of traditional neuropsychological reports. Although this manner of
formulation meets standards of medical necessity and, again is technically
accurate, it does not provide the specific information the epilepsy surgical team is seeking from the neuropsychologist. The neuropsychologist is
uniquely poised within the surgical team to provide information on the
functional integrity of various brain regions.

Although it is important that neuropsychologists not try to "fit" their
data into what is known about the patient in terms of lateralizing and
localizing dysfunction, it is equally important that they interpret cognitive findings in the context of known medical factors/epilepsy characteristics. Specifically, neuropsychologists generally no longer interpret test data
without placing neuropsychological findings in the context of other medical data, as doing so may lead to interpretations of data that are unhelpful
to the surgical team or even result in adverse surgical outcomes if taken at
face value. For example, it is well established that left-hemisphere lesions
during early childhood may disrupt typical cerebral organization, leading
to a functional reorganization of language and verbal memory. Neuropsychologists performing presurgical evaluations should be adept in recognizing and interpreting test performances that may indicate "crowding
effects." Signs of crowding often involve preserved language skills with
impaired visual spatial functioning in the context of a well-established left-
hemisphere lesion or seizure focus (Gleissner et al., 2003; Strauss, Satz, &
Wada, 1990). However, widespread deficits (i.e., impaired language skills
as well as visual spatial skills) may also suggest aberrant organization of
functioning. Neuropsychologists have the unique training to interpret such
findings.

Example 9: Presurgical Report—Summary

LESS DESIRABLE: DOCTOR A

The patient's overall neuropsychological profile suggests
multifocal deficits that are inconsistent with neuroimaging and EEG findings that document mesial temporal sclerosis and left temporal seizure onset. Whereas slowed motor

findings in the right hand suggest left-hemisphere deficits, impaired memory for visual information and poor
visual spatial skills in general suggest right-hemisphere
involvement.

MORE DESIRABLE: DOCTOR B

The patient's overall neuropsychological profile is complex. Whereas slowed motor findings in the right hand suggest left-hemisphere deficits, the patient's impaired memory for visual information and poor visual spatial skills
would typically be interpreted to implicate nondominant
hemisphere dysfunction. However, in the context of the
patient's known left mesial temporal sclerosis and left
temporal seizure onset, these findings may reflect the
effects of functional reorganization of language skills
(i.e., "crowding effect"). A Wada examination or fMRI is
recommended to confirm this interpretation.

COMMENT ON EXAMPLE 9

Dr. A, while correctly summarizing and succinctly describing the test findings, is failing to appreciate the functional implications of the data. In contrast, Dr. B conceptualizes the seemingly discordant findings in the context of what is known about the patient's epilepsy syndrome and makes
interpretive statements regarding functional organization/brain–behavior
relationships. Further, Dr. B makes appropriate recommendations for additional procedures that may confirm (or disconfirm) interpretations. Such
interpretations are important in presurgical evaluations as they help predict postsurgical outcomes; this patient would be at lower risk for cognitive morbidity (i.e., postsurgical decline in language function and/or verbal
memory) if functional reorganization of language is confirmed.

Example 10: Presurgical Report–Summary

LESS DESIRABLE: DOCTOR A

Consistent with the child's history of left temporal lobe
epilepsy, he shows prominent language deficits as manifested by a large split between the WISC-IV Verbal Comprehension Index and Perceptual Reasoning Index.

MORE DESIRABLE: DOCTOR B

The neuropsychological profile is strongly lateralizing
to the left hemisphere. Specifically, he shows prominent

verbal memory impairment relative to intact memory for
visually presented information, has word-finding deficits,
and motor skills are impaired in the right upper extremity.

COMMENT ON EXAMPLE 10

Dr. A makes the common mistake of basing decisions regarding the lateralizing nature of findings on discrepancies between indices of intelligence
measures. Despite the apparent face validity of this approach, indices on the
Wechsler intelligence tests have never been shown to provide reliable lateralizing data (Blackburn et al., 2007; Sherman, Brooks, Fay-McClymont,
& MacAllister, 2012), as intelligence tests are typically not developed with
brain–behavior relations in mind (Baron, 2004). Dr. B, in contrast, uti-
lizes findings that have more empirical support in implicating dominant
(left-) hemisphere dysfunction, mainly large (i.e., low-base-rate) disparities
between verbal and visual memory indices, naming deficits, and lateralizing motor impairment.

When considering follow-up evaluations, whether they occur after a
surgical intervention, are being performed to establish a new baseline several years after previous testing was conducted (even if no surgical intervention was performed in the interim), or are conducted in another situation wherein repeat testing has been requested (e.g., following a significant
medical event such an episode of status epilepticus), the key referral question generally relates to whether there has been change. Failure to address
this issue in the Summary section diminishes the value of the patient having
undergone the repeat testing and the value of what the neuropsychologist
can contribute to the medical team. In addition, it is critical that the neuropsychologist summarize information about change in a manner that is
streamlined and can be easily understood by members of the medical team.

Example 11: Presurgical Evaluation with Integration of Data from a Prior Neuropsychological Exam—Summary

LESS DESIRABLE: DOCTOR A

In comparison to his last neuropsychological evaluation,
the patient's performance on a construction task declined
from the average to borderline impaired range, as did his
ability on block design constructions, wherein performance
is now impaired. Attention skills are in the average
range. Although language skills were variable across time
(naming improved somewhat and fluency mildly declined),
the scores did not fall outside the high to low average range. Performance on measures of reasoning, problem

solving, and cognitive flexibility did not change. Verbal learning and memory are in the average to low average
range and are unchanged. Nonverbal memory was in the low
average range and is now in the very impaired range.

    In conclusion, the visuospatial processing deficits
with new impairment, as well as the decline in nonverbal
memory implicate nondominant hemisphere dysfunction and
suggest a right temporal lobe seizure focus.

MORE DESIRABLE: DOCTOR B

In comparison to neuropsychological test data obtained
three years ago, clear changes have taken place in higher
order visuospatial processing and nonverbal memory, while
other cognitive abilities remain largely stable. The pattern of changes suggests that the patient's continued
seizure burden has selectively disrupted nondominant temporal functions. The marked level of impairment seen at
this time suggests that he is at low risk for postoperative change following nondominant temporal resection.

COMMENT ON EXAMPLE 11

Dr. B collapses the results into an integrative statement that highlights the
most salient findings. The referral question is specifically addressed (vis-
à-vis do the combined data sets in this case facilitate an understanding of
focal cerebral dysfunction and by implication seizure localization), and a
statement on likely postoperatively cognitive morbidity (or lack thereof)
is included. Dr. A recounts the neuropsychological findings in an overly
detailed and even repetitive fashion. The level of detail provided in this
Summary section is certainly not needed, nor is it necessarily appreciated
by the non-neuropsychology members of the surgical team.

Recommendations

In making effective recommendations in a presurgical evaluation, one
should reflect on the unique information offered by neuropsychological
evaluations and consider this information in terms of what may be most
useful to the surgical team. That said, it is important to recognize that
many individuals presenting for possible surgery either (1) do not actually receive surgery for many months, or (2) are ultimately deemed poor
surgical candidates for various reasons and, therefore, never proceed to
surgery. As such, our approach is to provide appropriate recommendations
for all patients, regardless of possible interventions that may follow (with
caveats that the cognitive profile may change if surgery is undertaken). In

our experience, this is particularly important in child epilepsy presurgical evaluations wherein a given patient may benefit from several months of intervention, such as speech and language therapy or occupational therapy, either at school or through hospital/clinic-based services, before surgery can be scheduled.

Many recommendations made in presurgical epilepsy evaluations address procedures that may follow the assessment. For example, in cases of left temporal epilepsy (with left-hemisphere language dominance), all but the most cognitively impaired individuals may be at risk for memory or language decline upon resection or ablative surgery. In such cases, it is appropriate to recommend additional procedures to better lateralize language and/or exonerate memory structures; recommendations may include fMRI or the Wada procedure.

Further, the neuropsychologist is uniquely poised to discuss behavioral factors that are relevant in these complex cases. For example, many individuals with epilepsy, particularly children, have unmet psychiatric needs (Ott et al., 2003). In extreme cases, where mood is labile and behavior may be combative, these individuals may be at high risk for complications during special procedures. Accordingly, the neuropsychologist should alert the surgical team that the patient may be unable to tolerate certain procedures. For example, an emotionally labile patient is at increased risk for severe (i.e., potentially life-threatening) complications during invasive procedures, such as the Wada procedure where a catheter is placed in the carotid artery, or lengthy intracranial EEG monitoring where a combative patient pulling on the EEG leads may cause hemorrhage. In these cases, referral to a knowledgeable psychiatrist for psychopharmacological prophylaxis is warranted so that procedures may be better tolerated. Moreover, referral to behaviorally based psychotherapists can help the family better manage these individuals at home.

Other factors to consider when making effective recommendations involve the postsurgical period. For example, following neurosurgery, a patient with substantial cognitive impairment may have difficulties managing their medications or even may have difficulties with basic activities of daily living. Recommendations for a social worker consultation can be crucial in assuring that the patient is being discharged into an environment that will meet their medical needs. This may merely involve discussing postoperative needs with family members and ensuring that the family can meet the ensuing needs of the patient. In other cases, the social worker can help arrange for formal in-home nursing care services.

When patients are evaluated postsurgically, the neuropsychologist has a unique opportunity to reassess the needs of the patient and update recommendations. For some, cognitive changes will be documented upon postsurgical assessment. Here, recommendations for cognitive rehabilitation are typically made. Pharmacological interventions may also be helpful in these individuals, so recommendation for psychiatric consultation remains appropriate. Further, the neuropsychologist may make predictions regarding the ability of the patient to return to work and what supports may be helpful if this is to occur. As for all patients with neuropsychological deficits, the neuropsychologist should consider the patient's ability to live independently, or what level of support will be required if they are unlikely to be able to do so without risk. In patients for whom in-home safety is a concern, recommendations for social worker interventions are appropriate.

REFERENCES

Akanuma, N., Alarcon, G., Lum, F., Kissani, N., Koutroumanidis, M., Adachi, N., et al. (2003). Lateralising value of neuropsychological protocols for presurgical assessment of temporal lobe epilepsy. *Epilepsia, 44*(3), 408–418.

Baron, I. (2004). *Neuropsychological evaluation of the child.* New York: Oxford University Press.

Baxendale, S., Thompson, P., Harkness, W., & Duncan, J. (2006). Predicting memory decline following epilepsy surgery: A multivariate approach. *Epilepsia, 47*(11), 1887–1894.

Binder, L. M., Iverson, G. L., & Brooks, B. L. (2009). To err is human: "Abnormal" neuropsychological scores and variability are common in healthy adults. *Archives of Clinical Neuropsychology, 24*(1), 31–46.

Blackburn, L. B., Lee, G. P., Westerveld, M., Hempel, A., Park, Y. D., & Loring, D. W. (2007). The verbal IQ/Performance IQ discrepancy as a sign of seizure focus laterality in pediatric patients with epilepsy. *Epilepsy and Behavior, 10*(1), 84–88.

Brandling-Bennett, E. M. (2014). Developmentally delayed children and adults. In W. B. Barr & C. Morrison (Eds.), *Handbook on the neuropsychology of epilepsy* (pp. 275–300). New York: Springer.

Brodie, M., Shorvon, S., Canger, R., Halasz, P., Johannessen, S., Thompson, P., et al. (1997). Commission on European affairs: Appropriate standards of epilepsy care across Europe. *Epilepsia, 38*(11), 1245–1250.

Bronstein, J. M., Tagliati, M., Alterman, R. L., Lozano, A. M., Volkmann, J., Stefani, A., et al. (2011). Deep brain stimulation for Parkinson disease: An expert consensus and review of key issues. *Archives of Neurology, 68*(2), 165–171.

Castro, L. H., Silva, L. C. A. M., Adda, C. C., Banaskiwitz, N. H. C., Xavier, A. B., Jorge, C. L., et al. (2013). Low prevalence but high specificity of material-specific memory impairment in epilepsy associated with hippocampal sclerosis. *Epilepsia, 54*(10), 1735–1742.

Chelune, G. J., Naugle, R. I., Hermann, B. P., Barr, W. B., Trenerry, M. R., Loring, D. W., et al. (1998). Does presurgical IQ predict seizure outcome after temporal lobectomy? Evidence from the Bozeman epilepsy consortium. *Epilepsia, 39*(3), 314–318.

Duff, K. (2012). Evidence-based indicators of neuropsychological change in the individual patient: Relevant concepts and methods. *Archives of Clinical Neuropsychology, 27*(3), 248–261.

Gargaro, A. C., Sakamoto, A. C., Bianchin, M. M., Geraldi, C. D. V. L., Scorsi-Rosset, S., Coimbra, É. R., et al. (2013). Atypical neuropsychological profiles and cognitive outcome in mesial temporal lobe epilepsy. *Epilepsy and Behavior, 27*(3), 461–469.

Gleissner, U., Helmstaedter, C., Schramm, J., & Elger, C. E. (2004). Memory outcome after selective amygdalohippocampectomy in patients with temporal lobe epilepsy: One-year follow-up. *Epilepsia, 45*(8), 960–962.

Gleissner, U., Kurthen, M., Sassen, R., Kuczaty, S., Elger, C. E., Linke, D. B., et al. (2003). Clinical and neuropsychological characteristics of pediatric epilepsy patients with atypical language dominance. *Epilepsy and Behavior, 4*(6), 746–752.

Gleissner, U., Sassen, R., Lendt, M., Clusmann, H., Elger, C. E., & Helmstaedter, C. (2002). Pre- and postoperative verbal memory in pediatric patients with temporal lobe epilepsy. *Epilepsy Research, 51*(3), 287–296.

Gleissner, U., Sassen, R., Schramm, J., Elger, C. E., & Helmstaedter, C. (2005). Greater functional recovery after temporal lobe epilepsy surgery in children. *Brain, 128*(12), 2822–2829.

Harrison, P. L., & Oakland, T. (2003). *Adaptive Behavior Assessment System Manual* (2nd ed). San Antonio, TX: Harcourt Assessment.

Helmstaedter, C., & Elger, C. E. (2009). Chronic temporal lobe epilepsy: A neurodevelopmental or progressively dementing disease? *Brain, 132*(10), 2822–2830.

Hennessy, M. J., Elwes, R. D., Honavar, M., Rabe-Hesketh, S., Binnie, C. D., & Polkey, C. E. (2001). Predictors of outcome and pathological considerations in the surgical treatment of intractable epilepsy associated with temporal lobe lesions. *Journal of Neurology, Neurosurgery, and Psychiatry, 70*(4), 450–458.

Hermann, B., Meador, K. J., Gaillard, W. D., & Cramer, J. A. (2010). Cognition across the lifespan: Antiepileptic drugs, epilepsy, or both? *Epilepsy and Behavior, 17*(1), 1–5.

Hermann, B. P., Seidenberg, M., Schoenfeld, J., Peterson, J., Leveroni, C., & Wyler, A. R. (1996). Empirical techniques for determining the reliability, magnitude, and pattern of neuropsychological change after epilepsy surgery. *Epilepsia, 37*(10), 942–950.

Martin, R., Sawrie, S., Gilliam, F., Mackey, M., Faught, E., Knowlton, R., et al. (2002). Determining reliable cognitive change after epilepsy surgery: Development of reliable change indices and standardized regression-based change norms for the WMS-III and WAIS-III. *Epilepsia, 43*(12), 1551–1558.

Nakhutina, L., Pramataris, P., Morrison, C., Devinsky, O., & Barr, W. B. (2010). Reliable change indices and regression-based measures for the Rey–Osterreith complex figure test in partial epilepsy patients. *The Clinical Neuropsychologist, 24*(1), 38–44.

Ott, D., Siddarth, P., Gurbani, S., Koh, S., Tournay, A., Shields, W. D., et al. (2003). Behavioral disorders in pediatric epilepsy: Unmet psychiatric need. *Epilepsia, 44*(4), 591–597.

Sachs, B. C., Lucas, J. A., Smith, G. E., Ivnik, R. J., Petersen, R. C., Graff-Radford, N. R., et al. (2012). Reliable change on the Boston naming test. *Journal of the International Neuropsychological Society, 18*(2), 375–378.

Sawrie, S. M., Martin, R. C., Gilliam, F. G., Roth, D. L., Faught, E., & Kuzniecky, R. (1998). Contribution of neuropsychological data to the prediction of temporal lobe epilepsy surgery outcome. *Epilepsia, 39*(3), 319–325.

Sherman, E. M., Brooks, B. L., Fay-McClymont, T. B., & MacAllister, W. S. (2012). Detecting epilepsy-related cognitive problems in clinically referred children with epilepsy: Is the WISC-IV a useful tool? *Epilepsia, 53*(6), 1060–1066.

Sherman, E. M., Wiebe, S., Fay-McClymont, T. B., Tellez-Zenteno, J., Metcalfe, A., Hernandez-Ronquillo, L., et al. (2011). Neuropsychological outcomes after epilepsy surgery: Systematic review and pooled estimates. *Epilepsia, 52*(5), 857–869.

Soble, J. R., Eichstaedt, K. E., Waseem, H., Mattingly, M. L., Benbadis, S. R., Bozorg, A. M., et al. (2014). Clinical utility of the Wechsler Memory Scale—Fourth Edition (WMS-IV) in predicting laterality of temporal lobe epilepsy among surgical candidates. *Epilepsy and Behavior, 41*, 232–237.

Sparrow, S. S., Chicchetti, D. V., & Balla, D. A. (2005). *Vineland Adaptive Behavior Scales: Second Edition*. Bloomington, MN: Pearson.

Strauss, E., Satz, P., & Wada, J. (1990). An examination of the crowding hypothesis in epileptic patients who have undergone the carotid amytal test. *Neuropsychologia, 28*(11), 1221–1227.

Woods, S. P., Delis, D. C., Scott, J. C., Kramer, J. H., & Holdnack, J. A. (2006). The California Verbal Learning Test—Second edition: Test–retest reliability, practice effects, and reliable change indices for the standard and alternate forms. *Archives of Clinical Neuropsychology, 21*(5), 413–420.

Sample Neuropsychology Consultation Report

For illustrative purposes, this sample report includes an amalgamation of medical/psychosocial histories and score profiles commonly seen in individuals with temporal lobe epilepsy (the most common form of epilepsy) and is not reflective of the history and data from a particular patient.

Name:	XXXX XXXX	*Date of birth:*	XX/XX/XXXX
Age:	28	*Setting:*	Inpatient
Education:	16 years	*Medical record #:*	XXXXXX
Sex:	Female	*Referring physician:*	XX XX, MD
Handedness:	Left	*Date of evaluation:*	XX/XX/XXXX
Provider(s):	XXX XXX, PhD	*Trainee:*	XX XX, MA

Referral

Ms. XXXX was referred for neuropsychological testing as part of a comprehensive presurgical work-up of her epilepsy syndrome. The results will be used in surgical and treatment planning

Background

The following information was obtained during an interview with Ms. XXXX and from review of available medical records. Ms. XXXX has a history of seizures since age 14. While they were initially well controlled, in the last 3 years they have become refractory to multiple seizure medications. She currently experiences one to two seizures per week. Seizures are characterized by behavioral and speech arrest, and last approximately 2 minutes. Postictally, she is mildly confused with language disruption, but she returns to baseline in approximately 10 minutes. She is treated with Depakote, Keppra, and Lamictal.

Cognitive complaints: mild memory and word-finding issues over the last 2 years.

Past Neuropsychological Test Results

Patient denied having prior testing.

Other Medical History

- Frequent sinus infections.
- Other medications: Femcon, folic acid.
- Appetite/weight: Normal, no changes.
- Sleep: Normal, no changes.
- Alcohol/tobacco: No history of abuse; denied current use.

Surgical History

Sinus surgery.

Psychiatric History

Patient denied.

Family History

Patient denied a family history of neurological conditions. Her brother was diagnosed with ADHD.

Social History

Cultural/Social Background

Ms. XXXX is a Caucasian female who was born and raised in XXXX. She is single, never married, and has no children.

Educational History

Ms. XXXX graduated from college and completed some Master's-level courses. She did not endorse any difficulties with advancing through school.

Occupational History

Ms. XXXX has worked full time as an administrator in a small company. She has maintained this job for the past 6 years.

Behavioral Observations

- *Appearance*: Appropriate grooming and dress for context.
- *Behavior/attitude*: Cooperative, engaged.
- *Speech/language*: Fluent and normal in rate, volume, and prosody.
- *Mood/affect*: Neutral, range was full and appropriate.
- *Sensory/motor*: Performance was not limited by any obvious sensory or motor difficulties.
- *Cognitive process*: Coherent and goal directed.
- *Motivation/effort*: Normal.

Tests Administered

Wechsler Test of Premorbid Functioning (TOPF); Wechsler Adult Intelligence Scale–IV (WAIS-IV); Wechsler Memory Scale–IV, select subtests; Auditory Verbal Learning Test (AVLT); Rey Complex Figure Test; Verbal Fluency tasks; Boston Naming Test (BNT); Trail

Making Test (TMT); Stroop Color and Word Test (SCWT); Wisconsin Card Sorting Test-64 item (WCST-64); Ruff Figural Fluency Test; Grooved Pegboard Test; Beck Depression Inventory-II (BDI-II); Beck Anxiety Inventory (BAI); and Minnesota Multiphasic Personality Inventory-II-Restructured Form (MMPI-2-RF).

Test Results

General Intellectual Functioning

Normal general intellectual functioning with no evidence of decline from premorbid estimates.

- Premorbid estimate: TOPF, above average (SS = 112).
- Current general cognitive ability: VCI = 103; PRI = 117; WMI = 102; PSI = 92. All domains wnl; strong perceptual reasoning abilities.

Attention and Processing Speed

No deficits identified.

- Auditory Attention Span: 6 forward, wnl.
- Verbal Working Memory: 5 digits reversed and 6 digits sequenced,wnl.
- Mental manipulation of numeric information to perform oral arithmetic: wnl (ss = 11).
- Visual Search and Attention: Coding (ss = 8), Symbol Search (ss = 9), and TMT-A (25 seconds), wnl.

Executive Functions

Although many aspects of executive functioning were within normal limits, she demonstrated mildly inefficient problem solving and hypothesis testing.

- Simple, timed cognitive flexibility: TMT-B (50 seconds), wnl.
- Controlled behavioral inhibition: SCWT, wnl (CW T = 53).
- Cognitive flexibility, novel problem solving, and hypothesis testing: WCST-64, below expectations for this patient (two categories); error pattern suggested inefficient problem solving and use of feedback to modify responding.
- Verbal abstract reasoning: Similarities, wnl (ss = 11).
- Visual analogical reasoning: Matrix Reasoning, strong (ss = 16).
- Behavioral initiation and fluency: Verbal fluency (FAS raw = 45), wnl. Nonverbal fluency, wnl ($z = -0.6$).

Motor

No gross impairments detected.

- Dominant left hand: low average (66 seconds).
- Nondominant right hand: wnl (67 seconds).

Language Functions

While many areas of language functioning were within normal limits, Ms. XXXX demonstrated a weakness in aspects of word retrieval.

- Auditory comprehension: Able to respond appropriately to interview questions and follow test instructions without difficulty.
- Expressive vocabulary: Vocabulary, wnl (ss = 10).
- Fund of verbal semantic knowledge: Information, wnl (ss = 11).
- Visual confrontation naming: BNT, impaired (47/60).
- Verbal fluency: Animals (raw = 16), below expectations; FAS (raw = 45), wnl.

Visuospatial Functions

No deficits detected.

- Mental integration of visual stimuli: Visual Puzzles, wnl (ss = 12).
- Block construction: Block Design, wnl (ss = 11).
- Line drawing construction: Paper-and-pencil construction of a complex figure was wnl (35/36). Organized approach; figure contained all elements.

Learning and Memory

Although there were no gross deficits, there was a general pattern of stronger nonverbal memory than verbal memory ability. She particularly struggled with recalling more complex verbal information that was provided after a single learning trial.

Verbal

- Noncontextual: AVLT Total, low average ($z = -0.9$); Trial VIII, wnl (12/15); intact recognition (15 hits; 0 FPs).
- Contextual: Story IR, low average (ss = 6); story DR, low average (ss = 7); intact recognition (25/30). When compared to a more similar demographic peer group, performance was below expectations (LMI and LMII DemT = 35).

Nonverbal

- Passive learning of progressively more complex figures: VR I, wnl (ss = 11); VR II, wnl (ss = 10). Recognized 7/7 designs.
- Active learning: Complex figure delayed recall, wnl (18/36). Perseveration of features.

Mood/Self-Report

Significant affective distress was denied on self-report measures.

- Depression: Minimal symptoms (BDI-II = 6).
- Anxiety: Mild (BAI = 8).
- MMPI-2-RF.
    - Validity: Profile is considered valid.
    - Clinical: No clinically significant elevations.

Summary and Formulation

XXXX is a 28-year-old left-handed female with a history of medically refractory epilepsy who was referred for neuropsychological testing as part of a comprehensive presurgical work-up. General cognitive ability is well within normal limits, and there is no evidence of decline from premorbid estimates. No deficits were detected in the domains of attention, processing speed, motor functioning, or visuospatial skills. Although many aspects of executive functioning, language functioning, and memory were within normal limits, she demonstrated mildly inefficient problem solving and hypothesis testing, weaknesses in word retrieval, and inefficiency in new learning of verbal information. There is no evidence of a mood disorder at this time.

In conclusion, the cognitive profile is mildly localizing and lateralizing as there are elements that suggest relative left temporal involvement. That said, there were features seen during testing that suggested mild frontal systems disruption as well.

Although Ms. XXXX lives alone, she has arranged to have her mother stay with her for a week or two after surgery to help her and provide support in the immediate postacute period. She seems to have a good understanding of and appropriate expectations for the surgery. Taken together with her current asymptomatic mood profile, there are no obvious psychological risk factors for a poor outcome or need for presurgical mental health intervention.

CHAPTER 9

Evaluation for Treatment Planning in Rehabilitation

Kirk J. Stucky
Thomas J. Gola

Neuropsychologists frequently work in rehabilitation settings or offer consultation services for patients who are in need of rehabilitation services. Clinicians who work in these settings must have wide-ranging skills that allow them to provide services to patients with various conditions and at all levels of functioning from mild to profoundly impaired. It should be noted that rehabilitation psychology is a unique specialty with its own set of competencies and a separate board certification process (Hibbard & Cox, 2010). Consequently, not all neuropsychologists are adequately trained to provide services in rehabilitation settings. That said, many neuropsychologists are exposed to rehabilitation during internship and or postdoctoral residency and thus obtain cross training in both clinical neuropsychology and rehabilitation psychology. We maintain that in order to provide competent neuropsychological services in the rehabilitation setting, psychologists should have a thorough understanding of the core principles and competencies in both specialties.

The rehabilitation team typically consists of a physiatrist, nursing staff, therapy staff, social workers, and psychologists. In more integrated settings, the patient and family are also viewed as important team members. Ideally, the neuropsychologist functions as a *behavioral system engineer*, where incorporation of various factors impacting patient outcomes (e.g., neurological condition, neurobehavioral status, therapy/nursing teaching style, patient learning competencies, patient support systems and resources) are considered and effective intervention strategies are recommended to assist patients in meeting meaningful functional goals that maximize quality of life, community access, and social participation (Bennett, 2001; Butt & Caplan, 2010). In the following sections we discuss general rehabilitation report-writing recommendations. The chapter closes with a component analysis of the outpatient report and a sample report.

STANDARD REHABILITATION REPORT-WRITING RECOMMENDATIONS

Writing to the Audience

Readers of rehabilitation-oriented neuropsychological reports are interested in a report that offers information pertaining to the patient's current functional status and methods/recommendations to assist in restoring functional abilities. Consequently, most readers are disinterested in lengthy listings of specific test scores or detailed explanations of neuropathology and neuroanatomical systems. In contrast, information regarding specific functional goals and respective treatment strategies is most desired. There are various resources designed to assist in translating neuropsychological findings into lay terms (Postal &Armstrong, 2013). Furthermore, reports should avoid the use of terms primarily familiar to rehabilitation staff. For example, rather than describing the patient as requiring "moderate assistance for personal ADLs," the author might state, "When getting dressed and performing her morning routine, the patient requires assistance and redirection approximately 50% of the time secondary to her tendency to become distracted easily and/or forget what she is doing."

Goal Clarification and Concise Summarization

The report should facilitate the rehabilitation process by means of goal clarification. To do this, the report must provide insight into the "big picture" and where treatment energies should be directed. Thus, the report should include a summarization of the current team goals and how they complement or contrast with patient and family goals. For example:

```
Mrs. Jones is a 59-year-old female who sustained a large
stroke in the right MCA territory 1 year ago. The patient
and family were hopeful that she could return to driving
because she has become depressed and socially isolated.
In this evaluation she produced a panel of results marked
by moderate to severe visuospatial deficits, hemispatial
inattention, and left hemiparesis. Thus, there is a rela-
tively low probability that she will be able to return
```

to driving. Consequently, the family and treatment team should investigate and implement alternatives that will meet her transportation and socialization needs. Furthermore, psychotherapy may help the patient come to terms with her functional limitations, which will likely be persistent and continue to affect many of her day to day activities.

Focus on Function

Whether writing a report or directly communicating evaluation results to the team, one of the neuropsychologist's principal roles is to develop treatment strategies that the team can use to maximize rehabilitation outcomes based on the patient's unique composite of cognitive strengths and weaknesses, along with any behavioral or emotional barriers. Neuropsychologists must expand their focus from descriptions of brain–behavior relationships and differential diagnosis to practical application of assessment findings and creative problem solving. Rehabilitation-oriented evaluations are less about diagnosing a problem and more about how to address the problem(s).

Example 1: Focus on Function

LESS DESIRABLE

Objective neuropsychological assessment results indicate Mr. Smith is experiencing moderate to severe impairments in speed of information processing, memory acquisition, and retrieval. He also has very poor frustration tolerance, clear signs of executive dysfunction, and neurobehavioral disinhibition. These features strongly suggest diffuse injury affecting frontal and temporal lobe systems and are consistent with the consequences of his bacterial meningitis and subsequent development of sepsis. The patient meets criteria for major neurocognitive disorder due to bacterial meningitis.

MORE DESIRABLE

As the result of his bacterial meningitis, Mr. Smith currently has significant difficulty concentrating and retaining new information. He becomes easily frustrated, which at times leads him to refuse treatment or act out impulsively. The treatment team should use the following approaches to encourage optimal rehabilitation outcomes.

1. Treatment should be provided in a setting that minimizes distractions and is relatively quiet.

2. Instructions should be provided in short, clear, and concise statements. Mr. Smith should repeat the information/treatment instruction to ensure he has fully comprehended the instruction before he carries out the request.

3. Consider breaking the therapeutic task into component procedures and practice the first component until Mr. Smith performs it accurately before introducing the next component. This procedure uses an error-free shaping process.

4. Use compensatory techniques for poor learning and memory skills. A written chart of steps to perform in therapeutic tasks should be used. Additionally, maximize recognition skills by asking Mr. Smith to identify correct therapy task steps from multichoice cues. Also be sure that instructions and procedures are highly consistent between sessions to capitalize on procedural learning.

5. The pace of instructions should be slowed and given at a frequency of one instruction per 30-second interval. Allow Mr. Smith adequate time to respond and do not attempt to "speed up" the process by prompting for a quicker response. Keeping the pace of demands to this frequency will minimize displays of frustration and the possible inadvertent shaping of escape/avoidance response.

6. Begin and end therapy sessions with performance of tasks Mr. Smith is very capable of performing and introduce tasks that are more challenging in the middle of the session. This will serve to ensure that Mr. Smith positively anticipates his therapy sessions and his participation is reinforced by successful performance.

7. Staff should offer choices regarding what activity he chooses to perform first. This will allow him to be an active participant in the treatment process and promote a sense of autonomy.

8. Staff should also use highly probable activities (i.e., rest) to reinforce engagement in low-probability activities (i.e., walking 50 feet). Over treatment sessions, the duration/frequency/amount of engagement in the low-probability activity can be gradually increased.

9. Lastly, staff should consider using momentum schedules (e.g., starting with small, highly probable activity

and gradually increase demands to engage Mr. Smith in the
therapeutic activity).

The less desirable example provides information that the treatment
team is most likely well aware of, whereas the more desirable example outlines specific ways to address the cognitive, behavioral, and emotional deficiencies identified by the neuropsychological examination. When reports
are written without a focus on observable behavior and function, consumers often complain that they do not fully understand the report or cannot
easily apply the findings to their work with the patient.

It should be noted that neuropsychological measures were not designed
to directly measure specific functional abilities, and ecological validity has
often been called into question (Chaytor & Schmitter-Edgecombe, 2003).
Nonetheless, our reports seek to apply test findings to aid with treatment
planning, development of meaningful functional goals, and prediction of
outcome. The neuropsychologist should be familiar with tests shown to
correlate with or predict specific functional abilities, but should also ensure
that they do not overstate the meaning of test results.

Report Length

In concert with the above factors, the rehabilitation-oriented neuropsychological report should be specific and concise. Emphasis should be placed
on interpreting the test data for the purpose of defining functional implications and treatment strategies (Donders, 1999). Inpatient reports are
generally briefer (one to two pages in length) relative to more traditional
outpatient reports and should largely focus on treatment strategies and recommendations. Although a brief summary of the history and test results is
commonly provided, the bulk of the inpatient report focuses on integration
of the findings and recommendations. Additionally, inpatient reports are
often more narrowly focused on specific issues such as the determination
of decision-making capacity, the need for supervision, triage, and disposi-
tion planning, and, most importantly, ways to address specific barriers to
functional recovery or address strategies to facilitate recovery. For example:

Ms. Blue has a transcortical motor aphasia, and she was
unable to participate in more detailed bedside assessment. She was able to follow one- and two-step motor commands with 75% accuracy but had difficulty comprehending
more complex instructions. She was able to repeat words
and could sing overlearned songs (e.g., Happy Birthday)
in a limited fashion. As a consequence of aphasia, she
was unable to read or write short sentences. She did not
display apraxia or hemispatial inattention. More detailed

assessment will be considered in the future as improvements occur. Recommendations for her ongoing care have been provided below.

Outpatient reports can vary in length from 2 to 10 pages, depending on the patient's history, number of referral questions, and recommendations. Reports of greater length are likely too wordy and increase the probability of being unread. In community settings, patients are typically further along in their recovery, and more complex goals are often under consideration. Consequently, outpatient-based reports often provide more detailed information because they serve multiple purposes, and respective consumers typically have different needs. For example, the physician may be primarily interested in the summary and recommendations, while a teacher or speech therapist might want to closely review specific test results and behavioral observations. Further still, a vocational specialist might be interested in all of these elements as well as the patient's vocational and academic history.

Timeliness of the Report

Prompt turnaround is the norm in hospital settings. Patients are often experiencing steady or even rapid recovery over the course of a relatively brief length of stay (i.e., 1 to 3 weeks), and the neuropsychologist may only see the patient on a few occasions prior to discharge. Delayed report completion deprives the team of potentially useful information in guiding the treatment plan. Consequently, the inpatient report should be written and placed in the patient's chart within 24 hours. In rare cases, stat or urgent evaluations may be requested and expected within 4 to 12 hours (e.g., urgent determination as to whether a patient can leave the hospital against medical advice or refuse to undergo a potentially lifesaving procedure). Especially in inpatient settings, the advent of electronic medical records and organized templates or "smart text" features greatly facilitates timely report completion.

Outpatient reports rarely need to be finalized within hours or days of the examination. However, clinicians should always ask themselves, "If I was the referral source, caregiver, or patient, how long would I consider it reasonable to wait for the report and feedback?" and "What are the potential consequences if the report is not made available within X amount of time?" With the exception of urgent matters, in outpatient settings, finalization of the report after the completion of testing may feasibly require 1 to 2 weeks. In general, we do not provide the final report to referral sources or place it in the permanent medical record until formal feedback with the patient has occurred, but individual circumstances may allow for exceptions. It is rarely defensible for long delays in report completion (i.e., 2 to

3 months after testing). This is because patients with acute neurological conditions are often experiencing progressive improvements. In these situations, report delays effectively result in outdated recommendations in the context of achieved functional gains. The patient, family, and clinicians who read a delayed report may be disappointed or, worse yet, perceive it as being useless and out of touch with the patient's current needs.

Prognostic Statements

In inpatient settings, neuropsychologists should be very cautious in making broad prognostic statements due to the fact that accurate long-term outcome predictions are inherently challenging in the early stages of recovery. Although severe acquired brain injury can have devastating long-term effects, some individuals go on to have substantial and better than expected functional recovery (Sherer, Sander et al., 2002; Hart et al., 2003; Pastorek, Hannay, & Contant, 2004; Williams et al., 2013). Example 2 provides samples of less and more desirable prognostic statements.

Example 2: Prognostic Statements

LESS DESIRABLE

Ms. P. sustained a severe TBI requiring neurosurgical intervention, and she currently remains in a minimally responsive state. She will require 24-hour supervision and guardianship for the rest of her life. There are no prospects for return to work.

MORE DESIRABLE

Ms. P. is now 3 weeks post-severe TBI and remains in a minimally responsive state. There is a high probability that she will require 24-hour care and a guardian for the next 2 to 3 months. Weekly reassessment to monitor progress will continue.

The more desirable example speaks to the severe nature of the TBI but makes it clear that it is still relatively early postinjury. The summary note also makes some probabilistic statements that are easily defensible and consistent with the known outcome literature (Boake et al., 2001; Bercaw, Hanks, Millis, & Gola, 2011). Unlike the less desirable statement, the more desirable example does not make long-reaching predictions that the neuropsychologist cannot possibly know with a reasonable degree of scientific certainty.

Outpatient reports commonly address multiple issues and often contain broader prognostic statements when the recovery trajectory has plateaued, and the patient, caregivers, and treatment team are primarily focused on long-term planning. Fortunately, neuropsychological measures have been shown to have predictive value with regard to various functional concerns, including employment outcome, driving status, and supervision (Sherer, Novack, et al., 2002; Coleman et al., 2002; Vilkki et al., 2004). Additionally, it is often quite defensible and necessary to make long-term or broad predictions once neurorecovery has plateaued (Miller & Donders, 2003; Bryer, Rapport, & Hanks, 2006; Hanks et al., 2008). For example, a patient who displays moderate to severe executive dysfunction 2 years following an anterior communicating artery aneurysm rupture is unlikely to experience significant cognitive improvements but still might benefit from certain services. In situations like this, a helpful report would likely provide more long-term prognostic statements intended to help guide decision making and increase the patient's access to necessary services or benefits (e.g., long-term disability, supervision, and maintenance programs).

OUTPATIENT REPORT COMMENTARY AND COMPONENT ANALYSIS

There can be considerable variability in the format of outpatient neuropsychological evaluations, but certain central features are critical to a well-written rehabilitation-oriented report. In the following pages, we provide a brief discussion of each section in an outpatient report and highlight critical components. We do not repeat the standard recommendations for neuropsychological report writing outlined in Donders and Strong, Chapter 1, this volume, but instead refer the reader back to them, as they are certainly applicable to rehabilitation-oriented reports. Finally, a sample outpatient report is provided for consideration.

Identifying Information

Basic demographic and identifying information should be listed at the beginning of the report to give the reader quick access to core characteristics of interest, such as date of birth, handedness, level of education, and employment status. We also list the referral source and dates of evaluation.

Reason for Referral

Although specific referral questions can be nuanced and unique to the patient, the primary purposes of assessment with rehabilitation patients can be separated into five major categories:

- Suggesting treatment for rehabilitation-relevant problems.
- Identifying and suggesting realistic goals for community reentry.
- Identifying barriers to functional recovery and ways to address them.
- Measuring progress during recovery to assist in revising or updating goals.
- Determining the need for additional services.

In order to define the specific goals of the evaluation, the neuropsychologist often has to talk directly with referral sources to identify the primary referral questions, barriers to functional recovery, and other pressing issues. Typically, the reason for referral can be provided in two to three sentences. We also make a point of describing what the evaluation will be used for (e.g., vocational planning, school reentry, etc.). Sometimes the needs of the referral source and the patient/family goals are not the same. When this is the case, we list both sets of goals. For example:

> Mr. Daniels is a 44-year-old, right-hand-dominant, married white male referred for neuropsychological evaluation approximately 2 years after he sustained polytrauma and a severe traumatic brain injury. His physician requested assistance in treatment planning. The patient and his wife were interested in obtaining recommendations to improve his mood and participation in community activities.

Medical Records Review

The medical records review is placed before the self-report section in order to provide a concise and accurate summarization of the patient's medical and rehabilitation treatment history. We typically make an effort to highlight critical information that would likely be of interest to physicians and other treatment providers. When patients have had extended hospitalization, multiple injuries, and complications, we prefer to indicate this history in one or two short sentences rather than explain those details in depth. In the case of acute neurological injury, a summarization of injury parameters, length of hospitalization, and any issues impacting recovery is highly recommended. When available, objective data such as neuroradiologic studies and specific pathognomonic findings should also be noted (e.g., aphasia, apraxia, left-hemispatial inattention). This provides readers with a sense of what the patient's medical work-up revealed and how that pertains to their current status. Additionally, the accurate interpretation of neuropsychological test results always requires a complete understanding of injury parameters and medical history. An example of a concise medical history follows.

According to medical records from City Hospital, the
patient developed right-sided weakness and slurred speech
on [date]. Upon ED arrival, he was unable to speak but
remained alert and could follow simple motor commands. A
NIHS score of 11 was assessed. A Head CT revealed an acute
infarct in the left middle cerebral artery territory at
approximately the M2 segment. He was given tPA. Medical history was significant for hypertension, diabetes,
hyperlipidemia, and coronary artery disease. Three days
following admission, he was transferred to the inpatient
rehabilitation unit where he made progressive improvements such as ambulating short distances with a rolling
walker, but he was unable to use his right arm functionally due to ongoing hemiparesis. The patient also developed poststroke depression and was prescribed an antidepressant. He was hospitalized for a total of 26 days.
Afterward, he received outpatient physical, occupational,
and speech therapy.

It is always preferable to review medical records and to avoid primary
reliance on patient or collateral self-report to determine the medical history. However, in cases where formal medical records are not available for
review, we recommend making a qualifying statement such as the following:

Despite requests I did not receive formal medical records
at the time of writing this report. Consequently, the history was primarily based on patient and collateral report.
If alternative or contradictory information becomes available at a later date, the conclusions and recommendations
in this report may be subject to change.

It is important to include such commentary, as self-report can be inaccurate or potentially misleading. It is well known that individuals who
have sustained severe neurological injury often underestimate the severity
of injury or do not remember critical aspects of their rehabilitation. Additionally, the further someone is from their hospitalization, the less accurate
their recollection of specific details may be.

Medications

A separate listing of the patient's current medications is helpful for multiple
reasons. First, some medications can directly or indirectly affect cognition,
mood, or behavior. Second, listed medications often reveal what conditions
are being treated. Third, the patient may no longer be taking medications

prescribed while in the hospital or earlier in the course of rehabilitation. This section of the report can also be used to relay patient and collateral comments regarding perceived medication side effects or effectiveness.

Presenting Complaints

This section summarizes the patient's self-report as concisely as possible. Physical, functional, cognitive, behavioral, and emotional complaints are often discussed in separate paragraphs for organizational purposes. This section also identifies challenges the patient faces in performing daily activities, coping, and accessing resources. The order of the paragraphs can vary depending on the patient's primary complaints.

Collateral Report

Independent interview of family members and caregivers is preferable because they may confirm the patient's self-report or provide markedly different information. Conflicting reports are often found when patients have poor deficit awareness or there are competing agendas and or perceptions. Additionally, even upon direct questioning, patients may not disclose embarrassing aspects of their recovery or behavioral problems such as frequent temper outbursts, poor social skills, or safety issues.

History

Providing a thorough patient history can add significant depth and a more holistic perspective regarding the patient's overall situation. This broad section is broken into multiple parts, including medical/surgical, psychiatric, substance use, birth/developmental, educational, work, social, and functional histories. The length of the history section will be dependent on the individual's unique circumstances. As discussed in Donders and Strong, Chapter 1, this volume, the clinician should only detail information pertinent to the rehabilitation-oriented assessment, as it is unnecessary to provide an exhaustive description of the patient's entire known background. The relevant history may also explain or help the reader understand why the patient is experiencing a more complicated or atypical recovery.

Behavioral Observations

This is a standard section in most neuropsychological evaluations intended to concisely "paint a picture" of the patient. An exhaustive list of benign observations is rarely warranted, but the patient's overall level of participation and response to the testing environment should be discussed. When present, pathognomonic signs may be described here. Additionally, in a rehabilitation setting, it is often important to emphasize whether or not any accommodations were required during testing and whether or not the patient utilized adaptive equipment (e.g., wheelchair, walker, glasses, hearing aids). If the patient had specific physical limitations that impacted testing or standard test administration, these should be noted. Also, if any other factors may have negatively impacted performance such as drowsiness, pain, fatigue, emotional lability, and/or inconsistent test engagement, it should be noted as well. For example:

> Throughout the assessment, Mrs. Smith frequently repositioned herself in the chair and complained of back and neck pain. At times she stood up and walked around the room stating that she needed to stretch. This occasionally occurred during timed tests, which had a negative impact on her overall performance.

The behavioral observations section can also be used to summarize specific observations, which speak to the patient's mood or informative characterological features. This section might include commentary regarding the patient's emotional reaction to tests, such as the following:

> During problem-solving tasks, Ms. T became easily frustrated. Specifically, during a card-sorting task, she pounded her fist on the table, accused the examiner of trying to trick her, and eventually refused to continue despite encouragement.

The patient's awareness of or efforts to correct mistakes can also be informative. The patient's social skills or lack thereof may also be highlighted, especially if it coincides with known behavioral issues outside of the testing environment. Additionally, it is sometimes advisable to comment regarding how cognitive inefficiencies impacted the patient's ability to complete self-report questionnaires. For example:

> It should be noted that, while filling out written questionnaires, Mr. Q often asked about the meaning of sentences and seemed confused or would forget what the examiner just explained. Consequently, the examiner had to read most questions aloud to him several times before he could select an answer.

Procedures

This is an optional section in the report that contains a list of measures and procedures used in performing the assessment (e.g., clinical exam, specific tests, chart review). This section may be useful for billing or auditing purposes, or for other psychologists who read the report.

Neuropsychological Assessment Results

This section of the report is primarily written for clinicians or educators providing specific services such as cognitive rehabilitation, tutoring, or vocational services. Consequently, more complex terms may be used as long as they are helpful to those who are planning or providing treatment. We often inform patients and families that this is the technical part of the report and that they may not find it as useful as the summary and recommendations section. As much as possible, this section is used to describe the specific test performances and does not provide test interpretations or summative statements. Test scores should never be described as "impaired." We prefer the term "deficient" because multiple factors besides brain dysfunction can result in low test scores. It is our position that the neuropsychologist should wait until the summary section to interpret the test results and generate an opinion as to whether there is objective evidence of cognitive impairment. We have found this practice especially useful in circumstances where a patient earns a number of deficient scores as the result of non-neurological factors such as poor test engagement, low educational attainment, depression, and or premorbid cognitive limitations (e.g., learning disability).

In the test results section, there is no need to exhaustively describe tests and scores with the exception of those scores required by the referral source or those needed for the patient to gain access to certain services (e.g., schools, vocational rehabilitation). In some reports, the results section might also contain observations during specific tests, which would be useful to or enlightening for treatment providers. For example:

> Ms. V clearly displayed left-hemispatial inattention during design copying tasks. On coding and the Trail Making Test she displayed obvious problems with visual scanning. Thus, low scores on these measures were associated with visuospatial impairments as opposed to problems with speed of information processing alone.

Although these are not specific test results, these process-oriented observations add significant meaning to test findings and improve the reader's understanding of the patient's problems. When pathognomonic signs are present, they should be described specifically with regard to how they impacted performance.

The psychological assessment results section typically presents findings from self-report inventories. In rehabilitation, a wide variety of inventories are available to assess pain, adjustment to disability, coping style, and various cognitive and/or physical symptoms. Additionally, self-report measures for patients and collaterals can be summarized in this section (e.g., BRIEF). We strongly recommend inclusion of objective emotional status inventories, although these may not be indicated in all cases, especially for those individuals with severe cognitive impairments or in the early stages of recovery. Instruments such as the MMPI-2-RF or PAI can be helpful because individuals often experience significant injury- and noninjury-related emotional and behavioral issues that can cloud or complicate the clinical picture (e.g., somatization, dependency, symptom magnification). Incomplete or insufficient treatment planning can occur if these complicating factors are missed or not addressed in the report.

Summary

The summary and recommendations are the most critical sections of the report. In the summary section, our goal is to provide a concise page summary that is relevant and useful to all interested parties. We follow the general rule of "integration, not regurgitation," meaning that data from the history, behavioral observations, and test results section are condensed into the most meaningful components and are used to generate a cogent clinical impression. Specific test results or singular observations are not repeated. Instead, the summary describes the individual's current cognitive and emotional status in clear language, which in turn supports the specific diagnostic impression(s) and recommendations. It is important to stress that well-written reports identify the emotional and behavioral effects of the neurological condition versus adjustment-related factors. This may be one of neuropsychology's most unique contributions to the patient's overall care and treatment planning, considering that other clinicians are also likely assessing cognition in some fashion. A common format for our summary section includes:

- Three to four sentences introducing the patient, the presenting complaints, and primary referral questions.
- A short paragraph describing the patient's neurocognitive status.
- A short paragraph describing the patient's emotional/behavioral status and pertinent family/psychosocial issues.
- If necessary, a final paragraph that contains prognostic statements or emphasizes urgent needs.

At the end of the summary, we list appropriate diagnosis(es), both medical and psychological, in the order of importance. Neurocognitive and psychological diagnoses are often related to the medical condition when deemed appropriate (e.g., major neurocognitive disorder due to hemorrhagic stroke). It is also sometimes advisable to list other descriptive terms or language that do not specifically fit the *International Statistical Classification of Diseases and Related Health Problems* (ICD), or *Diagnostic and Statistical Manual of Mental Disorders* (DSM) format such as:

- Response bias and suboptimal test engagement.
- Normal emotional adjustment issues due to X medical condition.
- Psychological factors affecting medical condition and response to treatment.

For example:

> Mr. W is a 61-year-old, right-hand-dominant, married male who returned for neuropsychological evaluation. The patient sustained a right-hemisphere stroke [date] and went through a course of inpatient and outpatient rehabilitation. At the time of this assessment, he was interested in returning to driving.
>
> Neuropsychologically, he produced a panel of results marked by improved attention and concentration relative to the previous assessment. His verbal and visual memory was average. He continued to display impairments in spatial perception and visuospatial analysis, although overall performance was improved. At times he was somewhat inattentive, but his overall scores on measures of speed of information processing primarily fell within the average range. Some inefficiency in visual scanning was still noticeable, but there was no longer evidence of left-hemispatial inattention. Individuals with this pattern of cognitive impairment often have difficulty driving safely, but some individuals have been able to learn compensatory strategies and can drive safely in restricted or limited environments. Restoration of driving privileges should be based on the results of a driver's evaluation.
>
> Psychologically, Mr. W reported sadness, feeling bored and guilty. He admitted to suicidal thoughts but denied any plan or intent to act upon them. He also complained of reduced energy, fatigue, and irritability. He and his wife did attend marriage counseling but unfortunately did not find it very helpful. He was involved in some volunteer work and also plays golf one-handed. He will go to the bar and have a coke with his friends. The patient admitted that he sometimes misses drinking alcohol. He was trying to quit smoking. Although he has contact with

some friends, apparently family members have been
somewhat unreliable in providing him with transportation.
Recommendations for his ongoing care are listed and discussed below.

Diagnoses:

    Neurocognitive disorder due to right-hemisphere stroke
    Adjustment disorder with depressed mood

In the rehabilitation setting, it is not unusual to make some changes in the final report, depending on information obtained during the feedback session. For example, additional or contradictory information might surface, or the neuropsychologist may recognize that a specific recommendation is not practical or is no longer necessary. In these instances, prior to inclusion in the permanent medical record, the report should be modified to ensure that the final version is accurate, useful, and up to date. An example of a concise summary with recommendations can be found in Appendix 9.1 (pp. 250–252).

Recommendations

A well-written report translates findings and outlines practical ways to accomplish short- and long-term goals. We have found that most consumers appreciate recommendations that are clear, give specific direction, work within the patient's available resources, and can be readily added to the existing treatment plan. The neuropsychologist must think broadly and holistically about the patient needs and unique circumstances. In addition to addressing cognitive and emotional issues, rehabilitation-oriented reports should also offer suggestions and insights regarding other barriers to functional recovery such as pain, sleep disturbance, environmental factors, and psychosocial issues. In doing so, the report can provide the team, family, and patient with perspective regarding overarching themes and goals, ideally leading to more coordinated care.

To write good rehabilitation-oriented recommendations, neuropsychologists must be familiar with a broad range of evidence-based treatment literature, including the practical application of learning theory, behavioral management and modification, cognitive rehabilitation/remediation, nonpharmacological pain management, various psychotherapeutic interventions, stages of change, family systems, and behavioral activation. The clinician who knows how to apply these interventions is able to determine which ones will be most effective, when they should be delivered, and by whom. Thus, good recommendations tap the psychologist's broad knowledge, not just his or her understanding of brain–behavior relationships. Recommendations should strive to provide specific instructions or a prescribed recipe of care that details how therapy, nursing, or caretaking interventions should be taught or delivered. There are numerous resources outlining evidence-based treatment approaches that are helpful in this regard (Klonoff, 2010; Johnstone & Stonnington, 2001; Matthies, Kreutzer, & West, 1997; Sohlberg & Mateer, 2001).

We have generally found that it is best to provide specific recommendations in an independent section after the summary. We routinely list recommendations in the order of importance. For example, if pain management and problems with mood are the primary concern, we discuss recommendations regarding these issues first even if there are also significant cognitive impairments. Below we provide a list of common questions asked by referral sources and specific examples of rehabilitation-relevant recommendations separated into broad categories.

Treatment Justification

Psychologists often recommend but fail to provide justification for services and treatments. An accurate description of a patient's rehabilitation needs can act as a definitive document that justifies current and future rehabilitation services. Reports may also serve to discontinue or refocus treatment, as rehabilitation services that continue indefinitely with no meaningful change in function are not defensible. Exceptions to this rule are maintenance therapies, which are often less intense and intended to help an individual maintain therapeutic gains (e.g., range of motion, home exercise program).

Safety, Supervision, and Care Needs

What level of supervision is required and why? When does the patient require this supervision, and are the supervision needs different in different environments? Are there immediate issues of concern that warrant placement in a more supervised living situation (e.g., residential treatment program, behavioral unit)? What level of attendant care for cognitive and/or emotional concerns are required and why? Are specific replacement services required and why? Do caregivers need access to respite care? Examples of how one might address some of these questions are as follows:

```
Mr. X no longer requires 24-hour supervision. Based on
current test results, he should be capable of performing
advanced activities of daily living without significant
concern for safety. The residential treatment team should
```

begin the process of transitioning the patient to his
home with plans for outpatient therapy as needed.

Or

Mrs. Y was often unable to solve new problems or change
her behavior when it was clear a strategy did not work.
Her degree of impulsivity made it apparent that she continues to require direct supervision and a highly structured daily routine. A responsible adult should know where
she is and what she is doing at all times.

Rehabilitation Services

Does the patient require cognitive rehabilitation? What specific compensatory cognitive strategies and empirically based remediation activities
should be implemented? Is a home evaluation needed? Is a community-
based evaluation or approach necessary to address issues such as school
reentry, return to work, or driving? If the patient is ready for return to
work, does he require a functional capacity evaluation, job coaching, and/
or workplace accommodations? Examples of how one might address some
of these questions follow:

Mr. X should be using memory strategies such as task
lists, calendars, alarms, and other reminder systems. His
memory book should contain a detailed list of his functional goals and what he needs to accomplish in order to
graduate from the residential program and return home.
Time-limited cognitive rehabilitation should occur in the
home and community to promote generalization of these
skills to his everyday tasks and routine. I am hopeful
that this can be accomplished in 2 to 3 months through
his current program.

Or

Mrs. Y would benefit from reinitiating vocational interventions. She will likely remain unable to maintain a
full-time schedule, but she may be capable of performing some part-time work. Jobs should not require regular reading or high-speed performance. She could learn
and remember routines, but most likely would initially
require a job coach and monitoring. Jobs that require a
great deal of flexible thinking or stressful customer
interactions would not be a good match for her. She would

likely struggle in jobs that require advanced social skills or customer service. She could probably perform a job that was structured with very specific tasks and a checklist of duties. She does appear to have some problems with left-hand grip strength and psychomotor speed, which should also be taken into account during vocational assessment. Essentially, Mrs. Y will most likely perform best in an environment that is structured, has a steady pace, and does not require strong visual or reading skills.

Nonrehabilitation Services

What school reentry services, educational interventions, and/or specific accommodations should be implemented? Does the patient require pain management services or substance abuse treatment? Are psychological and/or psychiatric services indicated? Is there a need for additional consultations with other professionals, such as physical medicine and rehabilitation, neurology, or other pertinent disciplines? Here is an example of how one might address some of these questions:

He would benefit from outpatient psychotherapy with a psychologist familiar with post-TBI adjustment issues, cognitive rehabilitation, and community reentry. Ideally, this psychologist would work collaboratively with the patient, his wife, and the team to maximize functional recovery/ quality of life. Psychotherapy should focus on multiple issues, including:

- Helping him to accept some of his physical changes and consider using adaptive devices to compensate.
- Improving self-confidence and positive self-talk statements in the context of increased community/social activity.
- Encouraging exploration of community and/or volunteer activities that would give him a sense of purpose, meaning, and accomplishment.

Adaptive Equipment and Environmental Modification

A central principle in rehabilitation is that environmental factors interact with the person's deficiencies or condition to produce disability and/or limits to social participation. Does the patient need an assessment for specific equipment needs or adaptive strategies? Are modifications in the patient's home or community environment necessary to meet the patient's unique needs and limit the barriers to participation? When appropriate, the neuropsychological report should contain recommendations for altering conditions to allow for a more accommodating environment. For example, a patient with processing speed difficulties may be able to perform previous secretarial work skills accurately and reliably if the pace of work is reduced. Obviously, in some settings this type of accommodation might be possible, while in others it would not be feasible. A helpful conceptualization when writing neuropsychological reports is that barriers to functional recovery often involve a mismatch or conflict between the person's cognitive abilities and the unique environmental demands on that ability. For example:

> Though Ms. Y has mild residual cognitive impairments, I believe that she is capable of slowly phasing back into work as a nurse with several accommodations. First, she would be best suited for nursing assignments in which she can focus on one patient at a time (e.g., home care, private duty nursing). The employer has reportedly indicated that initially Ms. Y would be allowed to start part time and with a reduced patient load, which in my opinion will increase the odds of a smooth transition back to work. Second, by using her current compensatory strategies (e.g., notes, checklists, alarms), she should be able to accurately follow a structured plan of care. Third, an initial monitoring period with a senior nurse supervisor would be helpful. This individual should give Ms. Y feedback regarding her charting accuracy and consistency on the same day in order to facilitate learning. This would allow Ms. Y to further modify or fine tune compensatory strategies in the workplace. I believe that with these accommodations in place Ms. Y. should be able to resume independent nursing duties within 3 to 4 weeks.

Resource Utilization

Health-care disparities are prevalent. Some patients have a wide variety of readily available resources, while others have no income, insurance, social support, or housing. The neuropsychologist should take these realities into consideration when writing recommendations. Reports that recommend expensive treatments or programs that are unavailable in the community are essentially worthless and may give consumers the impression that the psychologist is out of touch with real-world practice. In situations in which patients need a certain type of treatment but there are no funding sources or community services available, the report should indicate this and offer alternative recommendations that might be carried out by family, friends, or other organizations (e.g., church, senior center). In limited-resource situations, rehabilitation-focused reports are also often valued for suggesting creative and novel solutions that are practical and possible, considering the individual's unique resources and level of support. Furthermore, well-worded recommendations can often increase the patient's odds of eventually gaining access to necessary services and represent an opportunity to advocate for services that are in the patient's best interest. It should also be noted that the lack of resources is not a valid reason to avoid making certain recommendations, but the neuropsychologist must remain mindful of those barriers and practical limitations. If there is significant concern that the lack of certain services will result in harmful ramifications or increase the patient's vulnerability to complications, this should be stated as well. Finally, the neuropsychologist must also remember to not suggest treatments that effectively try to advance the patient's skills beyond where they were premorbidly, recognizing that these goals are often unrealistic or impractical.

Scope-of-Practice Limits

Referral sources sometimes ask neuropsychologists to comment on or provide direction with regard to issues that may be outside their scope of practice. For example, physicians may ask if the patient's medications seem appropriate or if other agents warrant consideration. As a consequence of their hospital-based training, neuropsychologists and rehabilitation psychologists often obtain vast and detailed knowledge of various conditions, medications, and medical interventions. The neuropsychologist must be cautious when writing recommendations regarding things outside their scope of practice and ensure that they are not being directive but instead are suggesting or pointing out issues for consideration by other professionals. Example 3 provides sample language to this effect.

EXAMPLE 3: SCOPE-OF-PRACTICE RECOMMENDATIONS

LESS DESIRABLE

Mr. M should undergo a sleep study.

MORE DESIRABLE

I am concerned about Mr. M's reported poor sleep and excessive fatigue. His wife indicated that over the past 6 months he has been snoring much more loudly and at

```
times seems to stop breathing. I verbally informed Dr. Red
regarding this and will defer to her regarding the need
for a sleep study.
```

Note that the more desirable recommendation is designed to bring an important issue to the physician's attention and not direct or dictate medical care. Recommendations regarding concerns outside the neuropsychologist's scope or practice should ultimately defer to the physician's judgment regarding the need for a specific medical work-up or intervention.

Repeated Evaluation

A recommendation in the report for repeated evaluation may be perceived as self-serving. Neuropsychological reevaluation may or may not be warranted, depending on the patient's specific needs and circumstances. We generally advise against standard or automatic reevaluation dates in rehabilitation settings, preferring to conduct reassessment before or during functionally relevant transitions in the interest of answering specific questions. If, for example, at 6 months postassessment the patient has not made significant progress or shown response to treatment, there may not be a justifiable reason for reevaluation. Conversely, reassessment might be helpful in the same case if clinicians raise specific concerns regarding the development of complicating variables that the neuropsychologist is uniquely qualified to evaluate (e.g., depression, cognitive decline, somatization). We also support repeated neuropsychological evaluation at an earlier date if the patient has made better than expected functional gains and the treatment team is considering return to additional adult responsibilities ahead of the original anticipated schedule (e.g., transitioning into the community, work, or school). If repeated evaluation is recommended, the reason should be clearly stated and defensible. For example:

```
Older individuals with a history of severe TBI are at
increased risk for cognitive decline later in life.
Repeated neuropsychological reevaluation for comparison
purposes should be considered if changes in functional
abilities occur in the future.
```

SUMMARY

Rehabilitation-oriented neuropsychologists aspire to provide a unique perspective to the rehabilitation process by incorporating knowledge regarding the consequences of brain pathology and associated functional outcomes (Novack, Sherer, & Penna, 2010). A well-written report serves to define a treatment approach where deficiencies may be targeted for intervention, but also identifies how to instruct/teach the patient in ways that capitalize on the patient's remaining abilities. Neuropsychologists must be skilled in the application of evidence-based treatments to address the cognitive, emotional, and behavioral consequences of brain pathology. They must also be knowledgeable regarding the methods used by other members of the rehabilitation team to achieve outcomes and, most importantly, possess effective communication skills. A well-written neuropsychological report reflects all of these qualities and ultimately makes a meaningful contribution to the patient's overall plan of care. A sample neuropsychological report that illustrates these qualities has been provided in Appendix 9.1 (pp. 244–252).

REFERENCES

Bennett, T. L. (2001). Neuropsychological evaluation in rehabilitation planning and evaluation of functional skills. *Archives of Physical Medicine and Rehabilitation, 16*, 237–253.

Bercaw, E. L., Hanks, R. A., Millis, S. R., & Gola, T. J. (2011). Changes in neuropsychological performance after traumatic brain injury from inpatient rehabilitation to 1-year follow-up in predicting 2-year functional outcomes. *The Clinical Neuropsychologist, 25*, 72–89.

Boake, C., Millis, S. R., High, W. M., Jr., Delmonico, R. L., Kreutzer, J. S., Rosenthal, M., et al. (2001). Using early neuropsychologic testing to predict long-term productivity outcome from traumatic brain injury. *Archives of Physical Medicine and Rehabilitation, 82*, 761–768.

Bryer, R. C., Rapport, L. J., & Hanks, R. A. (2006). Determining fitness to drive: Neuropsychological and psychological considerations. In J. M. Pellerito Jr. (Ed.), *Driver rehabilitation and community mobility principles and practice* (pp. 165–184). St. Louis, MO: Mosby.

Butt, L., & Caplan, B. (2010). The rehabilitation team. In R. G. Frank, M. Rosenthal, & B. Caplan (Eds.), *Handbook of rehabilitation psychology* (2nd ed., pp. 451–457). Washington, DC: American Psychological Association.

Chaytor, N., & Schmitter-Edgecombe, M. (2003). The ecological validity of neuropsychological tests: A review of the literature on everyday cognitive skills. *Neuropsychology Review, 13*, 181–187.

Coleman, R. D., Rapport, L. J., Ergh. T. C., Hanks, R. A., Ricker, J. H., & Millis, S. R. (2002). Predictors of driving outcome after traumatic brain injury. *Archives of Physical Medicine and Rehabilitation, 83*, 1415–1422.

Donders, J. (1999). Pediatric neuropsychology reports: Do they really have to be so long? *Child Neuropsychology, 5*, 70–78.

Hanks, R. A., Millis, S. R., Ricker, J. H., Giacino, J. T., Nakese-Richardson, R., Frol, A. B., et al. (2008). The predictive validity of a brief inpatient neuropsychological battery for persons with traumatic brain injury. *Archives of Physical Medicine and Rehabilitation, 89*, 950–957.

Hart, T., Millis, S., Novack, T., Englander, J., Fidler-Shephard, R., & Bell, K. R. (2003). The relationship of neuropsychologic function and level of caregiver supervision at 1 year after traumatic brain injury. *Archives of Physical Medicine and Rehabilitation, 84,* 221–230.

Hibbard, M. R., & Cox, D. R. (2010). Competencies of a rehabilitation psychologist. In R. G. Frank, M. Rosenthal, & B. Caplan (Eds.), *Handbook of rehabilitation psychology* (2nd ed., pp. 467–476). Washington, DC: American Psychological Association.

Johnstone, B., & Stonnington, H. H. (Eds.). (2001). *Rehabilitation of neuropsychological disorders: A practical guide for rehabilitation professionals.* Lillington, NC: Psychology Press.

Klonoff, P. S. (2010). *Psychotherapy after brain injury: Principles and techniques.* New York: Guilford Press.

Matthies, B. K., Kreutzer, J. S., & West, D. D. (1997). *The behavior management handbook. A practical approach to patients with neurological disorders.* San Antonio, TX:Therapy Skill Builders.

Miller, L. J., & Donders, J. (2003). Prediction of educational outcome after pediatric traumatic brain injury. *Rehabilitation Psychology, 48,* 237–241.

Novack, T. A., Sherer, M., & Penna, S. (2010). Neuropsychological practice in rehabilitation. In R. G. Frank, M. Rosenthal, & B. Caplan (Eds.), *Handbook of rehabilitation psychology* (2nd ed., pp. 165–178). Washington, DC: American Psychological Association.

Pastorek, N. J., Hannay, H. J., & Contant, C. S. (2004). Prediction of global outcome with acute neuropsychological testing following closed-head injury. *Journal of the International Neuropsychological Society, 10,* 807–817.

Postal, K., & Armstrong, K (2013). *Feedback that sticks.* New York: Oxford University Press.

Sherer, M., Novack, T. A., Sander, A. M., Struchen, M. A., Alderson, A., & Thompson, R. N. (2002). Neuropsychological assessment and employment outcome after traumatic brain injury: A review. *The Clinical Neuropsychologist, 16,* 157–178.

Sherer, M., Sander, A. M., Nick, T. G., High, W. M., Jr., Malec, J. F., & Rosenthal, M. (2002). Early cognitive status and productivity outcome following traumatic brain injury: Findings from the TBI Model Systems. *Archives of Physical Medicine and Rehabilitation, 83,* 183–192.

Sohlberg, M. M., & Mateer, C. A. (2001). *Cognitive rehabilitation: An integrative neuropsychological approach.* New York: Guilford Press.

Vilkki, J. S., Uvela, S., Siironen, J., Ilvonen, T., Varis, J., & Porras, M. (2004). Relationship of local infarctions to cognitive and psychosocial impairments after aneurismal subarachnoid hemorrhage. *Neurosurgery, 55,* 790–803.

Williams, M. W., Rapport, L. J., Hanks, R. A., Millis, S. R., & Greene, H. A. (2013). Incremental validity of neuropsychological evaluations to computed tomography in predicting long-term outcomes after traumatic brain injury, *The Clinical Neuropsychologist, 27*(3), 356–375.

Sample Outpatient Neuropsychological Report

Please note: All identifying data in this report have been modified. Some aspects of the history are fictionalized in order to protect patient confidentiality. The test results, summary, and recommendations sections from the report remain in their original form.

Patient name: Catherine Blue	*Education*:	Bachelor of Arts
Age: 41	*Handedness*: Right
Date of birth: xx	*Gender*: Female
Referred by: xx	*Glasses*: Yes, near sightedness
Evaluated by: xx	*Hearing aids*: None
Dates of evaluation: xx	*Ambulation aids*: None
Location: xx		

Note: This report was written with the assistance of voice recognition software, which may have resulted in minor typographical errors.

Reason for Referral and History

Ms. Blue is a 41-year-old, divorced Caucasian female referred for neuropsychological evaluation after her discharge from the hospital. This assessment occurred approximately 3 months following severe TBI and was requested to assist in treatment planning, determine her need for ongoing supervision and her overall decision-making capacity.

According to available medical records, the patient's son found her unconscious at the bottom of her basement steps on [date]. It was suspected that she tripped and fell while carrying a laundry basket. It was believed that she might have been found several days following the fall, but the length of time since injury was not clear. EMS reported agonal respirations on the scene. She was taken to City Medical Center where workup revealed multiple facial fractures, respiratory failure, and pneumonia. A CT scan of the head revealed a left temporal lobe contusion, right temporal lobe epidural bleed, and high posterior subdural hematoma. Her Glasgow Coma Scale was 6. She required intubation. The neuropsychology service first evaluated Ms. Blue 2 days after admission, but she was sedated and unable to follow basic motor commands. Fortunately, she progressively improved. Serial testing with the orientation log indicated that the length of posttraumatic amnesia was approximately 23 days. Orientation testing was challenging secondary to the patient's expressive aphasia. She was prone to circum-locution and making numerous paraphasic errors, neologisms, and perseverative errors. A neuropsychological evaluation was conducted on [date] while she was on the inpatient brain injury rehabilitation unit. At that time, she displayed expressive aphasia and moderate to severe cognitive impairments. I recommended pursuit of guardianship and conservatorship. I also recommended outpatient brain injury rehabilitation and 24-hour supervision at the time of discharge [date].

Self-Report

At the time of this assessment, Ms. Blue was somewhat anxious and periodically tearful. She had no memory of the week before the fall injury, stating she only remembered the last 3 days of hospitalization. She identified that she was still having cognitive issues, especially when she felt under pressure or anxious. She was nervous about testing and concerned about what it might show.

Ms. Blue recently completed physical therapy. She reported some issues with increased heart rate after discharge from the hospital, but said her blood pressure was normal at her last PCP appointment. She stated that her PCP did not believe she needed to be on a blood pressure medication. She was exercising 2 to 3 days a week and lost 10 pounds since her discharge from the hospital. Ms. Blue is not following a formal physician-approved exercise program. Currently, her back pain comes and goes. She reported occasional balance issues when she initially gets up or tries to move too fast. She felt that she was sleeping relatively well. She took Trazodone until being weaned off by her PCP. She denied any changes in smell or taste.

Emotionally, Ms. Blue said she has experienced difficulty adjusting to her postinjury lifestyle. She was discharged home with supervision provided by her mother. Her 19-year-old son has also stayed with her to provide recommended supervision and assistance. She was grateful that people were looking out for her, but at the same time reported that it was stressful to be around family more often. She felt like people were disappointed in her or thought less of her. She said that sometimes her family did not appear to understand that she had a "bad head injury," and occasionally she did not like to think of herself in this way either. She occasionally has disagreements with her mother, which causes some stress. Ms. Blue was notably tearful and apologetic in describing her relationship with her mother. She reported a past history of some anxiety but denied ever receiving formal treatment.

Cognitively, Ms. Blue reported ongoing trouble "organizing my memories and thoughts." She described trouble concentrating and occasional difficulty expressing herself. In conversation, she periodically started a statement, then stopped herself and apologized before she started again. She was rather cautious in talking and voiced concern about the examiner's perception of her. She was receiving outpatient occupational and speech therapy, with goals of improving her thinking skills. She has been reading a lot and trying to look over her school lesson plans. She hoped to return to work in a few months, but knew that she was not ready to go yet. Ms. Blue was concerned about the way her fellow teachers and students might perceive her when she returned to work.

Functionally, Ms. Blue lives in her mother's basement with her son. She is independent in providing for her basic needs and performing basic household chores. She is not working or driving as per our restrictions. Ms. Blue is managing her own finances and reported that she was doing well with this. Since her injury, she has to write everything down or she will forget. She recognized that changes in her memory were significant.

Collateral Report

Ms. Blue's mother and son were also privately interviewed. They indicated that Ms. Blue had improved significantly since her discharge from the hospital, but expressed concern about her level of anxiety and sadness. The mother indicated that Ms. Blue had always been somewhat prone to worry but that lately she seemed much more anxious and tearful. Ms. Blue's son said his mother made occasional careless errors when paying bills. He reported that she would also sometimes misspell or use the wrong word in sentences, which was very unusual considering that she was an English teacher. Both the son and mother denied any safety concerns. They both felt Ms. Blue could be left alone in the home and that she was no longer at risk for falls or impulsive behavior like she had been in the hospital.

Medications

Ritalin 10 mg b.i.d. and Prozac 20 mg. Ms. Blue denied any side effects or concerns with regard to these medications.

Past Medical History

TBI as described above. Prior to injury, Ms. Blue reported a history of headaches that she described as minor. She did have a history of hypertension, which resolved after she lost 130 pounds following gastric bypass surgery in [year]. She was injured in a snow skiing accident when she was younger and underwent two lumbar laminectomies [year, year] secondary to back pain. She also underwent a cholecystectomy in [year].

Substance Use History

Ms. Blue denied any history of alcohol or illicit substance abuse. She does not use tobacco products. She drinks one or two cups of coffee in the morning most days.

Social/Educational/Work History

Ms. Blue earned a Bachelor's degree in education at the age of 27. She indicated that she was a good student overall and she denied any history of learning disability. She has worked as a high school English teacher for 10 years. Previously, she worked as a paraprofessional and waitress for four years before sustaining her back injury. At the time of her injury, Ms. Blue was taking graduate classes for a Master's degree in education. She was tearful, recognizing that most likely she would not be able to restart graduate school in the fall as she had planned. The patient divorced in [year] after eight years of marriage. Her 19-year-old son is from a previous relationship.

Behavioral Observations

Ms. Blue arrived on time for her appointment. She ambulated independently. She was pleasant and cooperative throughout the 6-hour testing session. Vision and hearing were adequate for testing purposes. She laughed spontaneously and impulsively at times. Slight word-finding difficulty was noted during conversation and testing. She often recognized when she spoke a word incorrectly and would pause until she found the correct word. She was self-critical, especially when working on memory tasks, and would sigh and say, "This is my problem." She occasionally needed encouragement due to becoming discouraged with her performance. Although she appeared to understand instructions as they were being read, she would forget portions of what she heard and often asked the examiner to repeat instructions. During conversation, Ms. Blue was slightly tangential or prone to circumlocution and would occasionally give extra details or share information after giving an answer. During this process, it was hard to determine her final answer, and the examiner had to ask clarifying questions. There was also some perseveration observed between her phrases and words used to answer previous questions. She was slow in thinking through problems, and she occasionally gave correct answers after time limits had expired. She also exhibited some indecisiveness and would hesitate to respond, going back and forth in her answer. She ruminated over past tests, and this seemed to interfere with her focusing on listening to instructions carefully after moving on to another task.

Neuropsychological Assessment Test Results

On the MMSE-2, Ms. Blue scored 29/30 possible points and was fully oriented. She performed adequately on formal and embedded measures of test engagement (WMT 100, 100, 100; Reliable DS 9; CVLT-2 recognition 13/16, forced-choice 100%). Thus, her participation in this assessment was deemed to be an adequate representation of her current neurocognitive function.

On achievement measures, Ms. Blue's performances fell within the average range. Her basic reading was average. She was able to solve written math problems accurately and earned an average score. However, when attempting to complete math problems without paper her scores were mildly deficient.

On intellectual tasks, Ms. Blue's subtest scores varied between the average and mildly deficient range. Her lowest index score was in working memory, but this was not significantly different relative to other scores and comparison with the normative sample. Her nonverbal and verbal skills appeared to be equally developed. Index scores fell within the low average to average range, which was considered to be somewhat below premorbid estimates of overall intelligence (WAIS-IV: FSIQ 90; VCI 98; PRI 96; WMI 80; PSI 89).

Ms. Blue completed several nonverbal tasks that required speed of information processing, psychomotor speed, and mental flexibility. On the Trail Making Test, she earned average to low average scores and did not make errors. On other speed of processing tasks, she earned low average to mildly deficient scores. Her basic auditory attention and concentration was average, but on tasks requiring sustained or complex attention her performance was mildly deficient. At times she seemed easily distracted and periodically required repetition of instructions.

Ms. Blue also completed learning and memory tasks. On a story memory task, her performance was moderately deficient. After a 30-minute delay, she recalled very few details, but in a recognition paradigm her performance improved to low average. On a word list-learning task, Ms. Blue was able to learn and retain new information slowly and displayed a low average learning slope. After a 20-minute delay, she recalled 8/16 words and 10/16 when given cues. Within a recognition memory paradigm, she correctly identified 13/16 words but made four recognition errors. These were low average to mildly deficient scores but represented significant improvements relative to the last hospital-based evaluation. It should be noted that subtle persistent word-finding difficulties most likely had a negative impact on her verbal memory performance. On visual memory tests, Ms. Blue displayed low average recall of simple figures after a 30-minute delay but average recognition memory for the same material. Her recall of a complex figure after a 30-minute delay was average. Her recognition of details from the same complex figure was low average. Overall, Ms. Blue was able to learn and retain new information with practice but persistent inefficiencies were apparent.

On tests of visual constructional abilities and organization, there was no evidence of impairment in spatial or form perception. Ms. Blue's copy of a complex figure was organized and accurate. Her performance was average when constructing block designs, and she earned average to high average scores on tasks requiring spatial relations.

On language tasks, there was no evidence of receptive aphasia. On a confrontation-naming task, Ms. Blue displayed mild dysnomia with occasional paraphasic errors. There was a significant improvement in her overall language skills relative to the last hospital-based evaluation.

On sensory-perception tasks, there was no evidence of finger agnosia. Her grip strength and finger tapping speeds were average bilaterally. Psychomotor and fine dexterity speeds were low average in the dominant right hand and average in the left hand. Bilateral motor planning and sequencing was unremarkable.

On tasks tapping executive function and problem-solving abilities, Ms. Blue was able to learn from mistakes but occasionally displayed impulsiveness. On several tasks requiring abstract reasoning, she earned average scores. On a card-sorting task, Ms Blue completed six categories and earned average overall scores. She was able to solve several complex verbal and nonverbal problems at a level generally consistent with her estimated premorbid intelligence, although it is possible that some low average scores were a regression from her baseline functioning. On word list generation tasks, her scores were mildly deficient for both categories and words starting with a specific letter. This may be due in part to mild persistent dysnomia. Overall, she displayed average to low average skills on measures requiring novel problem-solving and cognitive flexibility.

Emotional/Personality Function

On formal self-report inventories, Ms. Blue reported mild to moderate symptoms of anxiety and depression. She admitted to sadness, feeling discouraged, guilt, and crying spells. She denied suicidal thoughts, plan, or intent. She also complained of fatigue and reduced energy. Her ratings also suggested daily nervousness, concern about the future, and reduced overall self-confidence.

Summary

Ms. Blue is a 41-year-old, Caucasian female who sustained a severe traumatic brain injury with a hypoxic component as the result of a fall injury on [date]. She presented with complaints of persistent cognitive impairments and adjustment-related emotional issues. This examination occurred 3 months postinjury and was conducted to determine what level of supervision she required, whether she had the capacity to make her own medical decisions, and if she was ready to begin the process of return to work.

She produced a panel of neuropsychological test results marked by word-finding difficulties (i.e., dysnomia), mild verbal memory impairments, and declines in information-processing speed relative to her estimated premorbid level of functioning. There was a significant improvement in her overall language skills relative to the last hospital-based evaluation. However, it is noted that her dysnomia had a clear impact on verbal memory recall. Additionally, although the patient displayed mild impairments in sustained and divided attention, her problem-solving skills and reasoning abilities were consistently average. This suggests that systems involved with attention, concentration, and memory have been more impacted by the injury than her overall problem-solving skills and planning abilities. This is a positive prognostic sign, and considering that it has only been 3 months since the injury occurred, further improvement is expected with time and treatment.

Psychologically, Ms. Blue reported mild to moderate symptoms of anxiety and depression. She reported sadness, feeling discouraged, reduced self-confidence, and crying spells. She indicated reduced interest in things she used to enjoy but denied more significant symptoms of depression. Ms. Blue also complained of fatigue and reduced energy. All of these symptoms likely represent the combined effects of the TBI and emotional adjustment issues. Recommendations for her ongoing care are listed and discussed below.

Diagnoses

- Neurocognitive disorder due to TBI
- Traumatic brain injury
- Adjustment disorder with depression and anxiety

Recommendations

1. Ms. Blue could benefit from psychotherapy with a psychologist who specializes in the treatment of individuals with neurologic conditions. Psychotherapy should address emotional adjustment issues and help her develop more effective coping strategies (e.g., self-talk, relaxation strategies).

2. Cognitive rehabilitation with speech and occupational therapy should focus on establishing compensatory memory and organizational systems. Ms. Blue will need to write things down and learn to use task lists and an alarm system sufficient to establish more desirable habits. She will also need to learn to give herself adequate time and to try to focus on one task at a time to completion or a reasonable stopping point. I will discuss this during feedback.

3. Ms. Blue is currently on Ritalin, and I will defer to physicians regarding its continuation. Individuals with similar cognitive impairments often show benefit from a low-dose stimulant/dopamine agonist.

4. Ms. Blue is now capable of making informed medical and financial decisions. This does not mean that she will always make the best or most reasonable decision. I do not believe that she still requires guardianship and/or conservatorship, but for complex decisions she should take her time and consult with a trusted party.

5. There were no significant cognitive deficiencies identified in this examination that would preclude eventual return to driving. She should undergo a formal driver's evaluation that includes assessment of on-the-road decision making, visual scanning, and reaction time before restoring driving privileges.

6. Ms. Blue no longer requires 24-hour supervision. I believe that she can be left alone in a familiar environment for extended periods of time.

7. Ms. Blue reported that she was exercising 2 to 3 days a week but did not have a formal physician-approved exercise program. She sometimes has mild balance issues when she gets up and tries to move too fast. Physicians and her former physical therapist should review her current exercise program to ensure that it is safe and appropriate. Considering her report of occasional balance problems, fall risk precautions may be warranted.

8. I do not believe Ms. Blue is ready for return to work or resumption of her college studies at this time. However, she should increase the intensity of her daily chores and demands as tolerated. If possible, her daily life and therapy should

start to simulate a more challenging schedule and work-/school-related tasks. This should allow the rehabilitation team to gauge her abilities and move forward with her long-term goals.

9. When Ms. Blue is deemed ready for return to work or college, this should occur in a slow stepwise fashion. For example, she might initially take only one college class and utilize college assistance programs or tutoring. This should allow her and the rehabilitation team to gauge performance and increase responsibilities based on performance.

10. Neuropsychological reevaluation in 6 to 12 months if necessary to evaluate her progress and assist with treatment planning. Reassessment may be useful when the team believes she is ready to return to college or part-time work. I will remain available as needed.

Index

Note. *f* or *t* following a page number indicates a figure or a table.

Academic functioning. *See also* Eligibility
   for special education; Functional
   status; Intellectual functioning;
   Learning disabilities
  case examples, 45–52, 46*t*, 47*t*, 54–61,
   77–78
  eligibility for special education services,
   34–35
  medical complexity and, 77–78, 77*t*
  pediatric evaluations and, 31–32, 32–33,
   45, 46*t*, 47*t*, 54–61
  personal injury forensic evaluations and,
   160*t*
  psychiatric evaluations and, 119
  special education law and, 33–34
  writing for and collaborating with school
   professionals, 35–37
Activities of daily living
  personal injury forensic evaluations and,
   143
  rehabilitation settings and, 221
Adaptive equipment, 238–239
Adaptive functioning
  medical complexity and, 77*t*
  pediatric evaluations and, 32
Adjustment, 32
Age factors, 13–15, 119–120. *See also*
   Developmental history; Geriatric
   evaluations; Lifespan issues; Pediatric
   evaluations

Alzheimer's disease, 95. *See also* Geriatric
   evaluations
Ambiguous terminology, 8. *See also*
   Terminology used in reports
American Board of Clinical
   Neuropsychology (ABCN) criteria, 2,
   10–13
Anxiety disorder, 123
APA ethics code, 8, 9–10
Assessment. *See also* Forensic evaluations;
   Geriatric evaluations; Medical
   complexity; Pediatric evaluations;
   Postsurgical evaluations; Presurgical
   evaluations; Psychiatric comorbidity;
   Rehabilitation evaluations
  American Board of Clinical
   Neuropsychology (ABCN) criteria
   and, 10
  clinical neuropsychology and, 1
  developmental neuropsychological
   considerations, 31–33
  medical complexity and, 66–67
  rehabilitation evaluations and, 231–233
Attentional functioning
  attention-deficit/hyperactivity disorder
   (ADHD) and, 126–127
  case examples, 217
  medical complexity and, 75*t*–76*t*
  pediatric evaluations and, 32
  pre-and postsurgical evaluations and, 217

Attention-deficit/hyperactivity disorder
    (ADHD)
  lifespan issues and, 120
  neuropsychological characteristics of,
    124–126
Attorneys. *See also* Forensic evaluations
  criminal forensic evaluations and, 169
  overview, 144–145
  writing for and interacting with, 175–180
Audience
  criminal forensic evaluations and,
    175–180
  neurological/neurosurgical teams, 97–98,
    193–196
  neurologists, 97–98
  psychiatrists, 127–128
  rehabilitation settings and, 221
  school personnel, 35–37
  technical aspects of report preparation
    and, 6–7
Auditory Verbal Learning Test (AVLT),
    156–157

B

Background information. *See also* History
  case examples, 26, 77–81, 131–132
  medical complexity and, 77–81
  psychiatric evaluations and, 131–132
Basic activities of daily living. *See also*
    Functional status
  geriatric evaluations and, 98
  organization of reports and, 5–6
Battery length, 93–94
Behavioral observation. *See also*
    Observational data
  case examples, 27, 81–82, 102, 114,
    132–134, 199, 216, 247–248
  geriatric evaluations and, 92, 96, 102,
    114
  medical complexity and, 81–82
  pre-and postsurgical evaluations and,
    199, 216
  psychiatric evaluations and, 132–134
  rehabilitation evaluations and, 230–231,
    247–248
  report preparation and, 4
Behavioral system engineer, 220–221
Bipolar disorder, 123–124
Brain damage, 143. *See also* Traumatic
    brain injury (TBI)

C

California Verbal Learning Test–II
    (CVLT-II), 157
Capacity
  case examples, 183–186
  criminal forensic evaluations and,
    166–167, 173, 183–186
Capital punishment, 168–169, 188–189
Capitalization, 7
Care needs, 236–237
Causality
  criminal forensic evaluations and,
    167–168
  personal injury forensic evaluations and,
    145–146
Chart notes, 2
Children. *See* Pediatric evaluations; School-
    age children
Civil forensic evaluations, 166–169
Clarity, 2, 171–172
Classroom observations, 32, 35–36. *See
    also* Observational data
Clinical history, 2. *See also* History
Clinical interview. *See* Interviews
Clinical neuropsychology, 1
Clinical setting. *See* Practice setting
Cognitive flexibility
  attention-deficit/hyperactivity disorder
    (ADHD) and, 124
  pediatric evaluations and, 32
Cognitive functioning. *See also* Functional
    status; IQ
  attention-deficit/hyperactivity disorder
    (ADHD) and, 124–127
  bipolar disorder and, 123–124
  major depressive disorder and, 123
  medical complexity and, 64, 65, 67,
    68–69, 75t
  pediatric evaluations and, 32
  schizophrenia and, 121
Cognitive symptoms. *See also* Symptoms
  geriatric evaluations and, 98
  organization of reports and, 5–6
Collaboration
  criminal forensic evaluations and,
    175–180
  with neurological/neurosurgical teams,
    193–196
  with neurologists, 97–98
  with psychiatrists, 127–128
  with school personnel, 35–37

Collateral interview information
  case examples, 246–247
  rehabilitation evaluations and, 230,
    246–247
  report preparation and, 4
Comorbidities. *See also* Psychiatric
    comorbidity
  case examples, 132
  lifespan issues and, 14
  pre-and postsurgical evaluations and,
    198–199
  psychiatric evaluations and, 119, 120,
    132
Competency
  case examples, 181–183
  criminal forensic evaluations and,
    170–173, 178, 181–183
Complexity of a case, 6–8, 62–65. *See also*
    Medical complexity
Conclusions. *See also* Diagnostic
    formulations; Results section
  case examples, 104–106, 165
  geriatric evaluations and, 104–106
  personal injury forensic evaluations and,
    152–155, 165
Concussion, 31
Confidentiality, 9–10. *See also* Ethical
    concerns
Confirmation bias
  pediatric evaluations and, 43
  personal injury forensic evaluations and,
    156–157
Consent
  case examples, 180–181
  criminal forensic evaluations and, 176,
    180–181
  geriatric evaluations and, 95
Consistency of data, 156
Context, 10
Continuous performance tests (CPTs),
    124–125
Criminal forensic evaluations
  case examples, 180–188
  death penalty and, 168–169, 188–189
  overview, 166–169, 189
  referral questions and, 170–175
  report preparation and, 178–180
  writing for and interacting with
    attorneys, judges, and juries,
    175–180
Criminal responsibility, 143–144. *See also*
    Forensic evaluations

D

Data sources. *See* Sources of information
Daubert standard, 175–176. *See also*
    Criminal forensic evaluations
Death penalty, 167, 168–169, 188–189.
    See also Criminal forensic
    evaluations
Deep brain stimulation, 192, 195
Deficit syndrome, 121–122
Dementia. *See also* Geriatric evaluations
  overview, 94–95, 95
  psychiatric evaluations and, 119
  spectrum of MCI to dementia, 96–97
Depression
  neuropsychological characteristics of,
    122–123
  personal injury forensic evaluations and,
    160*t*
Detail to include in reports, 11–12
Developmental history. *See also* History;
    Lifespan issues
  geriatric evaluations and, 98
  lifespan issues and, 13–15
  medical complexity and, 66
  organization of reports and, 5–6
  psychiatric evaluations and, 119–120
Developmental neuropsychological
    considerations, 31–33
Diagnostic formulations. *See also*
    Differential diagnosis; Summary
    section
  American Board of Clinical
    Neuropsychology (ABCN) criteria
    and, 10, 12–13
  case examples, 49–50, 54–56, 104–106,
    205–210, 219, 250
  criminal forensic evaluations and,
    176–177, 178–179
  eligibility for special education services,
    34–35
  geriatric evaluations and, 93–94, 97–98,
    104–106, 111
  pediatric evaluations and, 40–41, 44,
    49–50, 54–56
  pre-and postsurgical evaluations and,
    205–210, 219
  psychiatric evaluations and, 119
  rehabilitation evaluations and, 233–235,
    250
  writing for and collaborating with
    neurologists and, 97–98

Differential diagnosis. *See also* Diagnostic
    formulations
    American Board of Clinical
        Neuropsychology (ABCN) criteria
        and, 12–13
    case examples, 104–106
    geriatric evaluations and, 96, 97–98,
        104–106
    neuropsychological characteristics of
        psychiatric disorders, 120–127
    writing for and collaborating with
        neurologists and, 97–98
Diminished capacity. *See* Capacity
Disability. *See also* Academic functioning
    compared to disorder, 34–35
    eligibility for special education services,
        34–35
    special education law and, 33–34
    writing for and collaborating with school
        professionals and, 35–37
Disagreements with other professionals,
    8–9
Disorder
    compared to disability, 34–35
    pediatric evaluations and, 41
Document review, 31–32

E

Educational risks and strengths. *See also*
    Academic functioning
    case examples, 56–58
    pediatric evaluations and, 41, 56–58
Eligibility for special education. *See
    also* Academic functioning; Special
    education law
    determining, 34–35
    overview, 33–34
    pediatric evaluations and, 40–41,
        42–43
    technical aspects of report preparation
        and, 40–41
    writing for and collaborating with school
        professionals and, 35–37
Emotional factors, 11
Emotional symptoms. *See also* Symptoms
    case examples, 116
    geriatric evaluations and, 98, 116
    organization of reports and, 5–6
Employment functioning, 118, 119. *See also*
    Functional status; Work performance
Environmental modifications, 238–239

Epilepsy. *See also* Medical complexity
    measuring reliable change, 197
    pre-and postsurgical evaluations and,
        192, 193, 195, 198–199
Ethical concerns
    geriatric evaluations and, 95–96
    overview, 2
    report preparation and, 8–10
Evaluations, 2–6
Evidence-based practice, 8
Executive functions
    attention-deficit/hyperactivity disorder
        (ADHD) and, 124–125
    bipolar disorder and, 123–124
    case examples, 217
    major depressive disorder and, 123
    medical complexity and, 69, 75t–76t
    pediatric evaluations and, 32
    pre-and postsurgical evaluations and,
        217
Expert testimony, 144–145. *See also*
    Forensic evaluations
Expressive language skills, 32

F

Family environment. *See also* Family
    functioning; Parents
    geriatric evaluations and, 92
    medical complexity and, 64–65
    pediatric evaluations and, 31–32
Family functioning. *See also* Family
    environment; Functional status
    medical complexity and, 68
    pediatric evaluations and, 31–32
Family history, 31. *See also* History
504 Plan
    eligibility for special education services
        and, 35
    pediatric evaluations and, 45
    special education law and, 33–34
Flynn effect (FE), 188–189
Follow-up section, 29
Forensic evaluations. *See also* Civil forensic
    evaluations; Criminal forensic
    evaluations; Personal injury forensic
    evaluations
    medical complexity and, 73–74
    psychiatric evaluations and, 119
Format of a neuropsychological report,
    1–2. *See also* Preparing and organizing
    reports

Formulations. *See also* Diagnostic
    formulations; Impressions;
    Recommendations; Summary section
    case examples, 205–210, 219
    pre-and postsurgical evaluations and,
        205–210, 219
Free and appropriate public education
    (FAPE), 33
Full scale intelligent quotient (FSIQ),
    125
Functional assessment, 94–95
Functional status. *See also* Academic
    functioning; Cognitive functioning;
    Intellectual functioning; Language
    functioning
    criminal forensic evaluations and,
        166–167, 170–171
    geriatric evaluations and, 94–95, 98
    organization of reports and, 5–6
    pediatric evaluations and, 31–32
    psychiatric evaluations and, 118
    rehabilitation settings and, 222–224

G

General Ability Index (GAI), 125
Geriatric evaluations
    case examples, 99–109, 100*t*, 113–117
    mistakes to avoid in, 111
    overview, 92–95, 93*t*
    pretest considerations, 95–96
    report preparation and, 98
    spectrum of MCI to dementia, 96–97
    writing for and collaborating with
        neurologists and, 97–98
Goal clarification, 221–222, 228
Grammar, 7
Gray Oral Reading Test—Fifth Edition
    (GORT-5), 46–47, 46*t*

H

Health Insurance Portability and
    Accountability Act (HIPAA), 9–10
History. *See also* Background information
    American Board of Clinical
        Neuropsychology (ABCN) criteria
        and, 10, 11–12
    case examples, 17–19, 26, 77–81,
        104, 131–132, 197–199, 215–216,
        244–245, 245–247

geriatric evaluations and, 92–93, 95–96,
    98, 104, 111
medical complexity and, 66, 77–81
organization of reports and, 5–6
pediatric evaluations and, 31, 38–39, 43
pre-and postsurgical evaluations and,
    197–199, 215–216
psychiatric evaluations and, 119–120,
    127–128, 131–132
rehabilitation evaluations and, 227,
    228–230, 230, 244–247

I

Identification
    medical complexity and, 69
    rehabilitation evaluations and, 227
Impressions. *See also* Diagnostic
    formulations; Recommendations;
    Summary section
    case examples, 28–29, 54–56, 205–210
    pediatric evaluations and, 54–56
    pre-and postsurgical evaluations and,
        195, 205–210
Impulse control, 125
Individualized Education Plans (IEPs)
    eligibility for special education services
        and, 35
    pediatric evaluations and, 32, 45
Individuals with Disabilities Education Act
    (IDEA), 33
Individuals with Disabilities Education
    Improvement Act (IDEIA), 33
Informed consent. *See also* Ethical concerns
    case examples, 180–181
    criminal forensic evaluations and, 176,
        180–181
    geriatric evaluations and, 104–106
Inhibition, 32
Inpatient report writing, 71–73, 72*f*,
    221–227. *See also* Medical complexity
Insanity defense. *See also* Criminal forensic
    evaluations
    case examples, 186–188
    criminal forensic evaluations and,
        186–188
    overview, 173–175
Instrumental activities of daily living. *See
    also* Functional status
    geriatric evaluations and, 98
    organization of reports and, 5–6
Integration of information, 5–6, 6*f*

Intellectual functioning. *See also* Academic
    functioning; Cognitive functioning;
    Functional status
    attention-deficit/hyperactivity disorder
        (ADHD) and, 125
    case examples, 217
    criminal forensic evaluations and,
        170–171, 188–189
    medical complexity and, 75*t*
    personal injury forensic evaluations and,
        160*t*
    pre-and postsurgical evaluations and, 217
    schizophrenia and, 121
Intelligibility, 2
Interpretations of test data. *See also*
    Psychometric test results
    American Board of Clinical
        Neuropsychology (ABCN) criteria
        and, 10
    case examples, 46–51, 46*t*, 47*t*, 75*t*–77*t*,
        163–164, 216–219, 248–250
    criminal forensic evaluations and,
        171–172, 177–178, 179–180
    medical complexity and, 69–70, 75*t*–77*t*
    pediatric evaluations and, 39–40, 46–51,
        46*t*, 47*t*
    personal injury forensic evaluations and,
        151–153, 157–158, 158*t*–160*t*, 163–164
    pre-and postsurgical evaluations and,
        216–219
    rehabilitation evaluations and, 231–233,
        248–250
    report preparation and, 15–16
Intervention, 69
Interviews. *See also* Collateral interview
    information
    case examples, 17–19, 26–27, 101, 131–132
    geriatric evaluations and, 102
    personal injury forensic evaluations and,
        147–149
    psychiatric evaluations and, 131–132
    report preparation and, 2, 4
IQ, 32. *See also* Cognitive functioning;
    Intellectual functioning

J

Jargon use. *See also* Terminology used in
    reports
    case examples, 81–82, 83
    criminal forensic evaluations and,
        171–172, 178

medical complexity and, 69, 74, 81–82,
    83
pediatric evaluations and, 43, 44
technical aspects of report preparation
    and, 7–8
Judges, 175–180
Juries, 175–180

L

Language functioning. *See also* Functional
    status
    attention-deficit/hyperactivity disorder
        (ADHD) and, 125
    case examples, 82–83, 218
    medical complexity and, 75*t*, 82–83
    personal injury forensic evaluations and,
        158*t*
    pre-and postsurgical evaluations and,
        218
Lawyers. *See* Attorneys
Learning. *See also* Learning disabilities
    case examples, 218–219
    medical complexity and, 75*t*
    personal injury forensic evaluations and,
        159*t*
    pre-and postsurgical evaluations and,
        218–219
Learning disabilities. *See also* Academic
    functioning; Disability
    eligibility for special education services,
        34–35
    special education law and, 33–34
    writing for and collaborating
        with school professionals and,
        35–37
Least restrictive environment (LRE), 33
Left ventricular assist device (LVAD)
    implantation, 192, 195
Legal factors. *See also* Criminal forensic
    evaluations; Forensic evaluations;
    Personal injury forensic evaluations
    overview, 143–144, 166–167
    psychiatric evaluations and, 119
Length of a neuropsychological report.
    See also Preparing and organizing
    reports
    inpatient report writing and, 72
    overview, 1–2
    rehabilitation settings and, 224–225
    technical aspects of report preparation
        and, 6–8

Lifespan issues. *See also* Age factors; Developmental history
  psychiatric evaluations and, 119–120
  report preparation and, 13–15
Long-term memory, 123. *See also* Memory

M

Major depressive disorder
  neuropsychological characteristics of, 122–123
  personal injury forensic evaluations and, 160*t*
Malingering
  criminal forensic evaluations and, 169
  personal injury forensic evaluations and, 153–155
  validity of a neuropsychological evaluations and, 5
Mandatory notifications, 176
Manual motor functioning, 158*t*
Manual tactile functioning, 158*t*
Medical complexity. *See also* Complexity of a case; Epilepsy; Medical history; Pediatric evaluations; Postsurgical evaluations; Presurgical evaluations
  assessment and, 66–67
  case examples, 74–89, 75*t*–77*t*
  family functioning and, 68
  inpatient report writing and, 71–73, 72*f*
  long-term prognostic issues and, 68–69
  overview, 62–65
  report-writing considerations, 69–74, 72*f*
Medical diagnosis, 40–41. *See also* Diagnostic formulations
Medical history. *See also* History; Medical complexity; Medical records
  geriatric evaluations and, 98
  organization of reports and, 5–6
Medical personnel, 70–71. *See also* Medical complexity
Medical records. *See also* Medical history; Record review
  geriatric evaluations and, 92–93, 95–96
  inpatient report writing and, 72
  outpatient report writing and, 73
  rehabilitation evaluations and, 228–229
  report preparation and, 3–4
Medications
  attention-deficit/hyperactivity disorder (ADHD) and, 125–126
  major depressive disorder and, 123

  rehabilitation evaluations and, 229–230
  schizophrenia and, 121–122
Memory
  attention-deficit/hyperactivity disorder (ADHD) and, 124, 125
  bipolar disorder and, 123–124
  case examples, 218–219
  criminal forensic evaluations and, 170–171
  geriatric evaluations and, 92, 94–95
  major depressive disorder and, 123
  medical complexity and, 75*t*
  pediatric evaluations and, 32
  personal injury forensic evaluations and, 159*t*–160*t*
  pre-and postsurgical evaluations and, 198–199, 218–219
  schizophrenia and, 121
Mental competency, 170–173
Mild cognitive impairment (MCI)
  geriatric evaluations and, 94–95
  spectrum of MCI to dementia, 96–97
Mild traumatic brain injury (mTBI), 31. *See also* Traumatic brain injury (TBI)
Mood
  attention-deficit/hyperactivity disorder (ADHD) and, 127
  case examples, 219
  pre-and postsurgical evaluations and, 219
Motor/visual-motor functioning
  case examples, 218
  pediatric evaluations and, 32
  pre-and postsurgical evaluations and, 218

N

Narrative reports, 1–2
Neurobehavioral status examination, 113
Neurological history. *See also* History
  geriatric evaluations and, 98
  organization of reports and, 5–6
Neurologists, 97–98
Neuropsychological tests. *See also* Psychometric test results
  American Board of Clinical Neuropsychology (ABCN) criteria and, 10
  case examples, 18*t*, 27–28
  pediatric evaluations and, 36–37, 39–40
  report preparation and, 4

Neurotoxic injury, 143
Norms, 93–94
Not guilty by reason of insanity verdict. *See also* Criminal forensic evaluations
  case examples, 186–188
  criminal forensic evaluations and, 186–188
  overview, 173–175
Notification, 176, 180–181
Novel ideas, 6–8

O

Observational data. *See also* Behavioral observation
  case examples, 19–20, 27, 102, 114, 132–134, 199, 247–248
  classroom observations, 32, 35–36
  geriatric evaluations and, 92, 96, 102, 114
  personal injury forensic evaluations and, 156
  pre-and postsurgical evaluations and, 199
  psychiatric evaluations and, 132–134
  rehabilitation evaluations and, 230–231, 247–248
  report preparation and, 3, 4
Older adults, 92–95, 93*t*. *See also* Geriatric evaluations
Opinions, 178–179
Organ transplants, 192. *See also* Medical complexity
Organization of reports. *See also* Preparing and organizing reports
  integration of information and, 5–6, 6*f*
  overview, 2
  technical aspects of report preparation and, 6–8
Organization skills
  attention-deficit/hyperactivity disorder (ADHD) and, 124
  pediatric evaluations and, 32
Outline, 5–6, 6*f*
Outpatient report writing
  case examples, 227–241, 244–252
  medical complexity and, 73
  overview, 227–241
  rehabilitation settings and, 221–227, 244–252

P

Pain scales, 160*t*
Paragraph organization, 7. *See also* Terminology used in reports
Parents. *See also* Family environment; Sources of information
  medical complexity and, 64–65, 67, 68
  pediatric evaluations and, 31–32
Pediatric evaluations. *See also* Medical complexity; School-age children
  case examples, 45–52, 46*t*, 47*t*, 54–61
  developmental neuropsychological considerations, 31–33
  eligibility for special education services, 34–35
  issues to avoid, 43–45
  overview, 45
  special education law and, 33–34
  technical aspects of report preparation and, 37–43
  validity and, 4–5
  writing for and collaborating with school professionals, 35–37
Performance validity tests (PVTs)
  major depressive disorder and, 123
  pediatric evaluations and, 32
  personal injury forensic evaluations and, 149–151, 156, 158*t*
  report preparation and, 3
Performance-based measures, 119
Personal injury forensic evaluations
  case examples, 158*t*–160*t*, 163–165
  interpretation of test data and, 157, 158*t*–160*t*
  mistakes to avoid in, 155–157
  overview, 143–146
  report preparation and, 146–155
Personality Assessment Inventory (PAI), 156
Physical symptoms. *See also* Symptoms
  geriatric evaluations and, 98
  organization of reports and, 5–6
Placement recommendations, 50–51. *See also* Recommendations; Treatment recommendations
Planning, 32
Postsurgical evaluations. *See also* Medical complexity
  case examples, 197–212, 215–219
  epilepsy and, 193
  measuring reliable change, 196–197

overview, 192
report preparation and, 197–212
writing for and collaborating with
neurological/neurosurgical teams,
193–196
Posttraumatic amnesia (PTA), 147
Posttraumatic stress disorder (PTSD),
126–127
Practice setting. *See also* Rehabilitation
settings
medical complexity and, 66–67, 71–73,
72*f*
overview, 1–2
pediatric evaluations and, 32
personal injury forensic evaluations and,
144
recommendations regarding, 237–238
technical aspects of report preparation
and, 6–8
writing for and collaborating with school
professionals and, 35–37
Prejudicial information, 176–177
Preparing and organizing reports
American Board of Clinical
Neuropsychology (ABCN) criteria
and, 10–13
case examples, 17–22, 18*t*, 26–29
criminal forensic evaluations and,
175–180
ethical and professional issues, 8–10
interpretation of test data and, 15–16
lifespan issues, 13–15
medical complexity and, 69–74, 72*f*
pediatric evaluations and, 37–43
personal injury forensic evaluations and,
146–155
pre-and postsurgical evaluations and,
197–212
prerequisites to, 2–6
psychometric issues and, 15–16
rehabilitation settings and, 221–227
technical aspects of, 6–8
writing for and collaborating with school
professionals, 35–37
Presentation. *See also* Reasons for referral
pediatric evaluations and, 39, 43
rehabilitation evaluations and, 230
Presurgical evaluations. *See also* Medical
complexity
case examples, 197–212, 215–219
epilepsy and, 193
measuring reliable change, 196–197

overview, 192
report preparation and, 197–212
writing for and collaborating with
neurological/neurosurgical teams,
193–196
Probative information, 176–177
Problem solving
pediatric evaluations and, 32
personal injury forensic evaluations and,
160*t*
Procedures, 231–232
Processing speed, 12
case examples, 217
personal injury forensic evaluations and,
159*t*
pre-and postsurgical evaluations and,
217
Professional considerations, 2, 8–10
Professional roles
report preparation and, 2
technical aspects of report preparation
and, 6–8
Prognosticating
case examples, 87–88
medical complexity and, 87–88
psychiatric evaluations and, 120
rehabilitation settings and, 226–227
Psychiatric comorbidity, 118–119, 120–127.
See also Comorbidities; Psychiatric
evaluations; Psychopathological
factors
Psychiatric evaluations. *See also* Psychiatric
comorbidity; Psychopathological
factors
case examples, 128–138, 129*t*–130*t*
neuropsychological characteristics of
psychiatric disorders, 120–127
overview, 118–119
writing for and collaborating with
psychiatrists and, 127–128
Psychiatrists, 127–128
Psychoeducation, 67
Psychological adjustment, 32
Psychological diagnosis, 40–41. *See also*
Diagnostic formulations
Psychological history, 98. *See also*
History
Psychological symptoms. *See also*
Symptoms
geriatric evaluations and, 98
organization of reports and, 5–6
Psychometric issues, 15–16

Psychometric test results. *See also*
    Interpretations of test data;
    Neuropsychological tests
    case examples, 27–28, 46–51, 46*t*, 47*t*,
        100*t*, 114–115, 129*t*–130*t*, 134–135,
        216–219, 248–250
    criminal forensic evaluations and,
        171–172, 177–178, 179–180
    geriatric evaluations and, 92, 95–96,
        100*t*, 111, 114–115
    pediatric evaluations and, 39–40, 46–51,
        46*t*, 47*t*
    personal injury forensic evaluations and,
        151–153, 158*t*–160*t*
    pre-and postsurgical evaluations and,
        216–219
    pretest considerations, 95–96
    psychiatric evaluations and, 129*t*–130*t*,
        134–135
    rehabilitation evaluations and, 231–233,
        248–250
    report preparation and, 2
Psychomotor speed, 123
Psychopathological factors. *See also*
    Psychiatric comorbidity; Psychiatric
    evaluations
    American Board of Clinical
        Neuropsychology (ABCN) criteria
        and, 11
    criminal forensic evaluations and, 170–171
    overview, 118–119
Psychosocial history. *See also* History
    geriatric evaluations and, 98
    organization of reports and, 5–6
Psychosocial risks and strengths, 41
Punctuation, 7
Purpose of the evaluation, 1–2

Q

Qualifiers, 8
Quality of life, 65

R

Reasons for referral. *See also* Referral
    questions
    case examples, 244–245
    geriatric evaluations and, 98
    rehabilitation evaluations and, 227–228,
        244–245

Recent/remote memory, 160*t*
Receptive language skills, 32
Recommendations. *See also* Treatment
    recommendations
    American Board of Clinical
        Neuropsychology (ABCN) criteria
        and, 10–11
    case examples, 21–22, 28–29, 50–51,
        54–56, 58–61, 85–89, 106–109,
        116–117, 136–138, 165, 210–212,
        251–252
    ethical and professional issues regarding,
        8
    geriatric evaluations and, 95, 106–109,
        116–117
    medical complexity and, 69, 85–89
    organization of reports and, 6*f*
    pediatric evaluations and, 41–42, 44,
        50–51, 54–56, 58–61
    personal injury forensic evaluations and,
        165
    pre-and postsurgical evaluations and,
        210–212
    psychiatric evaluations and, 128,
        136–138
    rehabilitation evaluations and, 235–241,
        251–252
    technical aspects of report preparation
        and, 6–8
Record review. *See also* Medical records
    access to records, 2
    geriatric evaluations and, 95–96
    medical complexity and, 80–81
    rehabilitation evaluations and,
        228–229
    report preparation and, 3–4
Reevaluation needs
    case examples, 209–210
    geriatric evaluations and, 93–94, 95–96,
        109–111, 110*f*
    measuring reliable change, 196–197
    pre-and postsurgical evaluations and,
        195, 196–197, 209–210
    rehabilitation evaluations and, 241
Reference groups, 10
Referral questions. *See also* Reasons for
    referral; Referral source
    American Board of Clinical
        Neuropsychology (ABCN) criteria
        and, 11
    case examples, 84–85, 128, 130, 215
    criminal forensic evaluations and,
        170–175, 176

geriatric evaluations and, 93–94, 95, 98, 111
medical complexity and, 74, 84–85
pediatric evaluations and, 32
pre-and postsurgical evaluations and, 215
pretest considerations, 95
psychiatric evaluations and, 118, 128, 130
rehabilitation evaluations and, 227–228
report preparation and, 2
school-age children and, 30
technical aspects of report preparation and, 6–8
Referral source. *See also* Referral questions
American Board of Clinical Neuropsychology (ABCN) criteria and, 10
personal injury forensic evaluations and, 144
rehabilitation evaluations and, 240–241
Rehabilitation evaluations
case examples, 221–241, 244–252
outpatient report writing and, 227–241
overview, 220–227, 241–242
report preparation and, 221–227
Rehabilitation settings, 220–221, 237–238. *See also* Practice setting; Rehabilitation evaluations
Reliability of tests and procedures. *See* Test reliability
Reliable change indices (RCIs), 196–197
Report cards, 32. *See also* Academic functioning; Record review
Resources, 239–240
Response bias, 235
Response inhibition, 124
Response to intervention (RTI), 34
Results section
case examples, 20–21, 102–103, 114–115, 200–205
geriatric evaluations and, 102–103, 114–115
pre-and postsurgical evaluations and, 195, 200–205
Rey Complex Figure Test, 157
Risk factors
American Board of Clinical Neuropsychology (ABCN) criteria and, 10
case examples, 56–57
geriatric evaluations and, 111
pediatric evaluations and, 41, 56–57

S

Safety
psychiatric evaluations and, 118
rehabilitation evaluations and, 236–237
Schizophrenia
case examples, 128–138, 129*t*–130*t*
lifespan issues and, 120
neuropsychological characteristics of, 121–122
School environment. *See also* Academic functioning
pediatric evaluations and, 31–32, 32–33, 42–43
special education law and, 33–34
School functioning. *See* Academic functioning
School performance, 5–6. *See also* Academic functioning; Functional status
School personnel. *See also* Teacher report
pediatric evaluations and, 32
writing for and collaborating with, 35–37
School psychologists, 35–37
School-age children. *See also* Pediatric evaluations
case examples, 45–52, 46*t*, 47*t*, 54–61
developmental neuropsychological considerations, 31–33
eligibility for special education services, 34–35
overview, 30, 45
special education law and, 33–34
technical aspects of report preparation and, 37–43
writing for and collaborating with school professionals, 35–37
School-friendly neuropsychological reports, 30
Scope-of-practice limits, 240–241
Self-report measures
case examples, 219, 245–246
pre-and postsurgical evaluations and, 219
rehabilitation evaluations and, 232–233, 245–246
Sensorimotor functions, 76*t*
Sentence structure, 7. *See also* Terminology used in reports
Set shifting, 160*t*
Setting, practice. *See* Practice setting
Social–emotional functioning
medical complexity and, 77*t*
pediatric evaluations and, 32

Sources of information, 92–93. *See also* Family environment; History; Medical records; Observational data; Parents; Psychometric test results; Record review; School environment; Teacher report

Special education law, 33–34, 35–37. *See also* Eligibility for special education

Specific learning disabilities (SLDs)
eligibility for special education services, 34–35
special education law and, 33–34
writing for and collaborating with school professionals and, 35–37

Stamina of patient, 93–94

Strengths
case examples, 57–58
pediatric evaluations and, 41, 57–58

Stroke, 3–4

Structured interviews. *See* Interviews

Summarizing data. *See also* Interpretations of test data; Summary section
case examples, 49–50, 85–88, 116–117
geriatric evaluations and, 111, 116–117
medical complexity and, 85–88
pediatric evaluations and, 49–50
rehabilitation settings and, 221–222

Summary section. *See also* Diagnostic formulations; Summarizing data
case examples, 103, 116–117, 135–136, 205–210, 219, 250
geriatric evaluations and, 95, 103, 111, 116–117
personal injury forensic evaluations and, 152–155
pre-and postsurgical evaluations and, 195, 205–210, 219
psychiatric evaluations and, 135–136
rehabilitation evaluations and, 233–235, 250

Supervision, 236–237

Supporting arguments, *6f*

Symptom validity tests (SVTs)
overview, 3
pediatric evaluations and, 32
personal injury forensic evaluations and, 149–151

Symptoms
American Board of Clinical Neuropsychology (ABCN) criteria and, 10
geriatric evaluations and, 98

interpretation of test data and, 16
lifespan issues and, 120
organization of reports and, 5–6
psychiatric evaluations and, 120
schizophrenia and, 121–122

T

Teacher report, 31–32. *See also* School personnel; Sources of information

Technical terminology. *See also* Terminology used in reports
case examples, 81–82, 83
criminal forensic evaluations and, 171–172, 178
medical complexity and, 81–82, 83
pediatric evaluations and, 43, 44
technical aspects of report preparation and, 7–8

Terminology used in reports. *See also* Jargon use; Technical terminology
criminal forensic evaluations and, 171–172
pediatric evaluations and, 43, 44
technical aspects of report preparation and, 7–8

Test findings. *See* Psychometric test results

Test reliability
criminal forensic evaluations and, 177–178
medical complexity and, 66

Test selection, 94

Testimony, 144–145. *See also* Forensic evaluations

Tiered research-based interventions, 34

Timeliness of reports, 225–226

TOMM, 156

Tone. *See also* Terminology used in reports
ethical and professional issues regarding, 8–9
pediatric evaluations and, 37–38, 44

Trail Making B, 157

Traumatic brain injury (TBI)
American Board of Clinical Neuropsychology (ABCN) criteria and, 12
pediatric evaluations and, 31
personal injury forensic evaluations and, 143, 146
psychiatric evaluations and, 120
record review and, 3–4

Treatment planning, 221–227, 228

Treatment recommendations. *See also*
  Recommendations
  American Board of Clinical
    Neuropsychology (ABCN) criteria
    and, 10–11
  case examples, 58–61, 108–109
  geriatric evaluations and, 108–109
  pediatric evaluations and, 41–42, 44, 58–61
  rehabilitation evaluations and, 235–241

V

Validity Indicator Profile (VIP), 156
Validity of findings
  criminal forensic evaluations and,
    177–178
  medical complexity and, 66
  personal injury forensic evaluations and,
    149–151
  report preparation and, 4–5
Verbal fluency, 124
Verbal learning, 159*t. See also* Learning
Verbal memory. *See also* Memory
  attention-deficit/hyperactivity disorder
    (ADHD) and, 125, 126–127
  bipolar disorder and, 123–124
  major depressive disorder and, 123
  personal injury forensic evaluations and,
    159*t*
Vigilance, 125
Vineland Adaptive Behavior Scales (VABS),
  177
Visual learning, 159*t. See also* Learning
Visual memory. *See also* Memory
  attention-deficit/hyperactivity disorder
    (ADHD) and, 125
  personal injury forensic evaluations and,
    159*t*

Visual perceptual functions, 76*t*–77*t*
Visual spatial skills, 32
Visuoperceptual/visuospatial functioning
  case examples, 218
  personal injury forensic evaluations and,
    158*t*
  pre-and postsurgical evaluations and,
    218

W

Wechsler Adult Intelligence Scale—Fourth
  Edition (WAIS-IV), 16
Wechsler Intelligence Scale for Children—
  Fourth Edition (WISC-IV), 12
Wechsler Memory Scale–IV (WMS-IV),
  94
Word choice. *See also* Jargon use
  case examples, 81–82
  criminal forensic evaluations and,
    171–172, 178
  medical complexity and, 81–82
  pediatric evaluations and, 44
  technical aspects of report preparation
    and, 7–8
Word Memory Test, 156
Work performance. *See also* Functional
    status
  geriatric evaluations and, 98
  organization of reports and, 5–6
  overview, 118, 119
Working memory. *See also* Memory
  attention-deficit/hyperactivity disorder
    (ADHD) and, 124
  major depressive disorder and, 123
  pediatric evaluations and, 32
  personal injury forensic evaluations and,
    159*t*